# Co-Creation in Tourist Experiences

The tourist experience is multi-faceted and dynamic, as tourists engage with its formation and creation. The tourists then become vital in creating value for themselves together with the service provider. Experience value cannot be pre-produced, but is co-created between host and guest(s) in the servicescape. The tourist managers can therefore only plan for and facilitate for value co-creation to take place.

This book responds to the need for a critical review of how firms can facilitate and dramatize for enhanced experience value for tourists. As the roles of participants and providers are changing rapidly, new knowledge in terms of how value creation and value co-creation can transpire needs to be generated. The aim of this book is therefore to accentuate the role and importance of the core elements in value creation processes, namely, the customer(s), the setting in which co-creation would take place, and the provider.

Bringing together scholars from diverse areas to address the nature of how the actors co-create values through interaction in different experience settings, the book also serves as a guide to the best practice of co-creation of tourist experiences. It will therefore appeal practically as well as theoretically to scholars and students of tourism, marketing, leisure, hospitality, and services management.

**Nina K. Prebensen** is a Professor at UiT – The Arctic University of Norway. She also holds a 20% position at the University College of South East Norway. She has published papers in various tourism journals. Her research particularly highlights the tourist decision and experience processes, where co-creation of value for hosts and guests are in focus.

**Joseph S. Chen** is Professor in Tourism, Hospitality and Event Management in the Department of Recreation, Park and Tourism Studies at Indiana University, Bloomington, USA. His research foci entail tourism marketing, tourist behaviors, social impacts of tourism, Arctic tourism and sustainability in hospitality and tourism.

**Muzaffer S. Uysal** is a Chair and Professor in the Hospitality and Tourism Management Department in the Isenberg School of Management at the University of Massachusetts, Amherst, USA. He is a member of the International Academy for the Study of Tourism and the Academy of Leisure Sciences. His current research interests center on tourism demand/supply interaction, tourism development and QOL research in tourism and hospitality.

# Contemporary Geographies of Leisure, Tourism and Mobility

Series Editor: C. Michael Hall, Professor at the Department of Management, College of Business and Economics, University of Canterbury, Christchurch, New Zealand

The aim of this series is to explore and communicate the intersections and relationships between leisure, tourism and human mobility within the social sciences.

It will incorporate both traditional and new perspectives on leisure and tourism from contemporary geography, e.g. notions of identity, representation and culture, while also providing for perspectives from cognate areas such as anthropology, cultural studies, gastronomy and food studies, marketing, policy studies and political economy, regional and urban planning, and sociology, within the development of an integrated field of leisure and tourism studies.

Also, increasingly, tourism and leisure are regarded as steps in a continuum of human mobility. Inclusion of mobility in the series offers the prospect to examine the relationship between tourism and migration, the sojourner, educational travel, and second home and retirement travel phenomena.

*For a full list of titles in this series, please visit* www.routledge.com/series/SE0522.

The series comprises two strands:

**Contemporary Geographies of Leisure, Tourism and Mobility** aims to address the needs of students and academics, and the titles will be published in hardback and paperback. Titles include:

**Routledge Studies in Contemporary Geographies of Leisure, Tourism and Mobility** is a forum for innovative new research intended for research students and academics, and the titles will be available in hardback only. Titles include:

# Co-Creation in Tourist Experiences

Edited by Nina K. Prebensen,
Joseph S. Chen and
Muzaffer S. Uysal

LONDON AND NEW YORK

First published 2017
by Routledge
2 Park Square, Milton Park, Abingdon, Oxon OX14 4RN

and by Routledge
605 Third Avenue, New York, NY 10017

First issued in paperback 2021

*Routledge is an imprint of the Taylor & Francis Group, an informa business*

*British Library Cataloguing in Publication Data*
A catalogue record for this book is available from the British Library

*Library of Congress Cataloging in Publication Data*
A catalog record for this book has been requested

ISBN 13: 978-1-03-224224-8 (pbk)
ISBN 13: 978-1-138-18330-8 (hbk)

DOI: 10.4324/9781315645919

Typeset in Times New Roman
By Swales & Willis Ltd, Exeter, Devon, UK

# Contents

vi  *Contents*

# Illustrations

## Figures

## Tables

# Contributors

**Eric S. W. Chan**, PhD, a certified hospitality educator (CHE), is Assistant Professor in the School of Hotel and Tourism Management at the Hong Kong Polytechnic University. His research interests include hotel environmental management, human resource management, and tourist behavior. He is Coordinating Editor of the *International Journal of Hospitality Management* (*IJHM*).

**Prakash K. Chathoth**, PhD, is Professor in the Department of Marketing and Information Systems, School of Business Administration, American University of Sharjah, United Arab Emirates. His research interests include topics related to strategic and service management/marketing with a particular emphasis on the service sector, notably the tourism and hospitality industry.

**Joseph S. Chen**, PhD, is Professor in Tourism, Hospitality and Event Management in the Department of Recreation, Park and Tourism Studies at Indiana University, Bloomington, USA. His research foci entail tourism marketing, tourist behaviors, social impacts of tourism, Arctic tourism, and sustainability in hospitality and tourism.

**Isabelle Frochot**, PhD, is a senior lecturer at the University Savoie Mont Blanc. She has specialized in the study of tourist behavior and her research interests focus on experiential consumption and its co-creation processes more specifically in the mountain tourism context.

**Ruhet Genc** is Associated Professor at the Turkish-German University's Economics and Administrative Sciences Department. He intends to see all issues from a management and strategy point of view. His research interests are sustainability, innovation, gastronomy, value creation, medical value tourism, tourist behavior, and quality of life.

**Sandra Gountas**, PhD, is Senior Lecturer at Curtin Business School, School of Marketing, Curtin University, Australia. Her research interests are mainly concerned with social marketing, societal issues, and quality of life.

**Robert J. Harrington**, PhD, is Professor in the School of Hospitality Business Management, Washington State University. His research areas include strategy management, hospitality innovation management, and food and wine. He is

Editor-in-Chief of the *Journal of Culinary Science & Technology* and author of *Food and Wine Pairing: A Sensory Experience.*

**Raija Komppula**, PhD, is Professor of Marketing and Tourism Business at the University of Eastern Finland, Finland. Her research interests include tourist experience, customer involvement in new service development, destination leadership, branding, small business, entrepreneurship, cooperation, and networks.

**Henna Konu**, PhD, is Project Manager and a researcher at the Center for Tourism Studies, University of Eastern Finland, Finland. Her research interests include service development, customer involvement, consumer/tourist experiences, experiential services, and wellbeing and nature tourism.

**Dominique Kreziak**, PhD, is a senior lecturer in consumer behavior at the University Savoie Mont Blanc, France. Her research interests range from tourism to upcycling and creative waste management.

**Timothy Lee**, PhD, is Professor at Ritsumeikan Asia Pacific University (APU) and Founding Director of the APRI-HOT (Asia Pacific Research Institute for Health-Oriented Tourism). His research interests include medical/wellness/health tourism, ethnic identity, cultural heritage tourism, and tourism development that incorporate East Asian values.

**Fevzi Okumus**, PhD, is Professor in the Hospitality Services Department at the University of Central Florida's Rosen College of Hospitality Management. His research areas include strategy implementation, strategic human resources management, crisis management, destination marketing, information technology, and developing countries. He is the Editor-in-Chief of the *International Journal of Contemporary Hospitality Management* (*IJCHM*).

**Nina K. Prebensen**, PhD, is a Professor at UiT – The Arctic University of Norway. She also holds a 20% position at the University College of South East Norway. She has published papers in various tourism journals. Her research particularly highlights the tourist decision and experience processes, where co-creation of value for hosts and guests is in focus.

**Zibin Song**, PhD, is Associate Professor in the Tourism School of Hainan University. His research encompasses human resources management, organizational behavior, tourism marketing, and tourism impact. He received both his master's degree (2003) and PhD (2010) from the School of Hotel and Tourism Management, Hong Kong Polytechnic University, Hong Kong.

**Muzaffer S. Uysal**, PhD, is a Chair and Professor in the Hospitality and Tourism Management Department of the Isenberg School of Management at the University of Massachusetts, Amherst, USA. He is a member of the International Academy for the Study of Tourism and the Academy of Leisure Sciences. His current research interests center on tourism demand/supply interaction, tourism development, and QOL research in tourism and hospitality.

**Kristin Woll**, PhD, is Associate Professor at the School of Business and Economics, UiT, Norway. Her current research focus is on psychological contracts, creativity, innovation, and tourism.

**Anita Zátori**, PhD, is a visiting assistant professor at the Hospitality and Tourism Department, Pamplin College of Business, Virginia Tech, and an assistant professor at the Tourism Center, Corvinus Business School, Corvinus University of Budapest. Her current research focus is on tourist experience phenomenology, tourist experience's contribution to well-being, and customer experience design.

# Preface

The tourism industry is a system of systems where hosts and guests meet with the intention of creating valuable experiences. These meetings happen in different places and settings, providing a plethora of examples of co-creation opportunities and practices. This book provides theoretical perspectives and cases of co-creation practices in various tourism settings. The chapters disclose how various types of experience value co-created by people also offer value potentials for firms, destinations and countries to become sustainable and competitive in the market place. Thus, this book is an attempt to provide a portfolio of studies that touch on the inner layers of tourist experience creation in different settings.

An examination of the chapters in the book reveals that the elements of the firm, tourists, and the settings are central to the process of tourist experience creation and shaping the nature of both personal and management outcomes. The key challenge for the tourism enterprise is to determine to what extent it can facilitate and stage the process of experience co-creation while still sustaining its business activities. The level of readiness and commitment expressed by the tourism enterprise would certainly influence its financial viability and future market share as we continue to see a major shift in today's dynamic, experience conscious consumers, placing significantly more value on engagement, involvement, and meeting higher order of needs such as personal growth, sense of wellbeing, mastery, competency, and self-development and discovery.

The book consists of thirteen chapters representing seventeen scholars around the globe. In order to develop a more focused theme on the book project, the editors held a book writing seminar in Bolzano, Italy (October 2015) for two days, made possible by the Norwegian Research Council. This gathering followed a similar structure that was employed while developing *Creating Experience Value in Tourism*, edited by the same authors of this current book, published by CABI in 2014. The first book, conceptual and theoretical in nature, covered a host of approaches to value creation, perspective-based definitions, and interpretations of how tourists, as customers, create value alone and with others. This book offered new and practical knowledge for tourism scholars and professionals to appreciate and understand the relevance of the concept of creating experience value to firms and organizations. On the other hand, this current volume *Co-Creation in Tourist Experiences* was crafted to provide examples of value co-creation along with theoretical underpinnings of the concept in selected settings with different experience activities, each bringing the uniqueness of the context and setting in understanding the underpinnings of tourist perceived experience value. This edited volume serves as a response to the need for practical examples of how firms can facilitate and dramatize for the tourist to partake in creating (co-creating) enhanced experience value for tourists. As the roles of participants and providers are changing rapidly, new practical knowledge in terms of how value creation and value co-creation can transpire need to be generated. In this vein, we believe that this books fills a gap in the scholarly literature of tourism. Our goal is not to be exhaustive in the coverage of settings or activities, but rather offer a selection of topics that would exemplify the best work of our contributors with respect to their selected settings and activities while adhering to the thematic focus of the book.

We believe that this book also serves as a state of the best practice of tourism experience creation and will be of great interest for practitioners as well as scholars and students of tourism. Researchers and practitioners in the field of tourism and hospitality as well as services in general will find this book very informative and useful in understanding the relevance and importance of consumer experience creation in business practices and developing marketing and management implications. The book is an exceptional offer to research areas and fields such as experiential marketing and management.

Nina K. Prebensen
Joseph S. Chen
Muzaffer S. Uysal

# Acknowledgments

We would like to thank our esteemed colleagues around the world for their full support for this project. A book like this would not have been possible without their help and outstanding contributions. We are grateful for sharing their time, talent, and expertise in crafting their valuable charters. We thank our industry partners for their participation and access services, staff, and customers. Through this access, valuable data and examples are recognised, collected and analysed, providing a platform for this book. We also thank the publisher and their staff. Finally, we thank our family members for their constant support. This book was written as part of the research project Northern InSights (http://www.opplevelserinord.no/), which is partly financed by the Norwegian Research Council, project no: 195306.

# 1 Tourist experience creation

## An overview

*Nina K. Prebensen, Joseph S. Chen and*
*Muzaffer S. Uysal*

## Introduction

An experience is illustrated as a steady flow of thoughts and feelings that take place during moments of consciousness regarding experience dimensions (Carlson, 1997; Csikszentmihalyi, 1990). Tourist experiences are believed to be multi-faceted, dynamic and evocative through interactive processes in which the tourist passively or actively engages. In other words, the tourist has to be present and partake in the formation and creation of these experiences. A refreshing question, in this regard, is how tourists participate in such processes. Answers to the question might help in providing theories concerning the creation and co-creation of tourist experiences and support tourism managers in facilitating creation of value for all actors involved.

The extant tourism literature (e.g. Prebensen & Foss, 2011; Uriely, 2005; Walls, Okumus, Wang, & Kwun, 2011) has urged in-depth examination to disentangle the complicity of experience formation, as such experiences come to life through interactions with both the physical environment and humans. Consequently, several frameworks are developed to assist managers and researchers in understanding how and why different factors play a role in experiential service. The present book follows the spirit offered through these works to grasp interaction processes providing experience value for the actors involved. The interaction processes are examined from different dimensions—that is, the formation, creation and co-creation of experiences providing various forms of value for the tourist.

The dynamic process of tourist experience formation has been recently brought to prominence through the work of Chen, Prebensen and Uysal (2016). They suggest a conceptual framework presenting the drivers affecting and moderating the creation of tourist experiences during the process of travel engagement: the Tourist Experience Driver Model (TEDM). This model deals with three trip stages (before, during, and after), capturing the different phases of the travel experience, and highlights different drivers modifying and shaping the tourist encounter as the tourist travels through time and space encapsulating various experience settings influenced by various drivers during the travelling process. Smith's (2003) holistic view of the tourism product included five elements: the physical plant, service, hospitality, freedom of choice, and involvement. Service providers need to acknowledge the alteration of perceptions, motivations, involvement, and knowledge amongst tourists going through the experience process. For tourism businesses catering to tourist demands at various stages of the trip, it is vital to focus on the interactions between tourists and service settings.

Tourism enterprises are service-centered entities, which stage and cater for diverse participant experiences. Staged experiences are expected to entice demand, increase market share and retain loyalty, and are rendered by service staff in specific experience settings that may include natural, cultural and built environments. The firm or the organization can, however, only create the environment and the circumstances in which consumers are able to have an experience (Mossberg, 2007). The firm needs to know what the tourists prefer in terms of quality levels of physical environment, service and interactions, for value co-creation to happen. Research needs to explore and figure out: (1) What is a valuable tourist experience? (2) What do we mean by interaction processes? (3) Who and what are/should be involved in such processes? (4) How should the firm respond to the customer demands in various trip phases? (5) How can the firm motivate the tourist to co-create experience value? (6) To what extent should the firm dramatize a tourist experience? (7) What elements of a tourist journey can influence tourist emotion and wellness? These questions are discussed in the present chapter to further explain what actually affects the perceived experiences amongst tourists.

A tourist experience is a blend of many dimensions that come together (Shaw & Ivens, 2002), in which each dimension may affect the tourist perception of the process and outcome of the experience differently. On that matter, Mossberg (2007) discussed dimensions within the individual that may involve the consumer emotionally, physically, intellectually, and spiritually. Involvement is further shown to influence value perception in tourist experiences positively (Prebensen, Chen, Woo, & Uysal, 2014). Experience dimensions may include physical surroundings (e.g. Berman & Evens, 1995; Bitner, 1992; Wakefield & Blodgett, 1996) and social environments, including interaction with employees and other customers (e.g. Arnould & Price, 1993; Silkapit & Fisk, 1985; Walls et al., 2011). Interactions with service personnel and other participants at destinations, along with the newly acquired perceptions of the setting, may evoke new tourist experiences. It is advantageous that tourism firms and destinations can carefully facilitate enhanced tourist experiences by motivating, involving, and educating the tourists to partake in value creation and co-creation processes.

*Experiential consumption*

There has been a great deal of discussion on the differences between manufacturing and service firms (e.g. Brush & Artz, 1999). Consumer researchers have articulated that service organizations are unique due to their special characteristics such as inseparability, perishability, heterogeneity, and inconsistency (variability). Tourist experiences include these four characteristics; however, they largely differ from traditional services. Prebensen, Vittersø and Dahl (2013) demonstrated, for instance, that time and effort regarding planning and going on a vacation positively affects overall trip satisfaction. As traditional service literature claims that time and effort should be regarded as a cost for the consumers, the study by Prebensen, Woo and Uysal (2014) showed that consuming a vacation differs from a service consumption in terms of the way the customer perceives the accumulated costs and benefits. In a similar vein, other studies on the subject validate this difference (e.g. Carù & Cova, 2007; Chen et al., 2016). Prebensen, Woo, Chen, and Uysal (2014) and Prebensen, Woo, and Uysal (2014) claimed, for instance, that in an experience-based consumption, participants are inclined to be present and partake in the production process more than in traditional services which are bought due to customers' unwillingness or lack of time or skill to do it themselves—for example, cleaning services, dentists, and lawyers. Another key difference between traditional services and tourism services is that for most traditional services the consumer is focused on the result of the service, whereas in tourism settings, services are being performed in the situation.

Prebensen and Rosengren (2016) examined the relative importance of the dimensions of experience value in four different hedonic- and utilitarian-dominated tourism services. Their study reveals that both hedonic and utilitarian value dimensions are present for different types of experience, as is the case in transport, accommodation, dinner and museum experiences. However, the structures of value dimensions differ between hedonic- and utilitarian-dominant services. The authors proposed that a tourist experience continuum may entail (1) air travel, (2) a hotel, (3) a restaurant, and (4) a museum, and presents a mostly utilitarian experience at the one end and a hedonic experience at the other. However, since they all are relevant elements of the overall travel experience, they should all be included to fully acknowledge the experience value and the potential mixed effects of the overall satisfaction. Surprisingly, functional value and value for money were found to have the strongest influence on satisfaction for both types of service. Prebensen and Rosengren (2016) claimed that for the tourism business to enhance experience value and tourist satisfaction, the service firms should focus on delivering functional values during the trip encountering stage while utilizing emotional values to attract visitors. Their study suggests including all relevant services in the utilitarian-hedonic continuum.

In order to acknowledge the process of creating and co-creating experiences, researchers have examined the processes and the outcomes of experience consumption separately (Prebensen, Woo, Chen, & Uysal, 2014). In their work, Prebensen, Woo, Chen, and Uysal (2014) highlighted the differences between motivation, value perception and satisfaction, even though they acknowledge overlapping tendencies. Motivation triggers the buying behaviour process; however, this may change over time during the experience process. During the trip, the tourist perceives the experience value, and after the experienced encounter the tourist evaluates the level of satisfaction, affecting future intentions. Figure 1.1 represents the phases of a trip experience with salient aspects as process and outcome variables, such as motivation, perceived value, satisfaction, and loyalty.

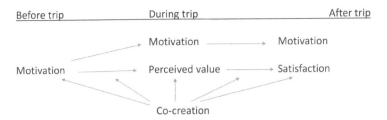

*Figure 1.1* Trip experience phases with overlapping tendencies

In experiential consumption hedonic and eudaimonic needs and emotions dominate the perceived experience value which are vital in managing long-term customer relationships (Pride & Ferrell, 2000). Definitions of value vary according to the context, target and goals (e.g. Babin, Darden, & Griffin, 1994; Dodds, Monroe, & Grewal, 1991; Holbrook, 2005; Holbrook & Corfman, 1985) and may manifest through different stages of trip. Thus, the context, target and goal are of vast importance to recognize and acknowledge tourist participation in creating meaningful experiences.

### Facilitating tourist experience co-creation

Tourism research has embraced theory from the service field which defines service as "a deed, a performance, and an effort" (Rathmell, 1966, p. 33). By doing so, tourism has more or less focused on the service provider as someone who produces valuable offers for the tourists to buy, to use and enjoy. This traditional view of the firm as the entity that produces value and the consumer as the entity that consumes value is discoursed strongly in contemporary perspectives on production and consumption processes (e.g. Prahalad & Ramaswamy, 2004; Vargo & Lusch, 2004). This logic claims that co-creation is about "shared creation of value by the company and the consumer" (Prahalad & Ramaswamy, 2004, p. 8), although in tourism literature the idea of the tourist being part of co-creation of experience is not new (e.g. Chon, 1989; Larsen, 2007; Mannell & Iso-Ahola, 1987; Uriely, 2005).

The service-dominant logic of marketing (Grönroos, 2006; Lusch & Vargo, 2006; Vargo & Lusch, 2004, 2006, 2008) recognizes the tourist role in creating experience value. This logic includes the idea that in the process of co-creating value, the tourists—in addition to firms and organizations—act as resource integrators (Arnould, Price, & Malshe, 2006; Vargo & Lusch, 2006), and that value is centered in the experiences of consumers (Prahalad & Ramaswamy, 2004). Hence, the foundational idea in the S-D logic is that the service encounter is an exchange process of value between the customer and the service provider. This perspective holds that the consumers and their skills and knowledge, depicted as operant resources, are able to contribute to value creation by integrating physical, social and cultural resources (Arnould et al., 2006).

The tourist experience value is not all about the tourist being present at the destination and mentally or physically partaking of and enjoying various experiences while staying there for an extended period of time (Prebensen, Kim, & Uysal, 2016; Sandström, Edvardsson, Kristensson, & Magnusson, 2008). Grönroos and Voima (2013) deployed the term "value-in-use" to portray customers' part in the co-creation process. Perceived experience value is defined by Prebensen, Woo, Chen, and Uysal (2014, p. 5) as "comprised of the benefits the tourist perceives from a journey and stay in a destination, including those assets or resources that the tourist, other tourists and the host bring to the process of co-creating experiences." The definition supports the idea that the firm and the destination can only facilitate the value coming alive through the tourist participation of creating experience value, signifying an interaction and co-creation process between actors in a specific situation surrounded by either a staged atmosphere or organically evolved environment.

One of the key functions of the tourism enterprise and destinations is to serve as a facilitator in the process of creating value. Co-creating vacation experiences relies on interactions with people (e.g. travel partners, other visitors, and service staff) and in the servicescape where the sellers and buyers interact and the service process takes place (Booms & Bitner, 1980). This interaction may lead to increased (or decreased) value for the tourists (Prebensen & Foss, 2011). In addition to being involved in the tourist experience, other reasons for co-creation may appeal, such as appreciating perceived control over the service delivery process (Bateson, 1985) and the feeling of choosing (including novel experiences), which offers higher levels of customization (Schneider & Bowen, 2010). Is the service delivery process about value creation via interactions between host and guest? Does it include guest interactions—for example, tourists sharing information? Could co-creation be defined as a visitor enjoying various activities provided by firms and organizations at the destination? Beyond the human dimension, could a process of enjoying nature and exercising by hiking in the trails be delineated as part of the co-creation construct? If so, could all sorts of interactions that a tourist is involved in during a trip account for co-creating value? In that case, scholars ought to discuss if the co-creation construct loses its usefulness as a theoretical underpinning.

Interaction has traditionally been regarded as an essential characteristic of tourism because of simultaneous production and consumption, explicated as "prosumption" by Toffler (1980). Tourists not only interact with other people, they also interact with natural and manufactured elements (Prebensen & Foss, 2011). The way the firm facilitates and plans for these interactions to happen shall ensure tourists' motivation, involvement, and learning to partake of the co-creation apparatus.

However, beyond what the firm can offer, some individuals are keen to produce their own experience, perhaps together with significant others—families, friends, other unknown tourists, local people and /or the service providers. Recognition that tourists are individualistic (active agents) rather than passive receivers of actions delivered by firms could be of vital importance for tourism management, marketing, and innovation research.

The firm can help the tourist to enjoy a valuable vacation: by utilizing tourist behavioral paths and pedagogical tools, a firm is able to design and facilitate valuable interactions for its clients. A central issue in tourism will therefore be how a firm can facilitate high quality interactions. Goffman (1959) used the dramaturgy metaphor as a theoretical framework to describe the relationship between what tourists do and value, and how interaction practices may be stimulated through staging, storytelling, and involvement.

Walls et al. (2011) revealed that consumer experiences are derived through a unique combination of responses to physical environment dimensions and human interaction dimensions. Their work confirmed previous research regarding the impact of physical environment and human interaction dimensions on emotions and behaviour (e.g. Mehrabian & Russell, 1974). Walls et al. (2011) suggested a framework of major constructs in tourist experience formation by including the physical environment such as ambience, multisensory factors, space/function, signs/symbols, and artefacts. Human interaction involves service providers and customers, where service providers contribute via attitude, professional behavior, proactive service and appearance. The customer interactive factors include demeanor, behavior, appearance and socialization, so the experience must include a mix of all these factors. Trip-related factors such as the purpose of the trip, the nature of the firm (e.g. hotel), the nature of the travel party and the experience continuum will influence the experience. Walls et al. (2011) showed how personal characteristics and trip-related factors play important roles in consumer experiences, pointing to the imperative of segmenting the market, tailoring and positioning services and amenities to the appropriate segments.

A vacation trip may be thoroughly pre-planned and arranged by a travel agency or tour operator. As tourists become more and more skilled, the tourists tend to plan the trip themselves. Despite preplanning, the tourists have to deal with a number of situations at the destination, necessitating coping behaviors and active participation to solve problems and/or to enhance value (e.g. Prebensen & Foss, 2011). A tourist journey includes a variety of products, services and experiences. Hence, to enjoy the vacation, the tourists are engaged in some activities (from either the service provider, the tourist or both) that help produce and consume ("prosume") experiences. The skills and knowledge and/or the ability to get information are subsequently expected to influence value creation and value co-creation processes.

### Tourist interaction as a facilitator of experience co-creation

Tourist interaction deals with involvement, contribution and creation, which may be of a direct or an indirect nature. In tourism, this is not only a premise for the industry to exist; it is also a tenet for the tourists to fulfil the various needs comprising their travel. Direct interaction is when the individual is in contact with another person or an object. Indirect interaction is when the individual is in contact with a person or an object through another party such as a tour operator or a medium such as the internet. Bolton and Saxena-Iyer (2009, p. 92) defined interactive services as "services that have some form of customer–firm interaction in an environment." Actors included in the service encounter—that is, the participants in value creation—refers to all individuals, whether customers or workers (Booms & Bitner, 1980; Noe, Uysal, & Magnini, 2010). The environment includes all aspects that facilitate or communicate the nature of the experience, before, during, or after its performance. Subsequently, tourists and hosts are part of an experience process in which both parties more or less willingly and actively engage for the purpose of creating value—that is, experience value for the customers, economic value for the firm, and social, economic, and sustainable value for the destination. For example, in their revelation of the perceived values of people interaction, Chen, Prebensen, and Uysal (2016) expounded that the social value is a significant factor motivating the tourist to interact with other tourists, service staff, and local residents.

The level of interaction—that is, interactivity—is delineated by Bolton and Saxena-Iyer (2009) along two dimensions, these being the extent of customer participation and the extent to which the service is technology enabled or delivered. Other researchers have suggested dimensions of interactive experience to include passive versus active participation and absorption versus immersion (Pine & Gilmore, 1999), and have suggested four realms of experience—that is, entertainment, educational, aesthetic, and escapist. Despite these efforts to acknowledge interactive experiences, few have actually explored interaction from the customers' viewpoint, which is tourist participation as a resource in enhancing value for the tourist and the firms in the service encounter. In sum, as noted by Ramirez (1999), the readers contemplate organizational structures and managerial arrangements to re-evaluate the process of value creation.

## References

Arnould, E. J., & Price, L. L. (1993). River magic: Extraordinary experience and the extended service encounter. *Journal of Consumer Research, 20*(1), 24–45.

Arnould, E. J., Price, L. L., & Malshe, A. (2006). Toward a cultural resource-based theory of the customer. In R. F. Lusch & S. L. Vargo (Eds.), *The service-dominant logic of marketing: Dialog, debate and directions* (pp. 320–333). Armonk, NY: M. E. Sharpe.

Babin, B. J, Darden, W. R., & Griffin, M. (1994). Work and/or fun: Measuring hedonic and utilitarian shopping value. *Journal of Consumer Research, 20*(March), 644–656.

Bateson, J. E. (1985). Self-service consumer: An exploratory study. *Journal of Retailing, 61*(3), 49–76.

Berman, B., & Evens, J. R. (1995). *Retail management: A strategic approach* (6th ed.). Englewood Cliffs, NJ: Prentice-Hall.

Bitner, M. J. (1992). Servicescapes: The impact of physical surroundings on customers and employees. *Journal of Marketing, 56*(2), 57–71.

Bolton, R., & Saxena-Iyer, S. (2009). Interactive services: A framework, synthesis and research directions. *Journal of Interactive Marketing, 23*(1), 91–104.

Booms, B. H., & Bitner, M. J. (1980). New management tools for the successful tourism manager. *Annals of Tourism Research, 7*(3), 337–352.

Brush, T. H., & Artz, K. W. (1999). Toward a contingent resource-based theory: The impact of information asymmetry on the value of capabilities in veterinary medicine. *Strategic Management Journal, 20*(3), 223–250.

Carlson, R. (1997). *Experienced cognition.* New York, NY: Lawrence Erlbaum Associations.

Carù, A., & Cova, B. (2007). *Consuming experience.* London: Routledge.

Chen, J. S., Prebensen, N. K, & Uysal, M. S. (2016). Tourist's experience values and people interaction. *Advances in Hospitality and Leisure, 12,* 169–179.

Chon, K. S. (1989). Understanding recreational traveler's motivation, attitude and satisfaction. *The Tourist Review, 44*(1), 3–7.

Csikszentmihalyi, M. (1990). *Flow: The psychology of optimal experience.* New York, NY: Harper & Row.

Dodds, W. B, Monroe, K. B., & Grewal, D. (1991). Effect of price, brand, and store information on buyers' product evaluations. *Journal of Marketing Research, 28*(August), 307–319.

Goffman, E. (1959). *The presentation of self in everyday life.* Garden City, NY: Doubleday.

Grönroos, C. (2006). Adopting a service logic for marketing. *Marketing Theory, 6*(3), 317–333.

Grönroos, C., & Voima, P. (2013). Critical service logic: Making sense of value creation and co-creation. *Journal of the Academy of Marketing Science, 41*(2), 133–150.

Holbrook M. B. (2005). Customer value and autoethnography: Subjective personal introspection and the meanings of a photograph collection. *Journal of Business Research, 58*(1), 45–61.

Holbrook M. B., & Corfman K. P. (1985). Quality and value in the consumption experience: Phaedrus rides again. In J. Jacoby & J. Olson (Eds.), *Perceived quality* (pp. 31–57). Lexington, MA: Lexington Books.

Larsen, S. (2007). Aspects of a psychology of the tourist experience. *Scandinavian Journal of Hospitality and Tourism, 7*(1), 7–18.

Lusch, F., & Vargo, S. (2006). *The service-dominant logic of marketing: Dialog, debate and directions.* New York, NY: M. E. Sharpe.

Mannell, R. C., & Iso-Ahola, S. E. (1987). Psychological nature of leisure and tourism experience. *Annals of Tourism Research, 14*(3), 314–331.

Mehrabian, A., & Russell, J. A. (1974). *An approach to environmental psychology.* Cambridge, MA: Massachusetts Institute of Psychology.

Mossberg, L. (2007). A marketing approach to the tourist experience. *Scandinavian Journal of Hospitality and Tourism, 7*(1), 59–74.

Noe, F. P., Uysal, M., & Magnini, V. P. (2010). *Tourist customer service satisfaction: An encounter approach.* New York, NY: Routledge.

Pine, J., & Gilmore, J. H. (1999). *The experience economy: Work is theatre and every business a stage.* Boston, MA: Harvard Business School Press.

Prahalad, C. K., & Ramaswamy, V. (2004). Co-creation experiences: The next practice in value creation. *Journal of Interactive Marketing, 18*(3), 5–14.

Prebensen, N. K., & Foss, L. (2011). Coping and co-creating in tourist experiences. *International Journal of Tourism Research, 13*(1), 54–67.

Prebensen, N. K., Kim, H. L., & Uysal, M. (2016). Cocreation as moderator between the experience value and satisfaction relationship. *Journal of Travel Research, 55*(7), 934–945.

Prebensen, N. K., & Rosengren, S. (2016). Experience value as a function of hedonic and utilitarian dominant services. *International Journal of Contemporary Hospitality Management, 28*(1), 113–135.

Prebensen, N. K., Vittersø, J., & Dahl, T. (2013). Value co-creation: Significance of tourist resources. *Annals of Tourism Research, 42*(July), 240–261.

Prebensen, N. K., Woo, E., Chen, J., & Uysal, M. (2014). Motivation and involvement as antecedents of the perceived value of the destination experience. *Journal of Travel Research, 5*(2), 253–264.

Prebensen, N. K., Woo, E., & Uysal, M. (2014). Experience value: Antecedents and consequences. *Current Issues in Tourism, 17*(10), 910–928.

Pride, W., & O. Ferrell (2000) *Marketing: Concepts and strategies.* Boston, MA: Houghton Mifflin Company.

Ramirez, R. (1999). Value co-production: Intellectual origins and implications for practice and research. *Strategic Management Journal, 20*(1), 49–65.

Rathmell, J. M. (1966). What is meant by services? *The Journal of Marketing,* 30(4), 32–36.

Sandström, S., Edvardsson, B., Kristensson, P., & Magnusson, P. (2008). Value in use through service experience. *Managing Service Quality: An International Journal, 18*(2), 112–126.

Schneider, B., & Bowen, D. E. (2010). Winning the service game. In *Handbook of service science* (pp. 31–59). Boston, MA: Harvard Business School Press.

Shaw, C., & Ivens, J. (2002). *Building great customer experiences.* New York, NY: Palgrave MacMillan.

Silkapit, P., & Fisk, G. D. (1985). "Participatizing" the service process: A theoretical framework. In T. M. Bloch, G. D. Upah, & V. A. Zeithaml (Eds.), *Services marketing in a changing environment* (pp. 117–121). Chicago, IL: American Marketing.

Smith, M. (2003). Holistic holidays: Tourism and the reconciliation of body, mind and spirit. *Tourism Recreation Research, 28*(1), 103–108.

Toffler, A. (1980). *The third wave.* New York, NY: Bantam Books.

Uriely, N. (2005). The tourist experience: Conceptual developments. *Annals of Tourism Research, 32*(1), 199–216.

Vargo, S. L., & Lusch, R. F. (2004). Evolving to a new dominant logic for marketing. *Journal of Marketing, 68*, 1–17.

Vargo, S. L., & Lusch, R. F. (2006). Service-dominant logic: What it is, what it is not and what it might be. In R. F. Lusch & S. L. Vargo (Eds.), *The service-dominant logic of marketing: Dialog, debate and directions* (pp. 43–56). Armonk, NY: M. E. Sharpe.

Vargo, S. L., & Lusch, R. F. (2008). Service-dominant logic: Continuing the evolution. *Journal of the Academy of Marketing Science, 36*(1), 1–10.

Wakefield, K. L., & Blodgett, J. G. (1996). The effect of the servicescape on customers' behavioral intentions in leisure service settings. *Journal of Services Marketing, 10*(6), 45–61.

Walls, A., Okumus, F., Wang, Y., & Kwun, D. J. W. (2011). Understanding the consumer experience: An exploratory study of luxury hotels. *Journal of Hospitality Marketing & Management, 20*(2), 166–197.

# 2 Creating emotional platforms

*Sandra Gountas*

## Introduction

Emotions play an important role in tourism experiences, starting with the very motivation for travel which is motivated by myriad conditions (Correia & do Valle, 2007). Many travel experiences are propelled by the need to escape, to relax, regain our self-identity, to enhance personal relationships, and perhaps reconnect with loved ones when the daily grind has made us forget to nurture meaningful relationships in our lives. Sometimes, we need to relieve stress accumulated at work, to recharge and rediscover ourselves through new experiences. Whatever the motive, the common life formula of preoccupation with work and familial responsibilities for the majority of the year interspersed with a few weeks free time (if we're lucky) creates a highly emotive platform from which our travel experiences begin. This is complicated further by most trips being taken with significant others whose satisfactions and happiness are also our concern. Planning a holiday is not an easy task, involving complex decision processes that evolve over time and include emotion and fantasy which departs from rational models of decision making (Decrop & Snelders, 2004). The consumption of many services such as leisure and tourism is funded by discretionary income. In this case, the associated act of consumption may be more highly charged with affective connotation than in the consumption of more staple products. Often, we have a situation where we are desperate to satisfy our own needs and those of others, and a "responsibility" to select travel experiences that will successfully meet a range of needs, tastes and wishes. However, many of us do this annually or more frequently, often planning far in advance of the event given the combination of needs, expectations, personalities, and so forth.

The complexity of tourism motivations are often categorised as push and pull factors. The push motivations are mostly related to personal, internal needs including those related to social interaction, while pull factors are more associated with external, cognitive factors such as destination attributes, and so on (Yoon & Uysal, 2005). Emotions are present in both push and pull situations. Most of us can relate to the notion that we are pushed by our own emotional state to take actions and decisions. Also, we plan tourism experiences in the hope of creating positive emotions. We may daydream about our forthcoming holidays a long time in advance and these episodes are assisted by the pull of promotional messages, perhaps seeking destination information, following blogs and more to the extent that our expectations are emotionally charged and may be very difficult to fulfil.

The theories of emotion that focus only on the internal and individual reactions to external stimuli do not present sufficient understanding of the processes that result in emotions. Although the cognitive, affective and physiological components of emotion are undeniably important, we should also consider that the social psychological approach as emotional functioning would always be partly due to social psychological considerations (Parkinson, 1996). Emotions arise negatively or positively according to the particular situation and our involvement level with the individual or group with whom we are interacting. Involvement level is a key variable, it is reasonable to suggest that family and close friends are often the cause of the most intense pleasure and pain that most will experience in the gamut of human emotions. As previously mentioned, close family and friends are often critical to our tourism decisions and enjoyment. Given the findings of a number of researchers it is surprising that relatively little attention is given to the social aspects of emotions (Parkinson, 1996). Social causes of emotions are likely to be particularly important in services marketing with many services taken with, and around other people. Contact with other people, in services, has been discussed in terms of affect and involvement (Price, Arnould, & Tierney, 1999). The concepts of affect and involvement are an inherent part of the individual's appraisal of satisfaction. Since participating in tourism services often involves risk and sacrifice (time, money, personal and social involvement) they can be considered a high-involvement, highly affective experience.

As most service experiences take place around and/or with other people, and involve interaction with the organisation's front stage person, it is essential to consider the social element in services marketing. In tourism experiences, we share our emotions with others who are part of each discrete experience, whether close, significant participants or complete strangers. Further to this, emotions derived by any given tourism experience may be recalled and recounted far beyond the time of the actual experience and, as a result, are dynamic (Lopez, Ruiz-de-Maya, & Warlop, 2014). Emotions experienced in the co-creation of tourism experiences may intensify, dilute, change direction or dissipate over time (Prebensen & Foss, 2011). Undoubtedly, they will influence our behaviour during the experience, our evaluation of the experience, and our intention to repurchase or recommend to others.

## Customer interaction with tourism service providers

The concept of co-creation is important in tourism services because they are often of a high-involvement nature. In co-creating a tourism service the customer may experience greater satisfaction and be able to more clearly articulate needs and desires in a way that enables the service provider to successfully fulfil the service promise. In co-creating tourism services, the customer may experience greater satisfaction, happiness, a heightened sense of personal achievement when things go well and also greater disappointment when problems occur (Heidenreich, Wittkowski, Handrich, & Falk, 2014). Co-creation may exist on the basis of one customer to one service provider but in complex services, such as tourism, the sum of the experience for both customers to service providers is more likely to be a many to many situation. "Many to many" situations require that all actors collaborate to create value for themselves and the others in a given network (Pinho, Beirão, Patrício, & Fisk, 2014).

Picture a bus full of cruise passengers participating in a shore excursion. Co-creation and cooperation is required from the start to the end of the process if the majority are to enjoy the day. A typical cruise excursion usually starts at a given meeting point where all participants are expected to arrive on time, announce themselves, collect a name badge from cruise personnel, wait to be asked to proceed out of the ship, escorted by another cruise staff, be checked at security, possibly go through immigration, find the correct bus, meet the tour guide, bus driver and cruise company escorts, negotiate with other passengers to secure a well-located seat. This represents many to many interactions within a very short time and the excursion has not even really started in the client's mind. This very process may set a positive collective mood or a negative one depending on how smoothly it is executed. Next, the tour guide will normally try to foster a positive mood and eager anticipation for the day to come. They need to ascertain the passengers' requirements, if they thirst for deeper knowledge of the location, special needs, patiently answer questions and respond appropriately. At some point, a destination will be reached and the passengers guided en masse to view the sights. The passengers may interact with local people keen to sell souvenirs, pose for photos, and argue about tips and more. Often time is limited before it's on to the next location, and on returning to the bus at the agreed time, most often someone is late and causes irritation to the other more compliant participants. This process may be repeated several times through the day, be further complicated by food, beverage, bathroom and shopping stops all aimed at providing equal levels of satisfaction for all. Consider the possible emotions that may emerge, change and subside endlessly throughout the day, multiplied by the number of actors involved. The single experience comprises myriad many to many interactions, each with potential to ruin the experience for any individual including the service providers involved and is only one of many that will happen during the course of a cruise or other style of holiday. This example illustrates the very delicate management required for successful co-creation. Every single interaction may make or break the day.

Much research focuses on emotions in service interactions and co-creation. Clearly, it would be useful if a service provider understands how emotional responses are created and the level of impact that a particular mood state had on the consumers' evaluation of the service received. Tracing the development of emotions and their influence on attitudes towards a service/product would contribute towards a solid foundation of understanding consumers' responses. In tourism service provision, it would be useful to understand the influence of actors' positive or negative emotions on the consumer and staff, and to develop strategies to anticipate and respond to mood states as part of the normal service process and in service recovery policy. Two very important concepts to consider are emotional contagion and emotional labour. Research suggests that emotional contagion takes place before mimicry and results in an emotional display (Verbeke, 1997). This reinforces the view that the social component of emotional development exists, is important and has consequences for all forms of human interaction.

Understanding the occurrence and influence of emotional contagion during service delivery is important. This is congruent with Dube and Menon's (2000) suggestion that the mimicry of expression and emotions is a two-way interactive process between the service provider and consumer. As mentioned, in the cruise shore excursion example, interactions are not confined to one actor and another. As people often travel in self-selected and random groups there will always be "many to many" interactions within tourism service provision.

Studying the effects of emotional contagion has a value for practitioners as appropriate service provider responses lead to greater consumer satisfaction than inappropriate responses (Dube & Menon, 2000). Hatfield, Cacioppo, and Rapson (1994) developed an emotional contagion hypothesis, which attempts to explain how emotions transfer through nonverbal cues. The authors suggest that there are psychophysiological processes that cause facial reactions that transmit emotions from one person to another or others, and refer to this process as an "emotional convergence". Individual differences will affect an individual's ability to "infect" others with emotions or to be "infected". This suggests that a level of trust or belief is needed for the emotion to be perceived as genuine or sincere and thus mimicked. In addition, women are more susceptible to emotional contagion than men which may be more due to socialisation than biological differences, but is worthy of consideration since there tends to be more women employed in service industries than men (Hochschild, 1983).

Giving and receiving emotions are not always straightforward (Bolton & Boyd, 2003). The ability to "infect" others, or be "infected" with emotions carries certain conditions. The major implications for tourism services and emotional contagion are:

1   The better we understand ourselves – how we think, feel and behave – the better the decisions we make about our lives. (This fits with the concept of consumer satisfaction as a contributing factor to life satisfaction posited by Fournier and Mick [1999] and Neal, Sirgy, and Uysal [1999].)

2   An understanding of the power and ubiquity of (emotional) contagion helps us correctly assess the factors that shape social interactions, allowing us better to deal with those interactions. (Personal power, manipulation of one's own feelings and the feelings of others in service industries is a key to the methods of development and delivery of service products [Hatfield et. al., 1994].)

3   It is necessary for people to "feel themselves into" others' lives if they are to truly understand them. (Hochschild [1983] discussed the way in which Delta airline crew were encouraged to visualise the passengers' attitudes, fears and problems in order to maintain a positive approach.) However, it is unlikely that all service providers have the experience, skills and temperament to maintain empathy for clients from very different backgrounds to their own (Hatfield et. al., 1994).

4   Knowledge of the power of contagion gives us a realistic perception as to how much we can expect to influence social situations. (If the service provider is aware of his or her own power and able to use it, they may reduce their own dissonance or longer term feelings of inadequacy when dealing with "difficult" clients.)

5   Knowledge of the power of contagion reminds us not to take more than we can cope with (Hatfield et. al., 1994). This may be very difficult to control in many tourism services where work is often seasonal, may exceed "normal" working hours and the providers may be young and possibly from poorer countries where the financial imperative encourages them to tolerate difficult working conditions.

Service employees are frequently expected to "perform" to scripts and standards determined by their employer which may not demonstrate knowledge and understanding of such concepts. Such standards often entail remaining cheerful, helpful and masking any outward sign of fatigue, all of which is very hard to achieve. Hatfield et al. (1994) refer to an "awkward" service incident involving themselves, a service provider and an "angry" client. The authors noticed the awkward and wooden stance of the customers whilst maintaining fake, pleasant smiles. This infers that attempts at masking emotions may be unsuccessful. The consumers, observed by Hatfield et al. (1994) were trying hard to control their facial expressions, without much success, as they still conveyed their discomfort through their body posture. This presents a conflict of interests for organisations and their service providers as service providers' emotion management may be essential to minimise the level of "transmutation of an emotion system" by the organisation (Hochschild, 1983). Yet it appears that attempts to fake emotions will not be successful, as the deception will be revealed implying that, although service providers are required to 'manage' their emotions, there will be limited success with such attempts.

Research in the airline industry has revealed four types of emotional management which are: "pecuniary management", an instrumental approach based on purely commercially driven feeling rules; "prescriptive management" which may be grounded in altruistic, status or instrumental motivations and is based on professional or organisational feeling rules; "presentational management" with the associated motivations being ontologically, security, or conformity driven and based on socially prescribed feeling rules; and "philanthropic management" which is motivated by the desire to present a gift to the recipient of the interaction and based on socially prescribed feeling rules (Bolton & Boyd, 2003). One would expect that only the "presentational" and "philanthropic" styles of emotion management would successfully allow positive emotional contagion to occur as these two styles are more likely to be underpinned by sincere motives. The findings of this particular study indicated that the airline's cabin crews perform all four types of emotion management and sometimes genuinely empathise with a passenger resulting in the sincere "presentational" and "philanthropic" emotion management (Bolton & Boyd, 2003).

Displays of emotions tend to reflect the current social construction of what appropriate display behaviour actually is, and what is deemed appropriate varies in different contexts (Fineman, 1993, p. 19). The author recalls travelling on a night flight and finding that she had been allocated a non-reclining seat even though she had requested leg room. Politely mentioning the situation to a flight attendant and asking for help resulted in the flight attendant giggling and covering their mouth with their hand. Fortunately, the author understood that this response was culturally acceptable to the flight attendant and did not infer lack of sympathy. However, the giggles could have resulted in a very angry response and, given the late hour and many tired and irritated passengers on board, resulted in an emotional contagion "rage" incident.

From the service provider's perspective, appropriate management of emotional displays is an imperative concurrent with the requirement that these displays appear to be authentic, genuine or sincere (Hochschild, 1983; Leidner, 1993; Bolton & Boyd, 2003). Customers do express a preference for receiving a "sincere" display from service providers (Grandey, 2003; Lynch, 1992; Bitner, Booms, & Tetreault, 1990; Hochschild, 1983). Service staff are generally required to manage their emotions as part of service delivery and most organisations are explicit about this requirement conceptualised as emotional labour. Furthermore, employees engaged in emotional labour are expected to appear genuine and this may result in acting to achieve the desired impression (Hochschild, 1983). In tourism services, there is often a blurred divide between work and personal life, where personal time is very connected to work life, such as the case of adventure tour guides (Carnicelli-Filho, 2013). This example may be applied to many tourism service roles particularly in situations where the service provider is living and working away from 'home' which is often the case. Take the example of a holiday representative living and working in a "foreign" location. Away from home, family and friends, new relationships with work colleagues are formed to replace those left behind. Depending on the location of the tourism service, the holiday representative may be living and working in a small geographical area, where there is no escape from clients, managers and other colleagues. This means that emotional performance and management are practised constantly. There may be little or no emotional downtime resulting in additional stress.

Many studies show negative consequences of emotional labour including job stress and a decrease in job satisfaction. However, emotional labour sometimes leads to greater job satisfaction and feelings of personal accomplishment with reduces negative impacts such as emotional exhaustion (Seery & Corrigall, 2009; Pugliesi, 1999). Work on emotional labour acknowledges that there are different aspects of emotions that comprise the variety of emotions used in work, including intensity, duration, surface acting and deep acting (Totterdell & Holman, 2003; Brotheridge & Grandey, 2002; Hochschild, 1983). "Service providers comply with expression norms or 'display rules' through surface acting, deep acting, and the expression of spontaneous and genuine emotion" (Ashforth & Humphrey, 1993). These displays are often manufactured in service interaction to comply with rules of appropriate behaviour and expression according to different situations and determined by management. There are many factors that affect desired impressions including service workers' personal characteristics, autonomy at work, and emotional exhaustion connected with the job role (Grandey, 2000; Wharton, 1993). Indeed, apparently conflicting emotions such as fear and pleasure can co-exist at the same time (Carnicelli-Filho, 2013). This is true for all actors in the service experience, customers and providers alike.

Unfortunately, negative emotions seem to be "caught" more easily and quickly than positive emotions in group situations. Customers may take courage from others' presence and be more critical and reactive in group situations than they might be alone. Such negative emotions are likely to escalate once a group is working together (Du, Fan, & Feng, 2014). Customers are also likely to catch unmanaged negative emotions displayed by the service providers (Carnicelli-Filho, 2013). All of this increases the difficulty level for service providers trying to calm and control a problem situation and has implications for management that will be discussed later.

Emotions often elicit a cognitive appraisal of the event which may provide a useful intervention the emotional state. For example, Arnould and Price (1993) found that participants in a white water rafting vacation resisted cognitive recall as they felt the magic was "best preserved if associated feelings and sensations are not examined too closely". It seems reasonable to suggest that clients adjust their cognitive evaluation of services consumption in order to avoid or minimise disappointments. A client may cognitively appraise a service situation, and choose to adjust/manipulate that assessment to avoid disappointment actively. In so doing, the client would choose to minimise or ignore aspects of the service delivery that fall short of expectations. In short, a deliberate attempt to keep "looking on the bright side". From the client's perspective, there is every reason to do this when we consider the sacrifice of time, money, dreams and the risks of service failure that is inherent in participating in many tourism services. Logically, such adaptive action must influence the level of overall satisfaction reported and it would be useful for tourism managers and providers to understand what behaviours from the service provider may elicit or contribute towards such a response. For example, does the perception of the service provider's sincerity positively contribute towards consumer satisfaction and associated variables? Conversely, will insincere displays of "pseudo-care" induce negative responses?

Although a positive, smiling disposition is often part of the service job and not always a true reflection of the service provider's mood state (Hochschild, 1983; Rafaeli & Sutton, 1987). However, as the concept of sincere and genuine behaviour does have an appeal for consumers (Bitner et al., 1990; Dubinsky, 1994; Lynch, 1992; Price et al., 1999) whether sincerity exists in the true sense may not be the point in question. Rather, whether the consumer believes that she or he has witnessed a "sincere" effort and if this makes any difference to the consumer's evaluative criteria may be salient (Hochschild, 1983). Such effort involves service providers' sensitive understanding of consumers' emotions. The emotional contagion hypothesis, which explores how emotions transfer through nonverbal cues (Hatfield, Caciopppo, & Rapson, 1994), is useful in understanding the effects of both sincere and insincere emotional displays in service interaction. The authors suggest that there are psycho-physiological processes that cause facial reactions that transmit emotions from one person to another or others, and refer to this process as an "emotional convergence". Emotion mimicry is more likely to occur when the interaction is between people who feel a bond, a connection or liking for each other. Therefore, a level of trust or belief is needed for displayed emotions to be perceived as genuine or sincere and thus mimicked. For conscious mimicry, the link between sincerity, emotional contagion, and service providers' emotions management display is particularly important to consider because, as mentioned previously, research has found that employees' "emotional displays are positively related to the customer affect and customer evaluation of the quality of service received" (Pugh, 2001, p. 1027).

Attempts to fake emotions are unlikely to be successful, as the deception will be apparent and conscious emotional contagion will not occur (Hennig-Thurau, Groth, Dwayne, & Gremler, 2006; Hatfield et al., 1994). Many authors consider genuine, sincere or authentic expression and effort in service provision an important element of consumer's service evaluation (Grayson, 1998; Mohr & Bitner, 1995; Bitner et al., 1990; Leidner, 1993; Hochschild, 1983). However, the routinisation of human interaction, in the form of script delivery, means that sincerity is compromised as it is surely impossible to "act" sincere even though such acting is a common requirement of service workers. This is part of the staged performance involving impression management. The notion of sincere service is inextricably linked with pleasing, quality service provision, as there is always an implicit requirement of service employees, in many services, to display positive emotions (Tsai, 2001).

Sincerity or authenticity of service provision is being questioned more frequently (Hennig-Thurau, 2006; Grandey, 2005; Grandey, Mattila, Fisk, & Sideman, 2002; Dubinsky, 1994; Lynch, 1992). Such questions may be a reflection of consumers' ever changing needs and demands and/or part of the marketers' search for ways to refine, improve and differentiate their service products. The value of authentic smiles' contribution to customer satisfaction has been tested with some mixed results (e.g. Hennig-Thurau, 2006; Grandey, 2005). Overall, authentic smiles have a positive impact on customer satisfaction but this depends somewhat on the context of the service and varies according to whether business is slow or fast at the moment of truth.

Research suggests that happy expressions perceived to be sincere elicit a more heuristic processing style than serious expressions and elicit trust and acceptance whereas expressions that are more sombre call for further cognition or evaluation (Ottati, Terkildsen, & Hubbard, 1997; Krull & Dill, 1998). Apparently sincere happy expressions are vital for many tourism services such as adventure guides, to engender confidence and trust in the service provider (Carnicello-Filho, 2013). Therefore, in the context of services marketing, it is possible that the perception of service provider happiness and sincerity will reinforce a positive correlation with satisfaction. A genuine display of emotions may moderate the relationship between displayed emotion and service quality perceptions (Pugh, 2001). If this is so, then perceived sincerity may have a value in terms of positive word of mouth, a relationship with company image and intention to repurchase.

Perceived insincerity in service provision has very practical consequences for the direct provider, which may affect the overall impression of the service received and the company providing it. A service display perceived to be insincere may subconsciously act as an assault on self-worth or value as an individual for both the provider and consumer. In addition to the personal level of suffering experienced by the service provider; "an emotionally exhausted person is less likely to be seen as sincerely warm and pleasant" (Grandey, 2003, p. 90). This may be something of a conundrum in tourism services that frequently force front line staff to work very long hours in difficult situations such as crowded airports during air traffic control strikes and other service failures. In tourism services, there are often times where customers experience intense emotions, but so do service providers. In general, people who are emotionally competent and intelligent will do better with coping themselves and in helping others to cope with difficulty (Delcourt, Gremler, van Riel, & van Birglen, 2016). The net effect of employing effective coping strategies is satisfaction for both customer and service provider. The well-trained, competent service provider.

The stress of acting (i.e. insincere display), as a service provider, has been widely recognised as a cause of emotional burnout or damage to personal well-being (Hennig-Thurau et al., 2006; Erickson & Wharton, 1997; Ashworth & Humphrey, 1993; Leidner, 1993). False displays may be detected and have a negative effect on consumer evaluation; insincerity has been noted to result in lower ratings being given to "guilty" staff in customer surveys (Grandey, 2003). There is possibly a greater cost to service providers, which is that inauthenticity may lead to depression (Erickson & Wharton, 1997). There are other practical considerations in that the service provider would be unlikely to satisfy a client's needs if they were to display or express insincerity or negativity. There may be tangible benefits of sincerity or authenticity for the service employee as research has shown that positively perceived displays in service providers results in higher rewards or "tips" (Pugh, 2001; Tsai, 2001; Tsai & Huang, 2002).

## Conclusion

So far, we have considered how tourists' motivations, expectations and personal circumstances affect their emotions during consumption. We have also considered the service provider's perspective and some of the issues in co-creating appropriate, positive emotions. The next question is: What can managers do to facilitate the best experience for all actors?

An optimum level of emotional interaction can be fostered in a number of ways as follows, not necessarily in order of importance.

- Manage expectations: Managers need to understand how expectations develop and avoid cynicism and complacency when considering customer's internal push factors. That way, the promotional pull can be developed to enhance customers' emotions and encourage co-creation of a realistic, positive experience. This means encouraging and guiding potential customers to contemplate their needs and desires and choose appropriate experiences to fulfil them.

- Consider the servicescape: Environmental conditions such as lighting, temperature, air quality, comfort, sounds and colours have a profound physiological effect on customers which creates and supports emotion states. Service providers are part of the servicescape and their personal appearance affects customers' assessment of the service provided and satisfaction levels with the experience and the company (Tu, Yeh, Gustin, Tsai, & Hu, 2011).
- Staff selection: Given the sensitive nature of tourists' motivation, the often difficult working conditions, and so forth, tourism providers are better if equipped with qualities such as empathy, resilience and stamina amongst others. The front line staff are the face of the organisation, a crucial part of the service "product". Yet the frontline providers are often the least qualified, lowest paid staff in organisations. Possibly, organisations who pay attention to staff are most likely to beat the competition.
- Staff training: Solid staff training can make or break the quality of service experienced by the customer. Going beyond service scripts and policies, frontline staff can be trained in emotional intelligence and empathy to help them "tune in" to their customers, learn how to spot potential emotional disasters early and disarm them, understand logistics in dealing with big issues such as group emotional contagion, and so on, will increase staff and customer satisfaction and ultimately have positive consequences such as greater profitability for firms.

As mentioned at the beginning of this chapter, the subject of emotions continues to provide fascinating study material and will do so into the future. Although, it is clear that emotions will continue to delight and frustrate us as service providers and customers, tourism experiences would be worthless without them!

## References

Arnould, E., & Price, L. (1993). River magic: Extraordinary experience and the extended service encounter. *Journal of Consumer Research, 20*, 24–46.
Ashforth, E. B., & Humphrey, R. H. (1993). Emotional labour in service roles: The influence of identity. *The Academy of Management Review, 18*, 88–111.
Bitner, M. J., Booms, B. H., & Tetreault, M. S. (1990). The service encounter: Diagnosing favourable and unfavourable incidents. *Journal of Marketing, 54*, 71–84.
Bolton, C. S., & Boyd, C. (2003). Trolley dolly or skilled emotion manager? Moving on from Hochschild's Managed Heart. *Work, Employment and Society, 17*, 289–308.
Brotheridge, C. M., & Grandey, A. A. (2002). Emotional labor and burnout: Comparing two perspectives of "people work". *Journal of Vocational Behavior, 60*, 17–39.
Carnicielli-Filho, S. (2013). The emotional lives of adventure guides. *Annals of Tourism Research, 43*, 192–209.
Correia, A., & do Valle, P. O. (2007). Why people travel to exotic places. *International Journal of Culture, Tourism and Hospitality Research, 1*, 45–61.

20    *Sandra Gountas*

Decrop, A., & Snelders, D. (2004). Planning the summer vacation. *Annals of Tourism Research, 31*, 1008–1030.

Delcourt, C., Gremler, D. D., van Riel, A. C., & van Birgelen, M. J. (2016). Employee emotional competence construct conceptualization and validation of a customer-based measure. *Journal of Service Research, 19*(1), 72–87.

Du, J., Fan, X., & Feng, T. (2014). Group emotional contagion and complaint intentions in group service failure: The role of group size and group familiarity. *Journal of Service Research, 17*, 326–338.

Dube, L., & Menon, K. (2000). Multiple roles of consumption emotions in post-purchase satisfaction with extended service transactions. *International Journal of Service Industry Management, 11*, 287–304.

Dubinsky, A. J. (1994). What Marketers can learn from the Tin Man. *Journal of Service Marketing, 8*(2), 36–45.

Erickson, R. J., & Wharton, A. S. (1997). Inauthenticity and depression: Assessing the consequences of interactive service work. *Work and Occupations, 24*, 188–214.

Fineman, S. (1993). Organizations as emotional arenas. In Fineman, S. (Ed.), *Emotion in organisations*. London: Sage.

Fournier, S., & Mick, D. G., (1999). Rediscovering satisfaction. *Journal of Marketing, 63*, 5–23.

Grandey, A. A. (2000). Emotional regulation in the workplace: A new way to conceptualize emotional labor. *Journal of Occupational Health Psychology, 5*(1), 95.

Grandey, A. A. (2003). When "the show must go on": Surface acting and deep acting as determinants of emotional exhaustion and peer-rated service delivery. *Academy of Management Journal, 46*, 86–96.

Grandey, A. A., Fisk, G. M., Mattila, A. S., Jansen, K. J., & Sideman, L. A. (2005). Is "service with a smile" enough? Authenticity of positive displays during service encounters. *Organizational Behaviour and Human Decision Processes, 96*, 8–55.

Grandey, A. A., Mattila, A. S., Fisk, G. M., & Sideman, L. A. (2002). *Is that smile for real? Authenticity of positive displays during service encounters.* Academy of Management, Denver Colorado.

Grayson, K. (1998). Customer responses to emotional labour in discrete and relational service exchange. *International Journal of Service Industry Management, 9*(2), 126–154.

Hatfield, E., Cacioppo, J. T., & Rapson, R. L. (1994). *Emotional contagion.* Cambridge, MA: Cambridge University Press.

Heidenreich, S., Wittkowski, K., Handrich, M., & Falk, T. (2014). The dark side of customer co-creation: Exploring the consequences of failed co-created services. *Journal of the Academy of Marketing Science, 43*, 279–296.

Hennig-Thurau, T., Groth, M., Dwayne, M. P., & Gremler, D. (2006). Are all smiles created equal? How emotional contagion and emotional labor affect service relationships. *Journal of Marketing, 70*, 58–73.

Hochschild, A. R. (1983). *The managed heart: Commercialization of human feeling.* Berkeley, CA: University of California Press.

Krull, D. S., & Dill, J. C. (1998). Do smiles elicit more inferences than do frowns? The effect of emotional valence on a production of spontaneous inferences. *Personality and Social Psychology Bulletin, 24*, 289–300.

Leidner, R. (1993). *Fast food, fast talk: Service work and routinization of everyday life.* Berkeley, CA: University of California.

Lopez, I., Ruiz-de-Maya, S., & Warlop, L. (2014). When sharing consumption emotions with strangers is more satisfying than sharing them with friends. *Journal of Service Research 17*, 475–488.

Lynch, J. (1992). Hear it from the heart. *Managing Service Quality*, November, 379–382.

Mohr, A. L., & Bitner, M. J. (1995). The role of employee effort in satisfaction with service transactions. *Journal of Business Research, 32*, 239–252.

Neal, D. J., Sirgy, M. J., & Uysal, M. (1999). The role of satisfaction with leisure travel/ tourism services and experience in satisfaction with leisure life and overall life. *Journal of Business Research, 44*, 153–163.

Ottati, V., Terkildsen, N., & Hubbard, C. (1997). Happy faces elicit heuristic processing in a televised impression formation task: A cognitive tuning account. *Personality and Social Psychology Bulletin, 23*(11), 1144–1156.

Parkinson, B. (1996). Emotions are social. *British Psychological Society, 87*, 663–684.

Pinho, N., Beirão, G., Patrício, L., & Fisk, R. P. (2014). Understanding value co-creation in complex services with many actors. *Journal of Service Management, 25*, 470–493.

Prebensen, N. K., & Foss, L. (2011). Coping and co-creating in tourist experiences. *International Journal of Tourism Research, 13*, 54–67.

Price, L., Arnould, E., & Tierney, P. (1999). Going to extremes: Managing service encounters and assessing provider performance. In J. Bateson & Douglas K. Hoffman (Eds.), *Managing Services Marketing*. Orlando, FL: Dryden Press, 249–266.

Pugh, D. S. (2001). Service with a smile: Emotional contagion in the service encounter. *Academy of Management Journal, 44*, 1018–1927.

Pugliesi, K. (1999). The consequences of emotional labor: effects on work stress, job satisfaction and well being. *Motivation and Emotion, 23*, 125–154.

Rafaeli, A., & Sutton, R. I. (1987). Expression of emotion as part of the work role. *Academy of Management Review, 12*, 23–37.

Seery, B. L, & Corrigall, E. A. (2009). Emotional labor: Links to work attitudes and emotional exhaustion. *Journal of Managerial Psychology, 24*, 797–813.

Totterdell, P., & Holman, D. (2003). Emotion regulation in customer service roles: Testing a model of emotional labor. *Journal of Occupational Health Psychology, 8*, 55–73.

Tsai, W. C. (2001). Determinants and consequences of employee displayed positive emotions. *Journal of Management, 27*, 497–510.

Tsai, W. C., & Huang, Y. M. (2002). Mechanisms linking employee affective delivery and customer behavioural intentions. *Journal of Applied Psychology, 87*, 1001–1008.

Tu, Y.T., Yeh, R., Gustin, L., Tsai, H., & Hu, S. M. (2011). Effects of hotel employees' uniform on customers' perceptions of employee performance and company image. *Journal of Travel and Tourism Research, 11*(1), 105–116.

Verbeke, W. (1997). Individual differences in emotional contagion of salespersons: Its effect on performance and burnout. *Psychology and Marketing, 14*, 617–636.

Wharton, A. S. (1993). The affective consequences of service work: Managing emotions on the job. *Work and Occupations, 20*, 205–232.

Yoon, Y., & Uysal, M. (2005). An examination of the effects of motivation and satisfaction on destination loyalty: A structural model. *Tourism Management, 26*, 45–56.

# 3 Designing and managing co-creative processes in a holiday environment
## The case of French Northern Alpine ski resorts

*Isabelle Frochot and Dominique Kreziak*

## Introduction

The aim of this chapter is to investigate the role of destinations and consumers in the co-construction process of the tourist experience. Whilst tourists' destinations offer a range of services, the overall value of the experience also involves consumers actively co-constructing their experience with this destination. Consumers deciding their choice, their holiday set-up and their behaviour when at the destination play a crucial role in developing a value out of their holiday. The destination is always present in this co-creation process with various degrees of intervention. Not only do visitors come with pre-formed images of the resort but they also develop personal strategies (actively using, choosing not to use, modifying and combining various components) aimed to create a satisfactory holiday.

Before looking at the co-creation dynamics, in the first instance it is essential to address the type of experience sought by tourists, looking at their deep need for escape but also at their push and pull motivations. This chapter investigates the experience within ski resorts but the notion of tourist destination will be taken broadly to encompass both elements of servicescape design that can be developed by service providers (design within private businesses such as restaurants and accommodation), and the more general natural and built mountain resources. The destination will be taken as a global value facilitator whose role is to design an environment conducive to satisfactory experience.

The co-construction process will be illustrated by evidence from consumer qualitative research conducted in several resorts and over different years of data collection. The outcome of the chapter will be to understand how mountain destinations can, through their design and planning strategies, meet consumers' expectations and engage a process of co-construction contributing to a successful experience.

## Background: the context of the ski industry in the French Northern Alps

Every winter, on average 7 million holidaymakers come to the French ski resorts, which represents 56 million day skiers and 44 million nights of winter in the

Northern Alps (SMBT, 2015). Unlike Northern American resorts, French resorts are the result of a complex mix of public and private management. The land is either public or private, the ski operators are often the result of a public service delegation contract, the accommodation is usually privately owned (large operators like Club Med or a multitude of owners) and the tourist offices are publicly funded but they can also develop their own direct booking systems. As a result, the governance of those resorts is complex since there is not one director that can impose a common drive. The tourist office, the resort DMO, directs the marketing strategy of the resort and its general management, but it has no ownership of the majority of all the private stakeholders. When holidaymakers reach the resort, they face a multitude of stakeholders and proposition of activities similar to most tourists' products.

However, in a ski resort context, there is a strong site unity, tourists are not mobile (they rarely leave the resort during their stay), and the major activity is skiing. Most consumers are unaware of the governance of those resorts and will often refer to "the resort" as they probably would for an integrated and privately owned resort. In recent years, the French ski industry has had to face a declining demand from the French consumers. In order to achieve high occupancy rates, resorts have turned to Northern European visitors such as Norwegian, Dutch, German and British visitors. Lately, the BRIC markets have become of interest to the French skiing industry on top of Middle-Eastern consumers.

In regard to the French market, the demand is also changing towards less skiing practice per day: contemporary tourists ski on average no more than 4 hours a day. While in the 1980s the demand was for all day skiing, contemporary tourists are keener to undertake intense skiing but intermediated with nice lunch breaks on the altitude cafés and other activities. In consequence, resorts have heavily invested in spa facilities and more recently they have developed vast water parks devoted as much to swimming as fun for all the family. Activities outside the main downhill activities have also developed, such as snow shoeing, zip lines, sledging, ski touring, and so forth. All those evolutions mean that ski resorts are facing an increasing diverse demand. On the ski-front, large investments have been devoted to snow cannons to guarantee snow coverage and even more importantly to ski lifts' modernisation. The improvements in ski lifts mean that consumers experience less queuing and thereby maximise their skiing time. Most high-altitude resorts have been built fairly recently in the 1960s and 1970s and cannot claim to have real authentic anchorage. However, beyond all the modernity and technology embedded in those resorts, a recent study showed that the size of the ski area is mentioned by half of the visitors as the prime factor of, but the landscapes come just after (37%) and the resort atmosphere is also mentioned by 28% of tourists (SMBT, 2015). This study also shows that the prime factor of dissatisfaction is the resort architecture, the traveling time (both 16%), the transport within resorts (15%), lack of non-ski activities (14%) and average après-ski (12%).

If the ski industry in the Northern French Alps is still successful, it has reached a turning point where it needs to understand how to adapt to the evolving consumer demand, how contemporary experienced tourists actively take a role in the construction of their holiday and how they can manage some elements of the service delivery to make this whole process even more successful.

## Literature review

### *The motivations in tourism consumption*

Motivations in tourism have always been conceived as two sides of a same coin: some motivations are to be found in the expectations of the experience (push factors) and others are attached to the characteristics of the destinations visited (pull factors).

Among the prime motivations repetitively identified in tourism studies (push factors), the need to escape always stands out as the prime motivator. This need has to be found in individuals' living conditions. Dann (1977) saw tourism as anomic: tourism consumption was seen as a way to escape from a meaningless life and society. Dann (1977) also perceived tourism consumption as an ego-enhancement activity that would allow individuals to compensate from the status deprivation they could experience in daily lives. Krippendorf (1999) even ascertained that holidays represented contemporary societies' safety valve, absorbing individuals' stress and frustrations with their daily lives. In other words, industrialisation caused both the reasons and the means for mass tourism to take place. It is commonly recognised that tourism consumption is first and foremost defined in opposition to daily stresses and frustrations (urban environments leading to overcrowding, pollution, noise, queuing, as much as the frustrations with contemporary working environments and the lack of quality family time). This differentiation from everyday life is often seen as common sense but it does have, however, many managerial implications in terms of resorts' development and the general tourism offer conceptualisation. It has perhaps been underestimated as a key player in the conception of tourism and is an element that has implications at various levels of the tourism offer, even the most minor ones.

At the same time, when on holidays, twenty-first-century consumers are, to a large extent, unable to leave their comfort completely. As a result, the whole tourism spectrum evolves between consumers who seek to remain in an environment close to home (at least in concept) and on the other end "true travellers" who will always seek real adventure and disconnection (Cohen, 2003; Plog, 2001). For ski destinations, consumers come mostly from urban areas and are in need for an extraordinary activity within a modern context. Hence, for tourism destinations it implies that the service delivery needs to integrate both this strong need for escape but, in most cases, respect the codes that shape contemporary demand.

Beyond the notion of escape, researchers have investigated in more details the dimensions of both push and pull factors. Crompton (1979) identified that the push factors included escape, self-discovery, rest and relaxation, prestige, challenge, adventure, excitement, family togetherness, and health and fitness. The pull factors were listed as encountering scenic beauty, historical areas, cultural attractions and events, sporting events, beaches, parks, recreation facilities, and shopping.

What helps researchers clarifying how both push and pull factors can be understood, from tourists' individual viewpoints, are motivational segmentation studies. Several authors have provided lists of motivations and in their broad lines, tourists' motivations can be seen as encompassing the need to escape and relax, to socialise (within one's family, with friends, other tourists or locals), to develop one's knowledge (culture) and capabilities (skills whether it relates to sport or other activities) (Crompton, 1979; Krippendorf, 1999). Among the segmentation techniques used, benefit segmentation, if benefits are defined on a psychological basis, provides some interesting results (Frochot & Morrison, 2000). Perhaps one element that is missing from these studies is the link between those motivations and the actual experience sought, and more importantly how service quality could find its place in this process: "One problem however with tourist services is that there is a rather unclear relationship between the objects and services purchased (ice creams, flights to Majorca, etc.) and a good holiday experience" (Urry, 1990, p. 23).

In that process, the role of consumers has been identified: "Since expected benefits are the outcomes of the visit to a park, we would expect visitor behaviour to be consistent with those benefits. Behaviour would reflect the visitor's way of organising the components of the setting the visitor controls to achieve those benefits" (McCool & Reilly, 1993, p. 4). Recently, the role of consumers in that process has been exemplified through the work produced on co-construction. The introductory chapter to this book provides all the theoretical framework to the concept of co-creation that will not be restated in this chapter. In summary, the vision of this chapter's authors is to consider that co-construction brings the foundations to understand how consumers interact, consciously or unconsciously, with the elements provided in order to construct their own holidays. Motivations play a driving force that gives the general direction to that process: depending on the types of motivations sought, different kind of experiences will be sought and supported by individual co-construction processes. In order to analyse fully those co-construction processes, it appears essential to study visitors while at the destination.

### *In situ experience: the need to follow and assess how consumers evolve along their holiday*

Experience has been the object of intense academic research, especially with the studies produced by Holbrook and Hirschman in 1982 and more recently with Pine and Gilmore's work on the experience economy (1999). Since then, researchers have been interested in the specificities of experiential consumption in various domains but tourism and leisure have provided a very interesting context in which experiences could be investigated. Indeed, tourism consumption provides a context whereby services are purchases for non-functional purposes, where hedonism is essential and where rationality is often replaced by more emotionally based and spontaneous processes.

Whilst experiential marketing considers that experiences need to be investigated, before, during and after consumption (Arnould & Price, 1993), most existing studies have investigated the experience within post-purchase studies that evaluate experiences' characteristics and evaluation after the purchase has taken place.

The authors of this chapter argue that more efforts should be conducted on analysing what takes place during the experience itself. Tourism holidays represent experiences that take place over a long period of time (at least one week), are longed for, and prepared several months in advance. They represent large parentheses where people clearly get away from their daily lives. The distance from home, the change of habits and activities practised, the simple change of scene, all mean that the tourist experience is unique. Satisfaction is often assessed after the holiday through various evaluations, often on a quantitative basis. Links to memories and loyalty have been identified; however what actually takes place during the holiday is of a different nature to post-purchase studies and deserves more attention.

Studying the experience is also precious when one aims to understand co-construction strategies that can only be fully understood when looking at how tourists construct their own holidays. It is understood that co-construction takes place right from the decision process and long after the holiday (satisfaction re-negotiation and memories' construction), but it is the object of this chapter to concentrate on what happens during the experience itself.

## Methodology

Over the years the two researchers have tremendously evolved in their research techniques. In their previous work undertaken in quantitative analysis, the researchers had experienced frustrations of not being able to reach consumers at the heart of their experience. Quantitative research was very useful but could not allow for a detailed analysis of the processes at stake during the experience. It was also questionable whether the researchers collected representative information. Indeed, a tourist would always answer a question, rank elements given, rate services, and so forth, but the researchers were not certain that those evaluations were truly representative of the real processes at stake when tourists experience holidays.

At the time, very little research had been conducted during the experience, so the researchers decided to use qualitative methods (focus groups in a project in 2006) that would be conducted during tourists' holidays. The complexities of the logistics in organising such groups moved the researchers to consider directly interviewing tourists in 2009, still during their holidays. Interviewing in situ proved to be very rich and efficient (only 10% of the tourists approached declined answering). Those interviews lasted on average 20 to 30 minutes and always took place towards the end of the week. This approach was somehow still frustrating as the researchers felt that they only grasped a global picture, summarising the whole stay and necessarily erasing a lot of details.

As a result, in their last two studies (2014 and 2015), the authors took the decision to interview tourists during every day of their stay. This daily interviewing technique has allowed researchers to collect extremely rich information. Every night, the researchers would meet up with the tourists to collect information about their day at the resort. The interview took on average one hour every night either in the tourists' accommodation or in a catering establishment. Tourists were awarded some small prize and were recruited through the Facebook contacts of the resort in advance. The richness of the information collected was very useful at understanding how visitors planned their stay and then organise their stay in situ daily. It gave information as to how they used, altered, and chose whether to participate in some activities with priceless justifications for their behaviour. Within this process, co-construction components could be identified in detail.

The only existing research that is close to this approach are the qualitative studies using diaries. Diaries are particularly interesting since they investigate tourists on a daily basis and collect fairly personal information on their tourist experience. Such approach has been developed through videos (Pocock, McIntosh, & Zahra, 2013) and by using written diaries (Prebensen & Foss, 2011). They have shown to be very useful at identifying precise co-construction processes in the holiday experience.

All the information gained from those various studies has been transcribed and content analysed. The content analysis aimed to find evidence of co-construction during the holiday process whether it related to projected images, the use/non-use of some facilities and activities, how tourists changed the use of some facilities/ activities and which strategies they developed to modify their perception of the reality. The objective of this analysis was to single out evidence of events where the consumers actively created their holiday with the resorts.

## Results

The results from these various studies has singled out four key domains where co-construction takes place: projected traditional images, perception of the mountain, satisfaction strategies, and the role of companions. For each of those four components, the researchers aimed to identify the strategies, conscious or unconscious, developed by consumers.

### *Co-constructing resorts' images: the role of projected images of mountain traditions*

One of the key findings of the results collected was the active role that consumers played in adapting their surrounding environment to their preconceived images. Mountains have very strong affective images among consumers visiting the resorts: they are very present in childhood through their association to Christmas, school teaching programs and the various tales and films taking place in that setting (Heidi or Belle and Sebastian novels for instance). This strong emotional link to childhood is one that tourists want to revive warmly. Those images are very stereotypical and bring in fairy tale images of a soft mountain: ideally, a small village made of wooden chalets, some pine trees surrounding a church and the whole picture covered by generous amounts of snow.

Necessarily, when consumers reach modern-day resorts (which was the case for the resorts investigated in our studies), the reality cannot really match this idealised image. As a result, consumers engage in a selective perception process and choose to select some iconic elements in the landscape and decide to ignore others. For instance, in La Toussuire resort, two women in their fifties picked up an image of a stereotypical mountain village as the picture best representing their resort. La Toussuire was a resort built in the 1960s and 1970s and is probably not the best example of alpine architecture, having the front part made of large concrete buildings of 5 to 8 floors. Recently some chalets were built but they cannot be seen from the front of the resort (where the interviews took place). The interviewees pointed to the fact that the resort might not quite match the picture chosen by the two interviewees but they confidently replied "Yes, but at the bottom on the right there is a church and behind those buildings you have some wooden chalets, and on other buildings they have recently added some wood panels, it is much better". In other words, consumers will pick on elements that match their preconceived images in order to not experience cognitive dissonance with their choice. They will clearly avoid seeing concrete buildings and will focus their attention on elements such as chalets or, at a minimum, the wood covering the buildings with alpine style balconies.

In Avoriaz resort, a 60-year-old man who had been coming to the resort for some years indicated that: "I can clearly see that this is a set of buildings but they are nicely disguised". Indeed, the resort has chosen to cover all its buildings with wood panels and this is what consumers expect to find when at the resort. This projection of images is not new in itself, Urry (1990) had already pointed to the fact that tourists tend to adapt reality to their preconceived images and the researchers found ample evidence of this mechanism during their studies.

Sometimes, the consumers interviewed have regrets about missing elements, however this is not necessarily conductive of dissatisfaction if it can be compensated by another major asset:

> When I see films with mountains with trees in them I think "okay, those trees are so, so beautiful" but because I realise the advantage of being so high and the reason you're so high is because you have no trees, or because you have no trees is because you're so high. I'm absolutely prepared to make that sacrifice because I'm less worried about the snow conditions when I come here because of the height and also because with the tree cover then you have less of a terrain to ski on. So, obviously trees would be lovely but I'm not going to go somewhere else just for the trees.
>
> (Kate, 45, Val Thorens)

The other conscious element that goes along with this feeling of being "in the mountains" is the constant need for tourists to immerse themselves in highly symbolical activities. The mountains have strong cultural specificities in terms of agricultural productions and are highly associated with specific food products such as cheeses (Comté, Beaufort, Reblochon, Mont d'Or, etc.) and charcuteries.

Resorts have clearly understood this need, and have invested in themed universe (bars, restaurants, shops) that provide those products in a mountain-themed setting. Consumers actively seek those elements and will even provoke situations that they clearly associate with the mountain universe and that will reinforce the feeling of being "in the mountains":

> On Thursday, we realised that it would be dangerous to ski due to low visibility. So we decided to go and sit on a terrace of a wooden chalet. It was themed with mountainous items: wood everywhere, materials with little snow flake stitches, a lot of red colour. We comfortably sat on the terrace, the waiter brought us a blanket and we ordered a big cup of hot chocolate. It was hot and comforting, we sat outside looking at the snow, but yet we were not cold thanks to the blanket and our clothes, it was so cosy and comforting.
>
> (Alyssia, 23, La Plagne)

Immersing themselves in that cosy mountain atmosphere is important to tourists for two reasons. First, as we have already mentioned, it brings tourists back to fond childhood memories and connects them directly with positive emotions. Second, it confirms that they are indeed spending their holiday in a mountain resort (i.e. a different environment) and, importantly, this helps them to cut free from their everyday lives. The more the resort reminds them of a setting different from their daily world, the better tourists will immerse in it and cut free from daily stresses. So the need to escape is often very present and expressed by consumers.

Sometimes, willingly or not, the immersion into the holiday and co-construction is improved by technological failure. For instance, tourists are delighted to find unexpected ways to escape totally from this world by cutting off:

> I work very hard so it's nice to have a week off, especially as the Internet doesn't work very well in the hotel and when I'm up the hill and my phone doesn't work. It just gets me away from work so I can concentrate on my kids
>
> (Kit, 42, Val Thorens)

Due to the similar problem another customer mentions: "I think not having Wi-Fi is really, really . . . it's like detached because we can't post and we can't talk to our family but it's also quite nice as well. I'm not getting disruptions from emails or tweets or Facebook or anything". Other consumers mentioned that they refused to switch on the TV while on holiday as it would send them back to the realities of their life and they preferred to stay in their holiday spirit, away and detached from it all.

### *The perception of mountains and their associated benefits*

At a second level, the mountain scenery is also one that helps the immersion even further. Tourists have immense respect for mountains and it elicits strong emotions when confronted with this landscape. It is altogether pure, wild, away from any signs of construction, respected but yet intimidating (the vast majority of tourists do not leave the groomed slopes). The mountains are not just perceived visually, they are also "felt" through various senses: freshness, pure air, brightness are all elements that also come in contrast to tourists' everyday lives (in winter, tourists often come from darker, polluted and crowded city environments). In this case, projected images are less evident because mountains are what they are and they do not need any artifice to be appreciated, but yet consumers know what to expect and are delighted to find it. As a result, the view is a commodity that is essential to their holidays, and having that view from the terraces and from the balconies of their accommodation is essential to them:

> It is spectacular, you know, the mountains and the snow and the sun and the . . . I just love it all, I love it all and I think about it and I hear . . . I can hear it all, you know, just the noise of the . . . your ski boots in the snow and the noise of the button as you are sitting . . . all these ridiculous elements.
>
> (Kate, 45, Val Thorens)

In regard to this mountainous landscape, elements of co-construction are perhaps less evident because tourists simply enter contemplation and are satisfied by the scope, pureness and beauty of this landscape. Their co-construction process means mostly finding locations where they can best appreciate this landscape (booking a flat with a view, choosing a café according to the view, etc.).

### Satisfaction strategies

Another form of co-construction strategy is one that is commonly encountered on holidays. It is not so much associated with the location but rather with the holiday spirit. When consumers arrive on the location of their holiday, they already know, intuitively and unconsciously, the spirit they will be in. They have gained this intuitive knowledge from their previous holidaying experiences and it is a feeling they have longed for. This spirit can be translated into a strong feeling of detachment which is defined in opposition to everyday life: no more hectic days, no more set times, no more obligations, and none of the everyday various stresses that urban life brings. As a result, they quickly transpose themselves into a frame of mind whereby they want to set themselves in a positive spirit. Their conception of "satisfaction" is redefined along the lines of this new context. This implies that they will be much less discerning about the service failures they might come across. For instance, in La Clusaz, a lady replied as follows: "(the interviewer): 'Are there any reasons of dissatisfaction that you have identified during your holiday?' The lady replies: 'No, we are not like that, everything is just great'". Or this gentleman in Avoriaz: "Me, overall I am on holidays, it is guaranteed relaxation, so I am not gonna get worked up about things". In other words, the consumers decide by themselves not to notice negative elements that they would probably view undesirably in their everyday life. Their objective is to enter this state of detachment and remain in it, therefore any elements that could potentially take them out of this feeling are disregarded or minimised. This is a strong co-construction process that questions the ways in which quality is usually assessed. Consumers' testimonies point to the fact that satisfaction is constructed with a true willingness to remain in a positive frame of mind and consciously (or unconsciously) choose not to notice some negative elements. This selective perception means that the ways in which quality is evaluated cannot be summarised by a list of items quantitatively evaluated through a questionnaire – the process is much more complex.

### *The role of companions*

The ski holiday is also a pathway to develop and reinforce social connections. The notion of socialising implies that tourists expect to live strong connecting and significant moments with the ones they love/care about.

The vast majority of tourists interviewed do not come alone. The usual group can be made of the family unit (parents and children) or a three-generation family unit (adding the grandparents), even a wider notion of families (with some cousins adding up to groups of 10 or 12 individuals). For those families, spending a week together is a way to get closer within a context: "that is much more fun than stuck at a table with lengthy family dinners at Christmas" (Florian, 44, Val Thorens). The resort is also seen as a place where the family can be reunited, wherever they come from geographically.

The parents also mention that skiing is an activity they can still share with their children, especially when they are teenagers, when most other activities are out of reach for them. Since the parents often learned skiing at an early stage, they can teach their children and see them progressing. When asked what was one of the strongest moments of their holidays, several parents mentioned skiing down a slope, turning back and seeing their children following them at a good pace, which produced both a feeling of togetherness and parents' pride:

> For me because I'm coming with my boys I actually work away from home . . . every two weeks of a month I'm away and then I'm at home for two weeks. So, for me it's special just to spend the two weeks with my boys. So, I want to come away and stay in a nice hotel, and we just want to ski all day. So, I'm not going to be going out to a bar and getting drunk or any of that, they're still too young for that so I need some nice accommodation as well. And I want loads of slopes, loads of opportunities, I want ski parks, they enjoy jumping and all that kind of stuff. So, I'm just looking for a big resort where I can enjoy myself with my kids. For me it's a good opportunity to be with my kids, concentrated for a couple of weeks . . . it's a good laugh, we enjoy ourselves; and it's a break.
>
> (Nick, 44, Val Thorens)

Indirectly, the other element that emanates from the studies is the memories that this holiday will create, memories of togetherness that can be produced by the skiing practice but also by creating special times, within the vicinity of the rented flat. For instance, many families mentioned the evenings as a time where they sit together and spend time with each other, often by playing a card game. These simple moments are also highly valued as these are times that are much less available in normal life and that also leave strong memories of family togetherness. These episodes are clearly co-constructed or even auto-constructed: the family consciously aims to create special times for togetherness with very simple but yet unifying activities. The fact of having time and with each other is already a major plus compared to everyday rhythms that often do not allow for these quality times.

Beyond family groups, another type of group is composed of males, often in their 20s up to their 40s. These groups are often comprised of 4 to 5 men, long-term friends, who visit outside any family connections. Their common interest is their shared passion for skiing: "We ski or snowboard intensely all day long, then in the evening we watch skiing videos then we might go to a nightclub, but usually we are too tired to go out in the evening" (a group of friends in their 20s in Val Thorens). Other older groups will use their holiday as a way to reunite and reinforce old friendships, they view their holiday as: "easy, uncomplicated, everything is easy, no conflicts, easy logistic, timing, eating . . everything runs smoothly, we have a good laugh and we always agree". For some tourists who have a family life outside the group, being together without their wives and children is synonymous with easiness, the logistics are simpler and they are with friends; they know and understand each other so well that the whole holiday is smooth: "With friends it's easier, we are only four people and then we sit down and drink and have fun like that and now we are most of the time together and the best skiers go together and then we change over" (Franz, 42, Val Thorens).

The other dimension of those groups of friends is to be able to match individuals with similar levels of sport practice. Indeed, the access to a good skiing holiday implies that friends have similar levels of competence, therefore the co-construction element starts from the selection of those friends right from the start of the holiday booking process. They will then identify, within the resort, slopes that they want to practice on and also bars and restaurants that will be in line with their group spirit.

### Which managerial implications?

Within the results collected through their studies, the researchers have identified several managerial actions that can boost positively the holidays' co-construction between tourists and resorts. Resorts should provide activities and resources that have strong significance for their customers but also that can aim to improve the tourist experience. Resorts have a lot to gain from understanding how their various products and activities feed the more general and personal holiday expectations of their clients. Some co-construction strategies directly use some of the elements designed by the resort, others will be developed in a more autonomous way, but in any case, those strategies improve the experience and are beneficial to the felt satisfaction with the holidays undertaken in the resorts.

In regard to resorts' theming, the results indicate that the mountain theme is essential to the visitors' experience: it is both a way to guarantee a distance from their everyday environment and to comply with their preconceived symbolical images of a mountain environment. Therefore, encouraging (and investing in) theming, both on the outside of buildings as much as inside is essential to the visitors. Some resorts, such as Méribel, have set up a new quality label that integrates, in its criteria, the mountain theming of rented accommodations' interior. This is clearly a path to follow along the necessity to invest in the outside look of the buildings. The results show that visitors do not have a precise discerning vision of the alpine style and are quite happy if the buildings, even modern ones, are at least covered in wood. Whether it implies for resorts to invest and encourage owners to cover the buildings in wood, or even integrate this request into their planning permissions is definitely a key factor of success for visitors.

On top of accommodation provision, the mountain theme is also one that is attractive through the products purchased and consumed: themed restaurants, souvenirs shops, and bars can all gain from investing in the mountain theme. Consumers clearly seek those elements to co-construct their fantasised mountain image. Visitors are also clearly attracted to local traditions that they see as being authentic and representative of the mountain universe and would be keen to participate in any event enhancing this dimension: meeting up with local inhabitants, getting to know better mountain life, encountering local farmers, learning about the early years of the resort creation, are all part of the demand that is also characteristic of the mountain visitors. Nowadays, tourists only ski a maximum of four hours a day, and one out of five tourists do not ski, therefore there is a lot of scope to develop complementary products to skiing that can enhance the perception of the mountain universe/atmosphere. People who do not ski still have a strong attachment to the mountain universe and are also in demand for products associated to it.

The emotional attachment to the mountains themselves is clearly identified but consumers are also intimidated by this environment, therefore the safe discovery of the mountains, away from the resort, can be improved by setting up interpretation walking paths and landscape interpretation tables. The view is clearly seen as an essential commodity in a mountain holiday and, from their conception, the resorts have maximised this view from the terraces and accommodation. Whilst the view might be seen as a given for tourists, most of the view is in fact "man-made". Local agriculture and forestry activities have shaped the mountains and several of the resorts investigated are located on the perimeter of the Vanoise National Park. The legislation of this park has heavily protected the landscape from any supplementary constructions or opening of new ski slopes. Beyond its prime mission to protect the natural environment, it has been beneficial to the landscape too, and ultimately to tourists. So, while the notion of co-construction between tourists and resorts is not so evident here, the co-construction between the resort (the territory) and other stakeholders is vital in the upkeep of this landscape.

In terms of socialisation, the identification of the role and place of groups within the skiing holiday has been clearly identified in the studies and has been clearly underestimated by resorts so far. Tourists groups come also to achieve togetherness while on holidays. One crucial element that they require is large accommodation, whether it might be large flats/chalets or contiguous accommodation, and what those groups need is proximity. To date, ski resorts can offer some large-scale accommodation (although the offer is limited) but are unable to guarantee the proximity of rented accommodation. Such guarantees could come as a major selling advantage since it is a crucial component to those groups.

## Conclusions

This chapter aimed to investigate the notion of co-construction in a mountain holiday context. The results from several studies have allowed the two researchers to identify different levels of co-construction processes, ranging from auto-construction up to a co-construction dynamic involving several stakeholders. In such a holiday context, co-construction takes its roots in the primary function of the resort (in this case, skiing), but the studies show that the co-construction process goes well beyond the main activity to include the more general setting of the mountains and their traditions. The symbolical dimensions of the mountains are very strong and carry with them various components that tourists will actively seek while at the destination. All these components give ample scope for resorts to strategically invest in components that will feed into this co-construction process. This study is set, however, within the very specific context of mountain resorts and it would be interesting to see how it compares to other tourism settings.

## References

Arnould, E. J, & Price, L. L. (1993). Rivermagic: Extraordinary experience and the extended service encounter. *Journal of Consumer Research, 20*(1), 24–45.

Carù, A., & Cova, B. (2007). *Consuming experiences.* Abingdon: Routledge.

Cohen, E. (2003). Towards a sociology of international tourism. *Social Research, 39,* 164–182.

Crompton, J. L. (1979). Motivations for pleasure vacation. *Annals of Tourism Research, 6*(4), 408–424.

Dann, G. M. (1977). Anomie, ego-enhancement and tourism. *Annals of Tourism Research, 4*(4), 184–194.

Frochot, I. V. & Morrison, A. (2000). Benefit segmentation: A review of its applications to travel and tourism research. *Journal of Travel and Tourism Marketing, 9*(4), 21–45.

Holbrook, M., & Hirschman, E. (1982). Hedonic consumption: Emerging concepts, methods and propositions. *Journal of Marketing, 46*(3), 92–101.

Krippendorf, J. (1999). *The holiday makers: Understanding the impact of leisure and travel.* Oxford: Butterworth-Heinemann.

Pine, J., & Gilmore, J. (1999). *The experience economy.* Boston, MA: Harvard Business School Press.

Plog, S. (2001). Why destination areas rise and fall in popularity: An update of a Cornell Quarterly Classic. *Cornell Hotel and Restaurant Quarterly, 42*(3), 13–24.

Pocock, N., & McIntosh, A. (2013). Long-term travellers return "home"? *Annals of Tourism Research, 42*, 402–424.

Prebensen, N. K., & Foss, L. (2011). Coping and co-creating in tourist experiences. *International Journal of Tourism Research, 13*(1), 54–67.

McCool, S. F., & Reilly, M. (1993). Benefit segmentation analysis of state park visitor setting preferences and behavior. *Journal of Park and Recreation Administration, 11*(4), 1–14.

SMBT. (2015). *Cadre marketing* (2014–2016). Une stratégie marketing au service de l'offre touristique du territoire, Savoie Mont Blanc Tourisme, Annecy.

Urry J. (1990). *The tourist gaze*. London: Sage.

# 4 Staging for value co-creation in nature-based experiences

## The case of a surfing course at Surfers Paradise, Australia

*Nina K. Prebensen*

## Introduction

Experiential and experience-based consumption entails interactions between actors and events in real time. Informed, involved, motivated and active tourists affect the value extracted from a vacation experience (Prebensen, Vittersø, & Dahl, 2013; Prebensen, Woo, Chen, & Uysal, 2014; Prebensen, Woo, & Uysal, 2014). The changing view or acknowledgement of the consumer as an active agent rather than a passive consumer challenges the tourism industry, firm by firm, branch by branch, and as a system. Based on concepts such as experience value, service encounters, value co-creation and service-dominant logic, this chapter explores and exemplifies how a tourism company can create the stage for its customers to participate in value-creation processes and improve the tourist experience value. The chapter uses a surfing course at Surfers Paradise in Australia as an experience setting to exemplify staging and facilitation of such an experience. An in-depth interview with one of the participants on a surfing course and observations of such experiences are used to exemplify different aspects of interactions in the surfing experience. The chapter reveals the importance of various aspects of interactions on the surfing course: the instructor, the setting and the surrounding nature, and other course participants. Surfing includes potential experiential value in terms of enjoyment, education and symbolic meanings for the tourist, and is therefore a good example to learn from in order to explore different aspects of value co-creation in tourism.

Tourist travel is about being in the process of the experience at the site. Even if the result of participating in a specific tourist activity is important, both research and the tourism industry need to acknowledge more fully the experience process before, during and after the journey (Chen, Prebensen, & Uysal, 2014). The process of being on the journey is core. Finishing the trip—that is, the result of travelling—is less interesting for most tourists than the travelling itself. However, finishing a concrete tourist activity during a journey may be as intriguing as the activity itself, depending on the purpose of joining in the activity. The activities that the tourist participates in may help tourism researchers and practitioners to understand important issues in tourism, such as how to enhance the tourist perceived experience value, satisfaction and well-being, and the relative importance of participating in value co-creation processes.

Marketing literature presents the importance of the service experience, signifying that service providers must encourage customers to participate in the service experience in addition to developing a theatrical environment for fun, excitement and entertainment (Mathwick, Malhotra, & Rigdon, 2001). Experiential value perceptions are strongly tied to interactions between direct usage and distant evaluations of goods and services, and these interactions provide the foundation for experiential value perception (Mathwick, Malhotra, & Rigdon, 2002).

Fesenmaier and Kim (2015) suggest a new approach for assessing travellers' emotions during a tourist trip, and find that the visitors exhibit substantial variation in emotions depending on the places visited, the activities joined, and the people met. The study concludes that the ability to measure travellers' emotions in real time and in natural settings leads to new knowledge about the relationship between travellers' emotions and the physical and social environments, which, in turn, provides a useful foundation for designing and managing a tourism experience.

Following the lead of experiential consumption and tourism researchers, Kim, Cha, Knutson, and Beck (2011, pp. 113–114) delineate consumer experiences as "holistic in nature and hence multidimensional, involving the customer on different levels, both psychological and physiological; . . . personal and individual; and, finally . . . elusive, difficult and indistinct." Consequently, tourist firms and destinations can only facilitate for experience value to happen. From the managerial standpoint, this chapter offers a platform for tourist companies to facilitate for enhanced value by motivating, involving and teaching the customer to participate in value-creation processes before, during and after the journey (Prebensen, Woo, Chen, & Uysal, 2014). Theoretically, the chapter supports existing conceptualizations of the value-in-use perspective (Grönroos & Voima, 2013). Furthermore, the chapter suggests new dimensions for firms to facilitate for enhanced experience value through enabling and facilitating the customer's participation in value-creation processes.

The present chapter first presents theories and empirical works amplifying the imperative of understanding the actors in interaction processes. A conceptual framework is suggested. The methodology is then presented, followed by the study case. Next, the chapter findings are outlined and validated by referring to existing research. Subsequently, a conclusion follows.

## Theory

### *The experience value encounter*

Following the lead of Shostack's (1985, p. 243) definition of the term "service encounter" as "a period of time during which a consumer directly interacts with a service," Bitner (1992, p. 70) embraces various aspects of the service firm with which the consumer may interact, including its personnel, its physical facilities, and other tangible elements as parts of the service encounter. In their book *Tourist Customer Service Satisfaction: An Encounter Approach*, Noe, Uysal, and Magnini (2010) suggest a theory of encounters. They build their work on important perspectives such as the interaction school (Schubert, Friedmann, & Regenbrecht, 1999). Schubert et al. (1999) claim that the social self is the creation of inter-subjective communication with the mind and the outside world. The present chapters follow the lead of these scholars.

Studies within tourism experiences (e.g. Prebensen, Vittersø, & Dahl, 2013) suggest that on-site experiences should be viewed from the perspective that some elements enhance the experience value while others may reduce it. This perspective is reflected in the dual factor theory, first presented by Herzberg (1959). The dual factor theory holds that people have two sets of needs: to avoid pain and to grow psychologically. Based on this thinking, Herzberg, Mausner, and Snyderman (2011) identified that there are factors (in job situations) that affect satisfaction positively (motivators) and negatively (hygiene factors). In the study by Prebensen, Vittersø, and Dahl (2013), the natural settings are of huge importance for tourists when visiting Norway. Even so, the study shows that the surrounding nature does not significantly affect overall satisfaction. The authors of the study therefore suggest that elements such as nature should probably be seen as some sort of hygiene factor in certain situations, such as after a while during longer vacations. Nature is important and may be a motivator in the early stage of the trip, adding to the positive experience value; after a while, however, the tourist may perhaps take nature for granted. In such situations, nature may influence satisfaction negatively if ruining or damaging the experience. Other researchers present similar discussions—that is, satisfiers versus dissatisfiers in tourist experiences (dual dimensions of satisfaction) (Alegre & Garau, 2010; Crotts & Pan, 2007; Crotts, Pan, & Raschid, 2008; Pritchard & Havitz, 2006; Tribe & Snaith, 1998; Truong & Foster, 2006).

Jennings and Weiler (2006) discuss how people engage with others who assist to mediate their experience. Interaction in tourism includes not only the physical manmade encounter between host and guest, but all physical surroundings such as the natural settings, cultural aspects and all individuals participating in the experience. The service provider may facilitate for all actors to take part in positive experience value creation. Jennings and Weiler (2006) propose that mediators for the tourist experience can be personal (e.g. other tourists, tourist providers, governments and host communities) and non-personal (e.g. signage, design, aesthetic and settingscape). All these aspects thus influence the perception of the experience. However, in a new setting in particular, the frontline employees such as guides or course teachers are delineated as the primary reflections of the firm (Maxham III & Netemeyer, 2003; Mossberg, Hanefors, & Hansen, 2014), influencing the tourist to a great extent. The roles taken by the various actors are therefore important to explore. Role actions are defined by Littlejohn (1983, pp. 62–63) as "beliefs about what should be done or should not be done to achieve an objective in a given situation." The interactions between host and guests are therefore in focus in the present chapter.

### Value co-creation as mental and physical participation in an activity or an event

Based on the service-dominant logic perspective of consumer behaviour (Vargo & Lusch, 2004, 2008), the process of creating value involving the participation of the customer is imperative (Prebensen, Vittersø, & Dahl, 2013). Customer participation is defined as "the degree to which the customer is involved in producing and delivering the service" (Dabholkar, 1990, p. 484). Prebensen, Kim and Uysal (2016) reveal that participation in value-creation processes moderates the relationship between perceived experience value and satisfaction. The Prebensen et al. (2016) study suggests that co-creation should be treated as mentally and physically participating in the tourist experience and that co-creation positively moderates the experience relationship between value and satisfaction.

The notion of co-creation in the present chapter is understood as the customer's mental and physical participation in the experience creation process (Prebensen et al., 2016). Physical participation is recognized as the customer's own perception of the degree of active participation in the activity experienced. Mental participation is identified as the customer's level of interest in an activity. It is expected that interest and physical participation in a tourist activity will moderate the effect of experience value and satisfaction—that is, the more active the participation, the stronger the effect of experience value and satisfaction, and vice versa.

### Employee as facilitator for value co-creation

The employees meet the customer's needs and are supposed to help the customer with their needs and problems, either by producing a service for them (e.g. providing fast food) or helping to solve a problem (e.g. teaching how to book a ticket). Both situations demand that the customer participate in a value-creation process— to a lesser extent in the first case than in the latter. Most tourist situations would include a collaborative approach in that the customer wants to participate in creating value, even though it may happen in various ways. Keng, Huang, Zheng, and Hsu (2007) show that these encounters positively influence the customer experiential value. In visiting a tourist destination where the tourist stays for a certain length of time, away from home, tourists interact with a number of people and a variety of firms and even with physical surroundings, manmade or natural—that is, nature, buildings and cultural attractions—and it is of huge importance to recognize this (Prebensen & Foss, 2011).

Tourist firms need to embrace the idea of staging host–guest encounters to co-create experience value for the customers. Goffman (1959) presented theoretical thoughts regarding impression management, holding that the service provider can and will affect the attitudes and behaviour of the customers. Impression management is therefore a critical part of the service provider's role, as he or she is interacting directly with the tourists. Literature on impression management claims that it is possible to create a positive impression by appearing both competent and likeable (Jones & Pittman, 1982; Tedeschi & Norman, 1985), as competence and expertise are revealed as important assets in interaction quality in service encounters (Czepiel, Solomon, & Surprenant, 1985; Grönroos, 1990; Noe et al., 2010), and employees manage impressions of competence by being efficient, available, accurate, and knowledgeable about products and services (Noe et al., 2010; Parasuraman, Zeithaml, & Berry, 1985; Zeithaml, Berry, & Parasuraman, 1991). Positive attitudes and a positive demeanour are also put forward as important aspects among service personnel (Czepiel et al., 1985; Grönroos, 1990; Noe et al., 2010) and are also shown to effect overall service quality (Diefendorff & Richard, 2003; Tsai & Huang, 2002). As interactions in the service encounter are vital to the evaluation of the experience for the tourist, tourism firms and destinations may manage employees in order to facilitate positive emotions and learning.

## *Mastering and motivation in experiential consumption*

People engage in physical activities based on three fundamentals: "self-efficacy, outcome expectations, and self-evaluated satisfaction or dissatisfaction" (Bandura, 1989, p. 1,176). The tourist thus makes a causal attribution to her own motivation and action within this "system of triadic reciprocal causation." Self-efficacy is further described as the individual belief in oneself regarding performing in a certain manner to attain certain goals (Bandura, 1977). In this attribution system, the tourist will judge her capabilities based on various mastery criteria—that is, the sense of competence within a certain activity, such as surfing—and the person's assessment of her ability to surf in comparison with the other participants. Perceived mastering is thus a core variable in this evaluative process.

Self-efficacy affects the level of motivation (positive relationship) (Bandura, 1989), revealing the level and amount of effort and time she will spend on meeting difficulties. Researchers focusing on consumer motivation (e.g. Vroom, 1964) claim that the term "motivation" concerns the energy, direction, persistence and evaluation activated by the individual. People can be motivated because they value an activity or because others or the situation convinces them to participate in the activity. Peoples' reflections on why they participate in activities such as surfing are about sense making of behaviours (by self or others) in society, defined as attribution (deCharms, 1968; Heider, 1958). Motivation can thus be intrinsically or extrinsically driven. Intrinsic motivation is defined as "the inherent tendency to seek out novelty and challenges, to extend and exercise one's capability, to explore and to learn," while extrinsic motivation refers to "the performance of an activity in order to attain some separable outcome" (Ryan & Deci, 2000, p. 70). Ryan and Deci (2000) also assert that externally driven motivation might include activities that are performed for instrumental reasons—for example, a tourist participating in surfing activities to tell others about it when arriving back home.

## A conceptual framework for staging tourist experiences

Researchers have discussed how firms may benefit from designing and managing their company based on different dramaturgy concepts (Clark & Mangham, 2004;

Gardner, 1992; Goffman, 1959; Grove & Fisk, 1997; Grove, Fisk, & John, 2003; Grove, Fisk, & Laforge, 2004; Haahti, 2003; Ritti & Silver, 1986). Traditionally, service encounters have been viewed from an adaptive performance perspective—that is, acted out by service employees—for customers (the audience) and by using two key dramaturgy concepts: scripts (the set of rules and instructions that deliver the service process) and improvisation (the aptitude to deliver a script) (McCarthy, Pitt, & Berthon, 2010).

To grasp host–guest interactions in joining an outdoor activity, a model suggested by Garrison, Anderson, and Archer (2000) is adopted. Garrison et al. (2000, p. 9) expose the experience as parts of two scales; conceptions (ideas) versus perceptions (awareness), and deliberation (applicability) versus action (practice). By combining these aspects, four dimensions are outlined as continuums: (1) the shared world (the action-perception continuum); (2) exploration (the perception-deliberation continuum); (3) reflection (the deliberation-conception continuum); and (4) discourse (the conception-action continuum).

In the starting phase of an experience, the shared world, the educator (here, the surfing instructor) explicitly communicates learning challenges or tasks to the surfing class. Garrison, Anderson, and Archer (2001, p. 10) claim that a critical role of the instructor is to "initiate, shape and, in some cases, discard potentially distracting events" to turn the learners' full attention towards the goal of the activity. The next continuum is about exploring. The participant is expected to shift and move between the private and the social exploration of ideas. The tourist is expected to move towards realization of the fundamental aspects of surfing. As the third phase, integration, approaches, the tourist starts to construct meaning from the new ideas and knowledge regarding surfing. The tourist is now expected to reflect on and discuss the surfing activity with fellow surfers and the instructor. The fourth phase is described by Garrison et al. (2000) as directed towards action—that is, trying to surf.

Chen et al. (2014) propose a model of the three phases of travelling and suggest how tourist firms can facilitate for different tourist values in the various phases of a tourist vacation. As customers vary in terms of their needs, motivations, involvement and skills (e.g. Prebensen, Woo, Chen, & Uysal, 2014), they need to be motivated and involved to learn how to act, based on their experience.

Deci and Ryan (1985, 2000) suggest a theory of "self-determination of motivation" that involves and embraces the dynamics of human needs, motivation and well-being within a given social context. There are three basic needs functioning as the basis for self-determination theory: autonomy (a sense of control and agency); competency (feeling competent with tasks and activities); and relatedness (feeling included or affiliated to others). By fulfilling these three needs, the tourist will experience a sense of self and achieve better psychological well-being. In contrast, the lack of fulfilment of the three basic needs is expected to generate disappointing experiences, promoting bad feelings and poor self-esteem.

Interactions in the host–guest encounter are outlined by combining the two perspectives: guest perception of self in the situation (autonomy, competency and relatedness) and host performance in the situation (initiating/shaping to get attention, exploring, in terms of private versus public, and integrating, by reflecting and discussing).

## Analysis

The aim of the current work is to develop an understanding of the meaning of interaction dimensions in a host–guest situation: a tourist activity at a destination such as joining a surfing class for the first time is chosen as a study case. As the qualitative research aims to address questions concerned with developing an understanding of the meaning and experience dimensions of humans' lives and social worlds (Taylor, Bogdan, & DeVault, 2015), participant observation and in-depth interviews are performed. Gadamer (1975) argued that in order to understand another person's experience, using the tool of language is vital. Therefore, the in-depth interview is a commonly used method in interpretive research to acknowledge the quintessence of a phenomenon and reveal meanings of participant experiences (McCracken, 1988; Wengraf, 2001). Observation is another primary tool to obtain data within an interpretive framework. According to Merriam (1998), observations are useful for qualitative researchers because observations take place in the natural setting where the phenomenon occurs, and the data from observations represent first-hand contact with the phenomenon.

As the present chapter aims to explore and exemplify the interactions between host and guest in novel situations, a case including one person buying and enjoying a surfing class is chosen as a study case. A teenager is chosen as the informant, as little research is performed on this tourist group. In addition, the researcher observed the surfing class and five other surfing classes during a week. Even though the study objective mainly is to exemplify an encounter situation, the work is intended to meet the requirements of validity such as authenticity, plausibility and criticality (cf. Golden-Biddle & Locke, 1993). To ensure the requirement of authenticity, the in-depth interview was performed over several hours and the results—quotations and reflections regarding what the researchers observed—were discussed the day after the interview with the informant. To obtain plausibility, the interviewee used theoretical underpinning to justify the data. A deeper look into the data helped to grasp important aspects, revealing new insights into the phenomenon. Last, criticality deals with the ability of the text to encourage readers to reconsider taken-for-granted ideas and beliefs. By studying the various interactions in one tourist setting, interaction aspects were closely studied. It also seemed plausible to divide the interactions into different interaction sets (see Table 4.1 below) where the host performance meets the tourist's perception. These thoughts are presented and discussed in the analysis and are also further validated by referring to existing research.

## The case: Surfing course at the Surfers Paradise, Australia

Helene (a teenager from Norway) and I (the author of this chapter and mother of Helene) walked along the surfers' strip for Helene to join a surfing class for beginners. I was supposed to observe the course from outside and then interview her after the class was finished. The surfing class started at 10.00 am and lasted for two hours.

## *Observation*

Helene bought a ticket at a small shed close to the beach. The shed had a sign indicating that it was the right spot for the surfing class. Helene was given a T-shirt with a logo (the name of the company). She put it on over her swimsuit. Then a man called the participants together in a circle. I could hear that he asked the participants to introduce themselves with their names and where they lived. The instructor walked away for approximately ten minutes. The participants stood in a circle. I heard them chat and laugh. Then the instructor approached them and they walked in pairs to pick up two surfboards (carrying them together down to the beach). They started practising surfing on the beach. Helene gave me looks: I could tell she was a bit embarrassed. Then they approached the sea. The sea seemed rough, with heavy waves. The pairs carrying the surfboards still seemed to stick together. Surfing seemed really troublesome. The instructor called them up to the beach and they continued practising on land. Then they went to the sea and the waves again. Suddenly, Helene managed to stand on the board for a few minutes. She seemed happy and proud. She was the first participant to manage the board. Soon, others followed. The instructor was present all the time, giving advice and applauding them for trying and mastering surfing. They seemed proud and happy.

## *In-depth interview*

Helene reported after the experience:

> We were a bit shy, but talked about our experiences regarding surfing, which was rather limited for most of us. The instructor then asked us to carry the surfboards to the beach (in pairs). I carried mine together with a woman from California. The boards were rather heavy. Down at the beach, we sat in a circle and the instructor started to tell us about surfing. He showed us the technique by utilizing the sand as a surrogate for the sea. We had to try on shore before taking the boards to the sea. It seemed fun, but we felt a bit silly practising surfing on the sand. Finally, we carried the boards to the sea and started practising real surfing. First, we just lay on our bellies on the board. This lasted for 15 minutes. Then we went on the beach to learn more . . . how to get up on the boards. So, back to the sea again. This was funny. I got on the board rather easily, while some people struggled a bit more. The nice feeling of surfing and of mastering the waves was magnificent.

## Discussion

The surfing class experience certainly exemplifies a lot of host–guest interactions and reveals a number of ways of facilitating for value co-creation with host and guest. The instructor, reflecting the host, is a mediator and facilitator for the experience. He is very important in organizing the whole experience. In addition, he builds trust and a social arena, making the participant eager to interact and to try surfing. Therefore, even if surfing and managing surfing to some extent are the core issues in taking a surfing class for two hours, the surfing instructor, other guests and the environment had a direct influence on the experience. Most of all, the perception of feeling safe in a social environment and mastering surfing impacted Helene's value perception.

The table below (Table 4.1) includes the fundamental tourist motivation for joining a tourist activity (vertical) and the firm's potential for engaging and motivating the tourist to learn, enjoy the activity and feel accepted in a social outdoor setting such as a surfing course (horizontal). The customer needs to feel in control of the situation and the activity. In the initial phase of the surfing course, the firm and the guide may apply artefacts such as marking the firm with a flag, a logo and some information. The participant pays for the course and receives a T-shirt with the logo of the company. The guide may welcome each participant and tell them where to meet in five minutes. The next step, the exploring phase, is the movement between a private and a public sense of situation. The guide asks the participants to present themselves and their country/place of origin. They are now asked to go together with a surfing partner of approximately the same height. The reason for this is that they are supposed to carry the surfboards together to the beach (five minutes' walk), which starts the integration phase. To enhance the sense of control for the participants, the course starts with practising surfing on land (on the sand).

To meet the need for competency—that is, feeling competent to surf—exercising is a core activity. The guide starts by informing participants about the course. This is related to the level of knowledge the course participants have—in this case, it is a course for beginners. Next, by wearing the same T-shirt, the participants feel included in the group. By practising surfing on land and then on the sea, they are feeling more competent. The participants seem to stick to the person they were carrying the surfboards with, indicating a social bond between the two. The surfers watch each other, and see that most of the participants struggle quite a bit; they share and laugh about their experiences. We see that by means of the stepwise progress, the participants feel related to the guide, to the other participants and, in particular, to the one picked out to help carry the surfboards. Feelings of competency and relatedness are in this case closely related. The last motivation is about trying—participating in the value-creation process. Here, the guide needs to inform, ask and answer questions. By giving the participants tasks such as presenting themselves and carrying the surfboards, they get a role "on stage" and start to feel responsible in the situation. These tasks help them relax and feel included in the group. As soon as the participants feel socially relaxed, they start talking and enjoying each other's company. They feel less embarrassed when practising on sand as they all are novice surfers and, at the same time, they now feel more socially integrated. The mastering experienced when standing on the surfboard on the waves is when skills and mastering meet, delineated as a flow feeling by Csikszentmihalyi (1975, 1990). Flow feelings refer to an optimal state

*Table 4.1* Host and guest interaction sets: examples from a surfing course at the Surfers Paradise beach, Australia

| | *Initiate/shape (to get attention)* | *Exploring (private versus public: socializing)* | *Integration (reflect/discuss)* |
|---|---|---|---|
| Sense of control/ agency | Applying artefacts such as signs, flags, certifications to signal quality; receiving a T-shirt with logo, then inviting tourist to group gathering. Asking questions, getting and giving information, payment, smiling. | Putting the tourist in the group— presenting themselves (names and residence). Picking a surfing partner and receiving surfboards. Practising on the surfboards. | Carrying the surfboards to the beach (two and two together). Training in surfing (on the beach). Surfing on sea. Enjoying, mastering the surfboards and the waves; mastering surfing. |
| Competency (feeling competent with tasks and activities) | Informing about the course (e.g. for beginners). | All surfers have the same t-shirt (group feeling). All in the same situation (beginners). | Mastering the board and the waves; watching the others; talking and laughing. |
| Realization | | The other struggles as well; when finally managing the surfing, mastering of the task occurs. | |
| Relatedness (feeling included or construing meaning) | The guide approaches the client. | Sticks to the co-surfer; knows where all the others come from. | Discussing if they are taking another course; discussing what went well/badly and how to improve. |

of mind in which an individual feels cognitively efficient, deeply involved and highly motivated, in addition to experiencing a high level of enjoyment. By following the steps presented in Table 4.1, the tourist firms may facilitate the tourist feeling a flow through co-creating the experience value.

The case shows a process of learning and enjoying facilitated by a surfing company and its employee. Learning, effort and enjoyment are close connected in Csikszentmihalyi's (1975, 1990) flow theory. By ensuring that the participants have control over the situation and master the surfing to a certain level (taking them back onto the beach), they perceive that the challenges posed by surfing are in balance with their perceived ability or skill to tackle the challenges. By initiating various activities to make the participants socialize and reflect, the tourists feel a sense of control, competence and relatedness, all of which are important aspects to feel good and to enjoy the surfing course. Surfing has experiential value in terms of enjoyment, education and symbolic meaning for the tourist, and is therefore a good example to learn from in order to explore different aspects of value co-creation in tourism. The surfing learner is motivated by autonomy (a sense of control and agency), competency (feeling competent in the tasks and activities) and relatedness (feeling included or affiliated with others) (Deci & Ryan, 1985, 2000; Ryan & Deci, 2000). By acknowledging these important motivators in tourism, the company can facilitate for enhanced experience value by initiating and getting attention, facilitating, teaching and motivating the tourist to move from a private to a public sphere, and by providing integration tactics through reflection and discussion. In line with the encounter theory of Noe et al. (2010), tourist firms need to understand how and why interaction processes should be managed, and recruit and train their employees to ensure customer satisfaction through value co-creation (Noe et al., 2010).

## Conclusions

The dramatizing and staging of a tourist experience have been outlined and discussed in tourism research as well as in marketing literature. Tourism researchers have to a larger extent taken the view that nature, culture and people are the foundations for travelling and as such a focal point in staging tourist experiences. People do not travel to buy a service: they travel to participate in creating experience value for themselves and their significant others. This work pinpoints that the tourist firm can only facilitate customer value, but facilitation and action taken seem to mediate the experience to a great extent. Tourists then co-create value with the service provider, with other tourists, and with the surrounding nature and culture. Co-creation in tourism does not necessarily indicate that a firm is present in value creation at all times—for example, in the aftermath of the surfing course, the tourist may enjoy surfing alone on the waves, enhancing her overall satisfaction with the destination and the journey and enhancing the felt well-being. The tourist, however, must always be present for value to transpire.

This chapter adopts concepts such as experience value, value co-creation, encounter theory and service-dominant logic as theoretical underpinnings in order to explore and exemplify how a tourism company can facilitate for its customers to participate in value-creation processes and, through that, improve the tourist experience. The chapter uses a surfing course at Surfers Paradise in Australia as the setting to exemplify staging and dramatizing in tourism. The author observed different types of surfing course and performed an in-depth interview with one of the surfers after the surfing course. The chapter reveals the importance of various aspects of the course: the instructor, the setting including the surrounding nature, and other course participants.

## References

Alegre, J., & Garau, J. (2010). Tourist satisfaction and dissatisfaction. *Annals of Tourism Research, 37*(1), 52–73.

Bandura, A. (1977). Self-efficacy: Toward a unifying theory of behavioral change. *Psychological Review, 84*(2), 191–215.

Bandura, A. (1989). Human agency in social cognitive theory. *American Psychologist, 44*(9), 1,175–1,184.

Bitner, M. J. (1992). Servicescapes: The impact of physical surroundings on customers and employees. *Journal of Marketing, 54*(2), 69–82.

Chen, J. S., Prebensen, N. K., & Uysal, M. S. (2014). Dynamic drivers of tourist experiences. In N. K. Prebensen, J. S. Chen, & M. S. Uysal (Eds.), *Creating experience value in tourism* (pp. 11–22). Oxfordshire: CABI.

Clark, T., & Mangham, I. (2004). Stripping to the undercoat: A review and reflections on a piece of organization theatre. *Organization Studies, 25*(5), 841–851.

Crotts, J. C., & Pan, B. (2007). Destination appraisals. *Annals of Tourism Research, 34*(2), 541–544.

Crotts, J. C., Pan, B., & Raschid, A. E. (2008). A survey method for identifying key drivers of guest delight. *International Journal of Contemporary Hospitality Management, 20*(4), 462–470.

Csikszentmihalyi, M. (1975). *Beyond boredom and anxiety*. San Francisco, CA: Jossey-Bass. [Reprinted in 2000 with a new introduction].

Csikszentmihalyi, M. (1990). *Flow: The psychology of optimal experience*. New York, NY: Harper and Row.

Czepiel, J., Solomon, M., & Surprenant, C. (1985). *The service encounter*. Lexington, MA: Lexington Books.

Dabholkar, P. (1990). How to improve perceived quality by improving customer participation. In B. J. Dunlap (Ed.), *Developments in marketing science* (pp. 483–487). Cullowhee, NC: Academy of Marketing Science.

Deci, E. L., & Ryan, R. M. (1985). *Intrinsic motivation and self-determination in human behavior*. New York, NY: Plenum.

Deci, E. L., & Ryan, R. M. (2000). The "what" and "why" of goal pursuits: Human needs and the self-determination of behavior. *Psychological Inquiry, 11*, 227–268.

deCharms, R. (1968). *Personal causation*. New York, NY: Academic Press.

Diefendorff, J. M., & Richard, E. (2003). Antecedents and consequences of emotional display rule perceptions. *Journal of Applied Psychology, 88*(2), 284–294.

Fesenmaier, D. R., & Kim, J. (2015). Measuring emotions in real time: Implications for tourism experience design. *Journal of Travel Research, 54*(4), 419–429.

Gadamer, H. G. (1975). Hermeneutics and social science. *Philosophy & Social Criticism, 2*(4), 307–316.

Gardner, J. S. (1992). The development of ski areas and environmental concerns: Banff National Park, Canada. In *Mountain Resort Development: Proceedings of the Vail Conference, Vail, Colorado, April 18–21, 1991* (p. 104). Centre for Tourism Policy and Research, Simon Fraser University.

Garrison, D. R., Anderson, T., & Archer, W. (2000). Critical inquiry in a texted-based environment. *The Internet and Higher Education, 2*(2–3), 1–19.

Garrison, D. R., Anderson, T., & Archer, W. (2001). Critical thinking, cognitive presence, and computer conferencing in distance education. *American Journal of Distance Education, 15*(1), 7–23.

Goffman, E. (1959). *The presentation of self in everyday life*. Garden City, NY: Doubleday.

Golden-Biddle, K., & Locke, K. (1993). Appealing work: An investigation of how ethnographic texts convince. *Organization Science, 4*(4), 595–616.

Grönroos, C. (1990). *Service management and marketing: Managing the moments of truth in service competition*. Lexington, MA: Lexington Books.

Grönroos, C., & Voima, P. (2013). Critical service logic: Making sense of value creation and co-creation. *Journal of the Academy of Marketing Science, 41*(2), 133–150.

Grove, S. J., & Fisk, R. P. (1997). The impact of other customers on service experiences: A critical incident examination of "getting along". *Journal of Retailing, 73*(1), 63–85.

Grove, S. J., Fisk, R. P., & John, J. (2003). The future of services marketing: Forecasts from ten services experts. *Journal of Services Marketing, 17*(2), 107–121.

Grove, S., Fisk, R., & Laforge, M. (2004). Developing the impression management skills of the service worker: An application of Stanislavsky's principles in a services context. *The Service Industries Journal, 24*(2), 1–14.

Haahti, A. (2003). Theory of relationship cultivation: A point of view to design of experience. *Journal of Business and Management, 9*(3), 303.

Heider, F. (1958). *The psychology of interpersonal relations*. New York, NY: Wiley.

Herzberg, P. (1965). The motivation to work among Finnish supervisors. *Personnel Psychology,* 11, 393–402.

Herzberg, F., Mausner, B., & Snyderman, B. B. (2011). *The motivation to work (vol. 1)*. London: Transaction Publishers.

Jennings, G., & Weiler, B. (2006). Mediating meaning: Perspectives on brokering quality tourist experiences. Working paper, Monash University.

Jones, E. E., & Pittman, T. S. (1982). Toward a general theory of strategic self-presentation. In J. Suls (Ed.), *Psychological perspectives on the self* (pp. 231–262). Hillsdale, NJ: Erlbaum.

Keng, C. J., Huang, T. L., Zheng, L. J., & Hsu, M. K. (2007). Modeling service encounters and customer experiential value in retailing: An empirical investigation of shopping mall customers in Taiwan. *International Journal of Service Industry Management, 18*(4), 349–367.

Kim, S., Cha, J., Knutson, B. J., & Beck, J. A. (2011). Development and testing of the consumer experience index (CEI). *Managing Service Quality: An International Journal, 21*(2), 112–132.

Littlejohn, S. W. (1983) *Theories of human communication*. Belmont, CA: Wardsworth Publishing Co.

Mathwick, C., Malhotra, N., & Rigdon, E. (2001). Experiential value: Conceptualization, measurement and application in the catalog and internet shopping environment. *Journal of Retailing, 77*(1), 39–56.

Mathwick, C., Malhotra, N., & Rigdon, E. (2002). The effect of dynamic retail experiences on experiential perceptions of value: An internet and catalog comparison. *Journal of Retailing, 78*(1), 51–60.

Maxham III, J. G., & Netemeyer, R. G. (2003). Firms reap what they sow: The effects of shared values and perceived organizational justice on customers' evaluations of complaint handling. *Journal of Marketing, 67*(1), 46–62.

McCarthy, I. P., Pitt, L. F., & Berthon, P. R. (2010). Service customization through dramaturgy. In F. S. Fogliatto & G. J. C. da Silveira (Eds.), *Mass customization: Engineering and managing global operations* (pp. 43–64). London: Springer.

McCracken, G. D. (1988). *The long interview*. Newbury Park, CA: Sage.

Merriam, S. (1998). Conducting effective interviews. In S. B. Merriam (Ed.), *Qualitative research and case study applications in education* (pp. 71–93). San Francisco, CA: Jossey-Bass.

Mossberg, L. E. N. A., Hanefors, M., Hansen, A. H., (2014). Guide performance: Co-created experiences for tourist immersion. In N. K. Prebensen, J. S. Chen, & M. Uysal (Eds.), *Value creation in tourist experiences* (pp. 234–247). London: CABI.

Noe, F. P., Uysal, M., & Magnini, V. P. (2010). *Tourist customer service satisfaction: An encounter approach.* New York, NY: Routledge.

Parasuraman, A., Zeithaml, V. A., & Berry, L. L. (1985). A conceptual model of service quality and its implications for future research. *Journal of Marketing, 49*(4), 41–50.

Prebensen, N. K., Kim, H. L., & Uysal, M. (2016). Cocreation as moderator between the experience value and satisfaction relationship. *Journal of Travel Research, 55*(7), 934–945.

Prebensen, N. K., Vittersø, J., & Dahl, T. (2013). Value co-creation: Significance of tourist resources. *Annals of Tourism Research, 42*(July), 240–261.

Prebensen, N. K., & Foss, L. (2011). Coping and co-creating in tourist experiences. *International Journal of Tourism Research, 13*(1), 54–67.

Prebensen, N. K., Woo, E., Chen, J., & Uysal, M. (2014). Motivation and involvement as antecedents of the perceived value of the destination experience. *Journal of Travel Research, 5*(2), 253–264.

Prebensen, N. K., Woo, E., & Uysal, M. S. (2014). Experience value: Antecedents and consequences. *Current Issues in Tourism, 17*(10), 910–928.

Pritchard, M. P., & Havitz, M. E. (2006). Destination appraisal: An analysis of critical incidents. *Annals of Tourism Research, 33*(1), 25–46.

Ritti, R. R., & Silver, J. H. (1986). Early processes of institutionalization: The dramaturgy of exchange in interorganizational relations. *Administrative Science Quarterly, 31*(1), 25–42.

Ryan, R. M., & Deci, E. L. (2000). Self-determination theory and the facilitation of intrinsic motivation, social development, and well-being. *American Psychologist, 55*(1), 68–78.

Schubert, T. W., Friedmann, F., & Regenbrecht, H. T. (1999, April). Decomposing the sense of presence: Factor analytic insights. In *2nd International Workshop on Presence* (Vol. 1999).

Shostack, G. L. (1985). Planning the service encounter. *The Service Encounter, 1*, 243–254.

Taylor, S. J., Bogdan, R., & DeVault, M. (2015). *Introduction to qualitative research methods: A guidebook and resource.* New Jersey, NJ: John Wiley & Sons.

Tedeschi, J. T., & Norman, N. M. (1985). A social psychological interpretation of displaced aggression. *Advances in group processes, 2*, 29–56.

Tribe, J., & Snaith, T. (1998). From SERVQUAL to HOLSAT: Holiday satisfaction in Varadero, Cuba. *Tourism Management, 19*(1), 25–34.

Truong, T.-H., & Foster, D. (2006). Using HOLSAT to evaluate tourist satisfaction at destinations: The case of Australian holidaymakers in Vietnam. *Tourism Management, 27*(4), 842–855.

Tsai, W.-C., & Huang, Y.-M. (2002). Mechanisms linking employee affective delivery and customer behavioral intentions. *Journal of Applied Psychology, 87*(5), 1001–1008.

Vargo, S. L., & Lusch, R. F. (2004). Evolving to a new dominant logic for marketing. *Journal of Marketing, 68*, 1–17.

Vargo, S. L., & Lusch, R. F. (2008). Service dominant logic: Continuing the evolution. *Journal of Academy of Marketing Science, 36*(1), 1–11.

Vroom, V. H. (1964). *Work and motivation.* New York, NY: Wiley & Sons.

Wengraf, T. (2001). *Qualitative research interviewing.* London: Sage.

Zeithaml, V. A., Berry, L. L., & Parasuraman, A. (1991). Understanding of customer expectations of service. *Sloan Management Review, 32*(3), 42.

# 5  Designing forest-based wellbeing tourism services for Japanese customers

## A case study from Finland

*Raija Komppula and Henna Konu*

## Introduction

Customer needs and expectations form the starting point for new service development. Price and Wrigley (2015) emphasize the importance of deep customer insight, especially when a new, national customer segment previously unfamiliar to the service provider is being considered as a potential market. Previous market research findings may help in building a broad picture of the potential market, but getting in touch with the actual customers would be the best way to learn to understand them (Price, Wrigley & Straker, 2015). When the potential customer target group is new and no previous experience of the behaviour of the customer is available, discovering methods of acquiring deep customer insight for new service development can be challenging. The purpose of this chapter is to introduce and evaluate methods of customer involvement in new service development for a new target group. First, it presents a short introduction to the theoretical underpinnings behind customer involvement in new service development, and then the development process in a form of a case study is presented phase by phase. Finally, it discusses the challenges and advantages of the methods of customer involvement that were applied in this case study.

The starting point for this study was the idea of developing forest-based wellbeing tourism services in Eastern Finland for Japanese clients, proposed by Japanese physician Fumio Hirano. He introduced to the Finnish partners the Japanese idea of "forest bathing" (*Shinrin-yoku*), a relaxation activity associated with visiting forests (Park et al., 2009) that has been shown to reduce stress (Tsunetsugu, Park & Yoshifumi, 2010). Several other studies have reported on the positive effects of forest-based activities on mental and physical health (Lee, Park, Tsunetsugu, Kagawa & Miyazaki, 2009; Lee et al., 2012; Li, 2010; Korpela, Ylen, Tyrväinen, & Silvennoinen, 2010; Morita et al., 2007; Morita et al., 2011; Ohtsuka, Yabunaka & Takayama, 1998; Park et al., 2008), and it is widely believed that coming into contact with forest environments is somehow beneficial to human wellbeing and comfort. In the Finnish context, forest-based wellbeing tourism might refer to culture, nature, peace and quiet in the countryside (Konu, Tuohino & Komppula, 2010). The location of the service offering would be in a rural environment, where acquiring a sense of one's own wellbeing through a peaceful environment and slow pace of life are core elements of a wellbeing holiday (Konu, 2010; Pesonen & Komppula, 2010; Pesonen, Komppula, Kronenberg & Peters, 2011).

According to Edvardsson, Kristensson, Magnusson and Sundström (2012), methods that permit potential customers to identify their own needs and ideas, and that are elicited in the natural use context, provide most concrete and immediately applicable information in service development. Magnusson, Matthing and Kristensson (2003) state that if customers are given the opportunity to deliberate at a location where user needs and information can be readily perceived, new ideas and solutions that were previously unthinkable may emerge. This chapter presents a case study of a new service development project with the aim of developing service modules that could be included in a forest wellbeing package tour for Japanese tourists. As the aim of the research was to acquire deep customer insight about the expectations and characteristics of a new and unfamiliar target group, the decision was made to apply a combination of diverse methods of customer involvement, some of them borrowed from service design.

## Theory

### *Customer involvement in new service development for new target groups*

According to Prideaux, Cave, Thompson and Sibtain (2012), tourist destinations should be active in searching for new potential markets; when such markets are identified, the tourist destinations should ensure that the supply-side pull factors match the demand-side push factors successfully. They continue by stating that developing new tourism markets requires a holistic understanding of consumer push factors and for the destination to able to respond to these by harnessing its pull factors to create a tourism experience.

As service-dominant logic (SDL) proposes, customers are co-creators of value (Payne, Storbacka & Frow, 2008; Vargo & Lusch, 2006) together with the service providers, which implies that customers should be involved in service development processes (Edvardsson et al., 2012). Tourism products are experience-centric services that engage customers emotionally, physically, intellectually or even spiritually (Shaw, Bailey & Williams, 2011; Stickdorn, 2009; Zomerdijk & Voss, 2010). Hence, customer involvement in tourism service development is particularly crucial when defining and designing the experience (Prebensen, Vitterso & Dahl, 2013). Although co-creation and customer involvement in service development in tourism has been recently pointed out by a few researchers (e.g. Prebensen & Foss, 2010; Prebensen et al., 2013; Shaw et al., 2011) only limited empirical evidence of the level of innovative activities in tourism and hospitality industries can be found in the literature (Hjalager, 2010). Hjalager and Nordin (2011) state that future research on tourism innovation should focus on topics related to user-driven innovation practices and methods. This case study is a small step in this direction.

Wetter Edman (2009) notes that some of the key principles of SDL – focusing on the needs, wants and expectations of the customer – are similar to those of service design (SD). Traditional market research methods – interviews, surveys and questionnaires – explore the how, what and where in relation to the customer or the product, but a need for a deeper customer insight when developing services for an unknown consumer group requires understanding of customers' why questions (Price et al., 2015). Price and Wrigley (2015) suggest that a design-led approach offers "an intimate shared understanding of the unspoken, latent current and future needs of the customer" (p. 1). According to Moritz (2005), "Service design is the overall experience of a service, as well as the design of the process and strategy to provide the service" (p. 39). Service design is about understanding customers' needs, expectations and behaviour, and developing and implementing solutions (Moritz, 2005). According to Mager (2009), service design is a holistic, interdisciplinary and human-centred approach that aims to integrate the customers into the exploration and development processes with the service providers.

Wetter Edman (2009) points out that the similarities between SDL and SD have given fruitful grounds for management and business in adapting service design methods and tools in developing products and services. According to Miettinen (2009), traditional research methods (surveys, questionnaires, interviews and experiments) serve their purpose well at supporting the design process. Nevertheless, adapted methods, such as observation and ethnography in a participatory setting, enable the researcher to understand the user's tacit knowledge in the use situation. Service designers often use innovative ways of collecting user information with a strong emphasis on visualizing, such as design workshops, collages, visual diaries, storyboarding and mind-mapping (Miettinen, 2009).

According to Cayla and Arnould (2013), ethnography has become a popular research approach in market research practice, and several large companies employ ethnographers in new product development projects or to explore new market opportunities. Nevertheless, according to them, research into ethnographic practices in the corporate world is still scarce. Cayla and Arnould (2013) discuss the advantages of ethnographic storytelling and the persona method as a means of provoking, inspiring and increasing organizational innovation, but they do not make any reference to service design or design-led methods. Hence, as Wetter Edman (2011) notes, the relation of service marketing and management to service design can be seen as complementary, especially in tools and methods for user involvement and co-creation.

A few attempts have been made to adapt service design thinking to the development of tourist services. One example of this is an application of mobile ethnography (myServiceFellow) in selected European tourism destinations, reported in a book edited by Stickdorn and Frischhut (2012). Another example is presented by Trischler and Zehrer (2012), reporting the findings of a study which applied "persona", "observation", "guided interviews" and "visualization" methods to evaluate service experiences at a theme park in Gold Coast, Australia. Price and Wrigley (2015) sought a deeper understanding of nationality segments in an airport context by utilizing shadowing, personas, touchpoint timelines, customer narratives, interviews and focus groups, as well as co-design workshops. Komppula and Lassila (2014) conducted a multiple case study in which they applied several methods of customer involvement, including focus group interviews, participatory observation, drama method, empathy-based method and contact point evaluation carried out with mobile devices. Their findings indicate that the qualitative methods produced an in-depth understanding of consumer needs and expectations, but they were demanding, time-consuming and required lots of expertise, which in many cases is not available to the smaller tourism entrepreneurs, who comprise the majority in the tourism and hospitality industry. Hence, Komppula and Lassila (2014) as well as Russo-Spena and Mele (2012) recommend that enterprises cooperate with a broad spectrum of collaborators, which would involve resource integration with several kinds of stakeholders (Payne et al., 2008) and improve the co-creation practices of innovation. Zehrer (2009) recommends that small tourism businesses act synergistically in cooperation with other tourism enterprises in adapting service design as a tool in developing the service experience.

### *The case study: the service development process*

The development project started in June 2011, when a network of eighteen entrepreneurs, the regional tourism marketing organization, representatives of the local municipality and other stakeholders were invited by University of Eastern Finland to attend the first meetings. The first phase of the project, a literature review, was conducted during summer 2011, and the group interviews with potential Japanese tourists took place in autumn that year. The findings of the literature review were presented to the entrepreneurs in February and the findings of the group interviews in October 2012. Based on these findings and additional training about the Japanese as customers, the entrepreneurs started to design product modules, which were then tested virtually among potential Japanese tourists in spring 2013. In May 2013, a group of members of the product development network travelled to Japan to meet with the initiators of the project and potential customers, as well as to get to know the Japanese forest bathing services. The findings of the virtual testing and the experiences of the trip were discussed with the entrepreneurs, and the final offering for the test group visit was created by the entrepreneurs. In August 2013, the experiences of the Japanese test group were studied utilizing an ethnographic method. The feedback of the findings of the ethnographic study were discussed with the members of the network in a seminar in November 2013.

   The phases of the research conducted in the development project are described in more detail in the following sections.

### *Phase one: literature review and market information search*

In the first phase, a literature review of Japanese culture and research on *Shinrin-yoku* and the effects of forests on human wellbeing was conducted in order to build a basic understanding of the potential segment. As Watkins and Gnoth (2011) state, it is widely accepted that an in-depth understanding of the characteristics of this market is required when developing new products for Japanese tourists.

From Japan, Finland attracts young females in particular for individual cultural trips to the capital region, while the elderly segment visit Lapland to see the Northern Lights (Finnish Tourist Board, 2013). The literature review gave an insight into the characteristics of the Japanese as consumers. Japanese consumers are relatively homogenous, co-operative and loyal, they greatly value harmony, and social obligations and reciprocity are emphasized (Synodinos, 2001). According to Wierzbicka (1997), conforming to group norms and building trust are important goals for relationship-oriented Japanese people, who promote a personality that is humble, self-limiting, adaptable, harmonious and passive. Synodinos (2001) also mentions the implications of a well-informed society and the importance of age and aesthetic values when approaching potential Japanese customers. Genestre, Herbig and Shao (1995) state that quality of service is highly appreciated in Japan, and for the Japanese the quest for status and prestige items is an important consideration. Customers are always treated with extreme courtesy and respect (Synodinos, 2001). Reluctance to give negative feedback is one specific feature of Japanese consumers, and connected to "reserved" behaviour, indirect speaking and to avoidance of giving personal opinions (Wierzbicka, 1997).

The Japanese have still relatively little free time compared to Europeans, and many people still do not take all the holidays to which they are entitled, but instead prefer to take time off during official public holidays (Synodinos, 2001). Nevertheless, Watkins and Gnoth (2011) state that a new movement towards travel and leisure activities has emerged: Japanese travellers are often inexperienced and travel in groups (Watkins & Gnoth, 2011), but in recent years, the amount of individually arranged travel has increased (Synodinos, 2001; Watkins & Gnoth, 2011). The top-ranking factors for Japanese travellers are outstanding scenery, historical or archaeologically interesting places, nice weather, high standards of hygiene or cleanliness and the availability of sufficient information before the trip (Watkins & Gnoth, 2011).

According to Watkins and Gnoth (2011), the middle-aged package tourist segment is in accordance with the existing literature on Japanese culture and travel styles, but the younger segment – Japanese backpackers – represent values that reflect a very personal search for meaning and fulfilment. The largest segment travelling from Japan to Europe are experienced female travellers aged fifty years and over, but the highest departure rate is among women in their twenties (European Travel Commission, 2013).

*The second phase: group interviews with SD methods*

In order to gain an in-depth understanding about the target group, a focus group method was chosen, as the outcome is richer than that of individual interviews (Hjalager & Nordin, 2011). As the budget for this study was limited, Japanese people currently living in Finland were invited as informants. Informants were sought via Finnish–Japanese associations and other stakeholders with connections to Japanese people living in Finland. Finally, five women and three men agreed to be informants.

Two focus group interviews were conducted, using methods borrowed from the service design approach. As Japanese people often find Western frankness in expressing their opinions immature, and as directly eliciting someone's preferences is deemed impolite (Wierzbicka, 1997), generative exercises were found effective in supporting the focus group interview. The topics were discussed in groups, and feelings or opinions were captured in "designerly artefacts" (Miettinen, 2009). In the first group meeting, with four informants (one male and three females aged 22 to 55, two students and two working people), a forest walk was undertaken, during which fifty-one photographs were taken. The participant was asked to explain why he or she chose to take the particular pictures they did. After the walk, there was an interview session that included building mindmaps. In the second group, (two males and two females aged 22 to 25 years, students) the research data was collected in an interview session with a mood board and mindmaps. The sessions were recorded on video and transcribed. Both focus group interviews lasted about four hours.

The transcriptions were organized, summarized, categorized and interpreted. The visual and verbal data were then analysed using content analysis. Following the guidelines from Roulston (2010), the data was organized into thematic groupings. In the artefacts, the number of triggers and the structure of the artefact were compared. From the presentation of the artefact, the length, the breadth and depth were analysed (Sanders, 2005). The recurring elements were collected in an Excel worksheet in order to gain an understanding of the basic elements needed for a functioning service product and then to identify the new ideas presented by the participants.

The persona method was adapted with the aim of illustrating the potential target segments found as a result of the literature review and the focus group interview. Personas represent user archetypes and lifestyles, and each profile should represent the composition of subpopulation of users (Moritz, 2005; Trischler & Zehrer, 2012). Personas are fictional user profiles, and they may include personalities, behaviours, details about specific interests, goals and even names (Miettinen, 2009). Brangier and Bornet (2011) posit that the persona method is often used to complement other user-centred methods. The strength of the technique is claimed to be its user-sensitizing impact, which enables the user to be better understood for further analysis and research (Trischler & Zehrer, 2012). Personas can shift the focus from demographics and other traditional segmentation criteria towards the actual wants and needs of the consumers (van Dijk, Raijmakers & Kelly, 2011), but as Brangier and Bornet (2011) note, interpreting the data is challenging, and the findings that emerge from the persona method may vary from researcher to another. According to Cayla and Arnould (2013), the persona method has become a common and widespread tool in ethnographic approaches to market segmentation. They state that personas help executives to make sense of the world of their customers and serve as a symbolic device that helps them to connect with their customers.

Four fictive personas representing possible segments in the target market were built from features provided by the informants and supported by the literature review. They do not represent a single person or informant; rather, they symbolize the main characteristics of a possible customer segment, leaving more detailed information aside. Seiko represents a young, female, well-educated target group with an active lifestyle and a high awareness of environmental issues. Sonny represents a young target group that appreciates adventurous activities. These two young segments would be interested in individual travel instead of travelling in a group. Monoke represents a segment that would travel with children and therefore would appreciate family friendly services. Sakiko would represent the elderly female target group with a preference for group travel.

The feasibility of the focus group method was discussed among the actors in the project. Using focus groups composed mostly of students and people who have already in a way absorbed in the context may reduce the credibility of the findings as a representation of pure Japanese opinions. Nevertheless, from the managerial point of view, using Japanese consumers living in Finland as informants was cost-effective. The conclusion was that the findings can be taken only as tentative reflections of potential Japanese tourists' expectations towards a Finnish forest-based wellbeing tourism offering. Although the focus group method combined with context mapping techniques was laborious and challenging in terms of interpreting the data, the findings concerning Japanese travel habits and the values behind them seemed to be substantiated by the literature. On the other hand, important details were raised concerning the similarities and differences between Finnish and Japanese people in terms of their relationship with forests, which might help Finnish tourism entrepreneurs in designing forest-based itineraries for Japanese target groups.

*The third phase: virtual testing*

Based on the findings of the focus group interview, the entrepreneurs developed service modules, from among which the representatives of the university chose fifteen activity service modules and five accommodation module descriptions, which were carefully translated into Japanese. Then, a web-based virtual testing environment was created in the platform, presenting the modules by giving a short written description and showing pictures or a video related to the module. This phase would correspond to a "service test drive", as suggested by Edvardsson, Enquist and Johnston (2010), which refers to giving potential customers the opportunity to get to know the service in a virtual "in-use" situation.

Convenience sampling was used, and the link to the test environment was sent to the Japanese partners in the development project, with a request to distribute the link in their networks. The respondents were asked to evaluate the service modules by describing the feelings the module raises in them, what they think is good and what should be changed, and for whom the service would be suitable. They were also asked to give a star rating on the attractiveness of each module. Altogether, 130 responses were received with star ratings. In addition, feedback on the test environment itself was received by e-mail.

The comments received about the modules brought forth four different themes and offered good ideas related to diverse modules. The first theme revealed travel motives and reasons for participating in particular kinds of services (being together with a family, relaxation, and gaining energy and strength). The second theme was comments on the diverse components and content of the modules. More practical information was sought related to the suitability and accessibility of the offering, for example. The comments and star ratings gave a very clear idea of which services were the most appealing. The third theme was ideas and suggestions for new services and additional themes for services. For example, in relation to a module that focused on farm tourism, the respondents pointed out that it is possible to visit farms anywhere in the world. They thought that it would be interesting to know more about the local wildlife. Fourth, suggestions for improving the module descriptions and the marketing messages of the offering were received. The respondents pointed out that the module descriptions should include more concrete and practical information. Some respondents provided alternative possibilities for some of the phrases used in the descriptions. They said that the offering could be more attractive to Japanese consumers with slightly different wording.

The findings of the virtual testing show that the information gained was varied, and the comments did not solely focus on evaluating the service modules; they also provided additional information. Although this was the first application of this virtual testing platform, it proved to successfully result in concrete suggestions for further development of the modules, and it gave us an understanding of which modules should be included in the actual test trip and which should be removed. Additionally, in technical terms, several ideas for further development of the method were received (see Konu, 2015b), and the platform was later applied to virtual testing in the domestic market.

*The fourth phase: ethnographic study during the test group visit*

After the virtual testing, the modules were further developed, and the final set of service modules were chosen for the external test of the offering. A test group of eight Japanese tourists and two representatives of a tour operator visited the destination in August 2013 for five days. The second author of this chapter travelled with the group and collected data by means of participant observation, group interviews and customer feedback surveys. Utilizing a variety of data collection methods is common in an ethnographic study (Fettermann, 2010) and enables the creation of a more comprehensive picture of the phenomenon under examination. The goal was to gather feedback from end users and intermediaries about the service modules and the entire offering. A detailed report of the ethnographic study is presented in Konu (2015a).

As it has been suggested that test customers should be interested and motivated to test the product and should represent the potential target market (Hoyer, Chandy, Dorotic, Krafft & Singh, 2010), the customers were selected to represent people interested in nature, nature activities and wellbeing. Based on the findings of the earlier phases of the study, the participants should also comprise different age groups and both genders, and they should show an interest in Finland. The responsibility for the final selection of the test customers was given to the project's collaborative partner in Japan, who sought out the test customers with help of the Finnish–Japanese Society. Additionally, representatives of the most important tour operator partner of the Finnish Tourist Board in Japan were invited on the test trip. In this case, the selected test customers paid for their flights to the destination and back, but the services at the destination were free for them.

The observation started at the airport when the test group arrived and continued until their departure. In addition to the researcher, an interpreter and a local Finnish tour guide were present for the duration of the trip. During the participant observation, the researcher focused on observing the customers and the interaction between service providers, customers and the environment. She also took a number of photographs to support the field notes.

At the beginning of the trip, the feedback surveys were delivered and the participants were asked to fill in the forms every day and to return the forms to the researcher. In the open-ended questionnaire, they were asked to describe what activities and/or things were the best during the day, what they would improve, and their overall assessment of the day. In addition, they were asked to evaluate each service module of that day by using a star rating, similar to the virtual testing phase. The Japanese test customers filled out the questionnaire in Japanese and the representatives of the tour operator in English. By the end of the trip, they had also completed an additional form to give an overall assessment of the whole trip. The Japanese comments and responses were translated into Finnish after the trip.

At the end of the test trip, two group interviews were conducted, one with two Japanese women and the other with two representatives of the tour operators. The interviews were carried out in English, but an interpreter was present in case there was a need for clarification during the interview. The interviews dealt with issues such as the most memorable experience and the best part of this trip for the interviewee, as well as what areas they would improve.

The overall data consisted of the field notes (26 pages), translated responses from the test customers (53 pages) and the two interviews. The analysis was written in the form of a trip description including a depiction of all activities day by day and activity by activity, telling the story of the whole week. The interpretation of the data was discussed with the interpreter and with the tour guide who had both experienced the whole trip. To increase the trustworthiness of the study (Creswell, 2014), the interpretations of the researcher were also discussed and checked with the informants.

The service providers received detailed, practical information for product development purposes. The data showed that some service modules were not seen as appealing to this target market, but features like the guided activities in a natural environment were the ones that brought the most positive emotional experiences among the test group. Some of the service modules divided opinions quite drastically, meaning that these service modules could be offered as optional services. Additionally, some service modules were more ready than others, meaning that more in-depth analysis of the customer journey and the touchpoints is needed as well as internal testing of the service processes. It was evident that the activities in some modules took longer than expected as the service providers had underestimated the time needed. As this was a test trip, the timetable was very tight because many activities and service modules needed to be tested. This felt rather exhausting for the test customers. For the final product, it is important to set a reasonable number of activities per day and also to leave some free time in the itinerary in addition to the guided activities. The tour guide also needs to be firm in guiding the group and keeping to the schedule. Information about the product and the service modules in it should be sufficiently detailed.

## Discussion and conclusions

The main purpose of this research was to gain deep customer insight of potential Japanese customers in order to develop new tourism services targeted at this new segment. This study responds to the call to use more qualitative, interpretative and interactive methods and approaches in order to increase the level of profound customer insight in new service development (e.g. Edvardsson et al., 2012; Price et al., 2015). This case shows that the methods used were effective in helping to identify the emotional responses of customers and in getting a deeper understanding of the wishes and needs of potential customers. Hence, our experiences during this project support the notions of Cayla and Arnould (2013), indicating that ethnographic stories and the development of narrative personas created a tool that enabled the entrepreneurs to immerse themselves in the narrative content of the study, describing the characteristics and behavioural features of the potential customers. According to Cayla and Arnould (2013), ethnographic stories are unique modes of market sensemaking and sensegiving, giving executives access to explanations of consumer behaviour. Having said that, they provide a reminder that ethnographic stories are always told from a specific point of view and for a specific audience, indicating that they are not trying to reach an objective truth. Cayla and Arnould (2013) also note that an ethnographic approach focusing on a few informants often conflicts with knowledge regimes that focus on scale and numbers.

During the new service development (NSD) process, the advantages and challenges of applying different methods in diverse NSD phases were identified. Despite the technical problems and a few shortcomings of the web-based platform in the virtual testing, the method enabled the provision of information in a manner that gave the potential customers an ability to "feel" the activities and the nature in the service modules, which is in accordance with the findings of Edvardsson, Enquist and Johnston (2010). Nevertheless, using other than traditional methods may be time-consuming and expensive for companies, and applying them may be problematic as companies may lack the knowhow to implement them (Konu, 2015c; Konu & Komppula, 2016). Hence, utilizing this kind of customer involvement method may require collaboration between tourism companies and research units that are familiar with these methods (Komppula & Lassila, 2014).

In addition to gaining information through the customer involvement activities, it must be noted that the trip to Japan by the entrepreneurs in order to get to know the source market was also an important phase of the new service development project. This trip gave them an opportunity to experience Japanese courtesy and hospitality in reality. Only a person's own experiences can demonstrate what the phrase "the customer is the king" really means in that market in practice, in the expression, gestures and movement of the service personnel. This highlights the idea of Edvardsson, Enquist and Johnston (2010) that emphasizes the importance of understanding the human interaction in the service experience. We conclude by arguing that, as the customer experience is at the core of tourism services (Zomerdijk & Voss, 2010), the customer should be involved actively in new service development in order to gain access deep customer insight.

## Acknowledgement

We want to thank the Forest Wellbeing project for enabling this research, and Lotta Snicker, whose contribution to gathering and analysing the data in the first two phases of the study was indispensable.

## References

Brangier, E. & Bornet, C. (2011). Persona: A method to produce representations focused on consumer's needs. In W. Karwowski, M. M. Soares & N. A. Stanton (Eds.), *Human factors and ergonomics in consumer product design: Methods and techniques* (pp. 38–62). Boca Raton, FL: Taylor & Francis Group.

Cayla, J. & Arnould, E. (2013). Ethnographic stories for market learning. *Journal of Marketing, 77*(4), 1–16.

Creswell, J. W. (2014). *Research design: Qualitative, quantitative, and mixed methods approaches*, 4th ed.. Los Angeles, CA: Sage Publications.

van Dijk, G., Raijmakers, B. & Kelly, L. (2011). What are the tools of service design? In M. Stickdorn & J. Schneider (Eds.), *This is service design thinking* (pp. 146–215). Amsterdam: BIS Publishers.

Edvardsson, B., Enquist, B. & Johnston, R. (2010). Design dimensions of experience rooms for the service test drives: Case studies in several contexts. *Managing Service Quality, 20*(4), 312–327.

Edvardsson, B., Kristensson, P., Magnusson, P. & Sundström, E. (2012). Customer integration within service development: A review of methods and an analysis of insitu and exsitu contributions. *Technovation, 32*, 419–429.

European Travel Commission. (2013). Market Insights, Japan, September 2013. European Travel Commission Market Intelligence group. www.etc-corporate.org/reports/market-insights-japan?page...id.

Fetterman, D. M. (2010). *Ethnography, step-by-step*, 3rd ed. Los Angeles, CA: Sage Publications.

Finnish Tourist Board. (2013). Semi-annual report, Japan, 2013. Available at: http://www.visitfinland.fi/wp-content/uploads/2013/06/Japan-Market-news_2013-21.pdf (accessed 10 October 2013).

Genestre, A., Herbig, P. & Shao, A. T. (1995). What does marketing really mean to the Japanese? *Marketing Intelligence & Planning, 13*(9), 16–27.

Hjalager, A. -M. (2010). A review on innovation research in tourism. *Tourism Management, 31*(1), 1–12.

Hjalager, A. -M. & Nordin, S. (2011). User-driven innovation in tourism: A review of methodologies. *Journal of Quality Assurance in Hospitality & Tourism, 12*(4), 289–315.

Hoyer, W. D., Chandy, R., Dorotic, M., Krafft, M. & Singh, S. S. (2010). Consumer cocreation in new product development. *Journal of Service Research, 13*(3), 283–296.

Komppula, R. & Lassila, H. (2014). Co-creating tourism services: A multiple case study of methods of customer involvement in tourism. In H. Pechlaner & E. Smeral (Eds.), *Tourism and leisure: Current issues and perspectives of development in research and business* (pp. 287–303). Wiesbaden, DE: Gabler-Springer.

Konu, H. (2010). Unique value creating destination product attributes of the Nordic countries: Finnish perceptions. In *Proceedings of the Academy of Marketing Conference 2010: Transformational Marketing, Proceedings*. Coventry, UK: Coventry University.

Konu, H. (2015a). Developing a forest-based wellbeing tourism product together with customers: An ethnographic approach. *Tourism Management, 49* (August 2015), 1–16.

Konu, H. (2015b). Developing forest-based well-being tourism products by using virtual product testing. *Anatolia, 26*(1), 99–102.

Konu, H. (2015c). Developing nature-based tourism products with customers by utilizing the Delphi method. *Tourism Management Perspectives, 14*, 42–54.

Konu, H. & Komppula, R. (2016). Customer involvement in a new service development process: Developing the "feelgood in Lapland" tourism offering. *Anatolia: An International Journal of Tourism and Hospitality Research*, 27, DOI:10.1080/130329 17.2016.1144625.

Konu, H., Tuohino, A. & Komppula, R. (2010). Lake Wellness: A practical example of a New Service Development (NSV) concept in the tourism industry. *Journal of Vacation Marketing, 16*(2), 125–139.

Korpela, K. M., Ylen, M., Tyrväinen, L. & Silvennoinen, H. (2010). Favorite green, waterside and urban environments, restorative experiences and perceived health in Finland. *Health Promotion International, 25*(2), 200–209.

Lee, J., Park, B. J., Tsunetsugu, Y., Kagawa, T. & Miyazaki, Y. (2009). Restorative effects of viewing real forest landscapes, based on a comparison with urban landscapes. *Scandinavian Journal of Forest Research, 24*, 227–324.

Lee, J., Li, Q., Tyrväinen, L., Tsunetsugu, Y., Park, B.-J., Kagawa, T. & Miyazaki, Y. (2012). Nature therapy and preventive medicine. In J. Maddock (Ed.), *Public health: Social behavioral health* (pp. 325–350). InTech Europe. DOI: 10.5772/2242.

Li, Q. (2010). Effect of forest bathing trips on human immune function. *Environmental Health and Preventive Medicine, 15*, 9–17.

Mager, B. (2009). Service design as an emerging field. In S. Miettinen & M. Koivisto (Eds.), *Designing services with innovative methods* (pp. 28–42). Keuruu, FI: Otava Book Printing Ltd.

Magnusson, P. R., Matthing, J. & Kristensson, P. (2003). Managing user involvement in service innovation: Experiments with innovating end users. *Journal of Service Research, 6*(2), 111–124.

Miettinen, S. (2009). Designing services with innovative methods. In S. Miettinen & M. Koivisto (Eds.), *Designing services with innovative methods* (pp. 10–25). Keuruu, FI: Otava Book Printing Ltd.

Morita, E., Fukuda, S., Nagano, J., Hamajima, N., Yamamoto, H. & Iwai, Y. (2007). Psychological effects of forest environments on healthy adults: *Shinrin-yoku* (forest-air bathing, walking) as a possible method of stress reduction. *Public Health, 121*, 54–63.

Morita, E., Naito, M., Hishada, A., Wakai, K., Mori, A., Asai, Y., Okada, R., Kawai, S. & Hamajiva, N. (2011). No association between the frequency of forest walking and blood pressure levels of the prevalence of hypertension in a cross-sectional study of a Japanese population. *Environmental Health Preventive Medicine, 16*(5), 299–306.

Moritz, S. (2005). Service design: Practical access to an evolving field. KISD. Available at: http://stefan-moritz.com/welcome/Service_Design (accessed 10 January 2016).

Ohtsuka, Y., Yabunaka, N. & Takayama, S. (1998). *Shinrin-yoku* (forest-air bathing and walking) effectively decreases blood glucose levels in diabetic patients. *International Journal of Biometeorol, 41*, 125–127.

Park, B. J., Tsunetsugu, Y., Morikawa T., Ishii, H., Furuhashi S. & Hirano, H. (2008). Physiological effects of *Shinrin-yoku* (taking in the atmosphere of the forest) in mixed forest in Shinano Town, Japan. *Scandinavian Journal of Forest Research, 23*, 278–283.

Park, B. J., Tsunetsugu, Y., Morikawa T., Kasetani, T., Kagawa, T. & Miyazaki, Y. (2009). Physiological effects of forest recreation in a young conifer forest in Hinokage Town, Japan. *Silva Fennica, 43*(2), 291–301.

Payne, A. F., Storbacka, K. & Frow, P. (2008). Managing the co-creation of value. *Journal of the Academy Marketing Science, 36*, 83–96.

Pesonen, J. & Komppula, R. (2010). Rural wellbeing tourism: Motivations and expectations. *Journal of Hospitality and Tourism Management, 17*(1), 150–158.

Pesonen, J., Komppula, R., Kronenberg, C. & Peters, M. (2011). Understanding the relationship between push and pull motivations in rural tourism. *Tourism Review, 66*(3), 32–49.

Prebensen, N. K., Vittersø, J. & Dahl, T. I. (2013). Value co-creation significance of tourist resources. *Annals of Tourism Research, 42*: 240–261.

Prebensen N. K. & Foss L. (2010). Coping and co-creating in tourist experiences. *International Journal of Tourism Research, 13*(1), 54–67.

Price, R. & Wrigley, C. (2015). Design and a deep customer insight approach to innovation. *Journal of International Consumer Marketing*. DOI:10.1080/08961530.2015.1092405.

Price, R. A., Wrigley, C. & Straker, K. (2015). Not just what they want, but why they want it. *Qualitative Market Research: An International Journal, 18*(2), 230–248.

Prideaux, B., Cave, J., Thompson, M. & Sibtain, J. (2012). Recognizing new market opportunities and selecting appropriate segments: Targeting Chinese outbound tourists. *Journal of Vacation Marketing, 18*(4), 287–299.

Roulston, K. (2010). *Reflective interviewing. A guide to theory and practice*. London: Sage Publications.

Russo-Spena, T. & Mele, C. (2012). "Five Co-s" in innovating: A practice-based view. *Journal of Service Management, 23*(4), 527–553.

Sanders, E. B.-N. (2005). Information. Inspiration and Co-creation. Paper presented at *The 6th International Conference of the European Academy of Design*, March 29–31 2005. Bremen, GE: University of Arts. http://u.osu.edu/sanders.82/files/2015/02/InformationInspirationandCocreation_Sanders_05-19uvmzz.pdf (accessed 10 January 2016).

Shaw, G., Bailey, A. & Williams, A. (2011). Aspects of service-dominant logic and its implications for tourism management: Examples from the hotel industry. *Tourism Management, 32*(2), 207–214.

Stickdorn, M. (2009). Service design in tourism. In S. Miettinen & M. Koivisto, (Eds.), *Designing services with innovative methods* (pp. 246–265). Keuruu, FI: Otava Book Printing Ltd.

Stickdorn, M. & Frischhut, B. (2012). *Service design and tourism: Case studies of applied research projects on mobile ethnography for tourism destinations.* Norderstedt, GE: Books on Demand GmbH. http://www.experiencefellow.com/pdf/Stickdorn Frischhut2012.pdf (accessed 10 January 2016).

Synodinos, N. E. (2001). Understanding Japanese consumers: Some important underlying factors. *Japanese Psychological Research, 43*(4), 235–248.

Trischler, J. & Zehrer, A. (2012). Service design: Suggesting a qualitative multistep approach for analyzing and examining theme park experiences. *Journal of Vacation Marketing, 18*(1), 57–71.

Tsunetsugu, Y., Park, B. J. & Yoshifumi, M. (2010). Trends in research related to "Shinrin-yoku" (taking in the forest atmosphere of forest bathing) in Japan. *Environmental Health and Preventive Medicine, 15*, 27–37.

Vargo, S. L. & Lusch, R. F. (2006). Evolving to a new dominant logic for marketing. In R. F. Lusch & S. L. Vargo (Eds.), *The service-dominant logic of marketing: Dialog, debate and directions* (pp. 1–28). Armonk, NY: M.E. Sharpe.

Watkins, L. J. & Gnoth, J. (2011). Japanese tourism values: A means–end investigation. *Journal of Travel Research, 50*(6), 654–668.

Wetter Edman, K. (2009). Exploring overlaps and differences in service dominant logic and design thinking. In S. Glatworthy, J-V. Nisula & S. Holmlid (Eds.), *Proceedings of 1st Service Design and Service Innovation Conference, ServDes.2009, DeThinkingService ReThinkingDesign* (pp. 201–300). Linköping, SE:Linköping University Electronic Press. http://www.servdes.org/pdf/2009/wetteredman.pdf (accessed 10 January 2016).

Wetter Edman, K. (2011). Service design: A conceptualization of an emerging practice. Licentiate thesis. University of Gothenburg. ArtMonitor Doctoral Dissertations and Licentiate Thesis No. 28. Faculty of Fine, Applied and Performing Arts, University of Gothenburg.

Wierzbicka, A. (1997). *Understanding Cultures through Their Key Words: English, Russian, Polish, German and Japanese.* New York, NY: Oxford University Press.

Zehrer, A. (2009). Service experience and service design: Concepts and application in tourism SMEs. *Managing Service Quality, 19*(3), 332–349.

Zomerdijk, L. G. & Voss, C. A. (2010). Service design for experience-centric services. *Journal of Service Research, 13*(1), 67–82.

# 6  Innovation potentials through value proposals

## A case study of a museum in Northern Norway

*Nina K. Prebensen*

## Introduction

Museums as providers of cultural heritage reflect knowledge, change and creative innovations in society. Heritage is delineated by Hewison (1987) as derived from past images of history transmitted into current reality. Cultural heritage also contributes to form the history and identity of places, inducing place attachment feelings of locals. The interpretation of cultural heritage, and the different meanings that people find in it, assist people in creating their own identity as members of a bigger entity to which they belong. Cultural heritage is defined as "a human creation intended to inform" (Feather, 2006). The present chapter aims to study one museum from a customer perspective and to utilize tools to highlight innovation potential for museums to attract different customer segments and co-create experience value for all parties involved in the experience process.

Museums have different purposes, such as collecting and preserving cultural pieces, conveying history and facilitating for visitors to visit and learn about their cultural heritage. Public museums are also economic and commercial entities, ensuring proper income in order to cover their costs. Museums commercialize ideas through facilitating and attracting customers to visit them and experience their products and services. To attract visitors to pay for their visit, museums need to acknowledge the motives and purposes of various types of visitor (customers). As tourism literature shows the imperative of tourist motivation, involvement and knowledge in the tourist perceived experience value (e.g. Prebensen, Woo, Chen, & Uysal, 2014; Prebensen, Woo, & Uysal, 2014), firms should develop strategies and perform activities that motivate, involve and teach the tourist. This process of facilitating and co-creating experience value with the tourists may begin before the physical journey starts, continuing throughout the travel and after the tourists have arrived back home (Chen, Prebensen, & Uysal, 2014). Museums need to focus on the various types of user and their needs throughout the whole process of the customer experience—that is, before, during and after the physical museum visit. Ryan and Hsu (2011) suggest that visitors to a museum may have various motives for their visit, such as (a) a search for facts; (b) motives of relaxation; (c) social interaction with family and friends; and sometimes (d) simply having a place to take children on a rainy day.

Researchers have expressed a desire to enrich the literature on the foundations of individual experiences—that is, experiential consumption practices—through systems (Frochot, 2004; Larsen & Mossberg, 2007; Prebensen & Foss, 2011). In particular, the dynamic nature of service research and the current paradigm shift have reoriented our understanding of experiential consumption towards the experience as an interdisciplinary concept (Sfandla & Björk, 2013). Nowadays, memorable experiences often happen when tourists can share their experiences with others. Recent studies highlight the role of social platforms and network effects in accelerating and dissolving the integration process, according to an ecosystem conceptualization of market opportunities (Lusch & Nambisan, 2015). As a result, facilitating platforms where tourists can express themselves, learn and interact with the museum and the locals, and where all together may design and co-create the tourism products and adapt their consumption in a personalized way, constitutes a strategic tool for destinations as well as for the museum and other firms.

The process of commercialization has been outlined as the completion part of the innovation process (Garcia & Calantone, 2002), and materialized by Österwalder and Pigneur (2010) within the business model framework. The core notion of a business model is to analyse an idea according to different market segments which will provide different economic outcomes. The present chapter uses innovation system tools to exemplify various value proposals for customer groups for a museum. The chapter then provides new ideas in terms of how to co-create value with customers within the tourism system, in tourism experiences where the customers are present.

## Theoretical perspectives

### *Value co-creation*

Customer participation in creating value is one of the key premises in new perspectives in marketing (Vargo & Lusch, 2004). Prahalad and Ramaswamy (2004, p. 5) claim that "armed with new connective tools, consumers want to interact and co-create value". Co-creation is the process during which consumers take on an active role and co-create value together with the company (Prahalad & Ramaswamy, 2004; Prebensen, Vittersø, & Dahl, 2013). The acts of collecting information on a museum, travelling there and visiting are all parts of this co-creation process. However, the potential for value creation resides in much more than these simple actions.

Grönroos and Voima (2013) discuss the concepts of value creation and co-creation, and refer to value creation as customers' creation of value-in-use, while co-creation is a function of interaction. They further claim that both the firm's and the customer's actions can be categorized by spheres (provider, joint, customer), and their interactions are either direct or indirect, leading to different forms of value creation and co-creation. Subsequently, a museum creates value by collecting and preserving cultural items and historical events. As soon as the customer then visits the museum and enjoys and learns from the work that has been done, co-creation of value processes starts, delineated as value-in-use by Grönroos and Voima (2013). From this, the actors do not need to be present for value co-creation to take place. Facilitating information on homepages and social media where customers interact is another example where the firm or the institution has created value before the customer arrives, facilitating for value co-creation.

### Innovation tools: business canvas model

Because many museums face economic challenges, they need to develop new business models. The reasons for this struggle may reflect low visiting of the attraction by residents and/or tourists and inappropriate pricing, promotion, distribution or product/experience strategies.

A business idea by itself has no economic value until the customers adopt it. Even after the customers have adopted the idea, it may not provide revenue for the firm. This points to the fact that different customer segments will provide the company with different returns. Porter (1990, p. 45) claims that innovation is the attempt "to create competitive advantages by perceiving or discovering new better ways of competing in an industry and bringing them to market". It should be noted that a new idea might be slightly different from the existent business model in the firm or completely new. Dewar and Dutton (1986) distinguish between incremental and radical innovation, dependent on the degree of change—that is, minor versus major changes. Innovation can therefore include different levels of change from the existent business and it may include various dimensions such as technology, methods, services and new ways to reach a market (Garcia & Calantone, 2002).

Chesbrough and Rosenbloom (2002, p. 529) advocate that a business model should include the following functions:

- articulate the value proposition (i.e. the value created for users by an offering based on technology);
- identify a market segment and specify the revenue generation mechanism (i.e. users to whom technology is useful and for what purpose);
- define the structure of the value chain required to create and distribute the offering and complementary assets needed to support the position in the chain;
- detail the revenue mechanism(s) by which the firm will be paid for the offering;
- estimate the cost structure and profit potential (given the value proposition and the value chain structure);
- describe the position of the firm within the value network, linking suppliers and customers (including identifying potential complementors and competitors);
- formulate the competitive strategy by which the innovating firm will gain and hold an advantage over its rivals.

## The business model canvas

The business model canvas (BMC) is a conceptual instrument that helps firms to make decisions in terms of commercialization (Österwalder & Pigneur, 2010). The BMC is a tool or a platform that includes decision points such as objects, concepts and their relationships, expressing the logic underlying the business. By dividing the value creation process into canvases, it helps the firm to analyse customer relationships, the creation process and financial aspects.

The BMC is structured in nine building blocks: (1) customer segment; (2) value proposition; (3) channels; (4) customer relationships; (5) revenue streams; (6) key resources; (7) key activities; (8) key partnerships; and (9) cost structure. Each block comprises a set of questions to validate the model and verify its internal strength. Four main areas are proposed: product, customer, infrastructure, and finance. The second building block describes the value proposition of the business. This block includes the products and services delivered to the market. Building blocks 1, 3 and 4 are about customer engagement, defining the targeted audience, the demands, how customers perceive the value delivered, and what type of relationship the company upholds with each segment of customer. Building blocks 6 and 8 denote the functions of logistics and production, and express the relationships between key partners (e.g. employees, suppliers or partners) and the firm. Building blocks 5 and 9 refer to the sustainability of the firm, the cost structure, and how the firm is going to earn revenue. Building block 6 is about key resources.

The BMC model starts with an analysis of various customer segments and their needs and wants, which helps decide whether there is a market potential for the product/service. By pointing out different market segment potentials, this is a starting point for the next steps in the model. Then, by combining the market segments with value propositions for the respective segments, an evaluation can be made of what value propositions the firm can offer the various segments. Choosing one segment at a time and analysing what communication, distribution and sales would be appropriate is the next step. Following this, a customer relationship evaluation should be performed, including how to establish and maintain a relationship with the segment. When the value proposition is successfully offered to customers, revenue streams will occur, followed by an evaluation of the key resources that are required to offer and deliver all elements so far highlighted. Then, key activities that need to be performed should be outlined and discussed in terms of whether they should be delivered by the company itself or be acquired from outside the firm. All these elements put together will result in a cost structure.

Marketing literature (Kotler & Armstrong, 2010) reveals that a number of different customer segments exist, these being the mass market, niche market, segmented market, diversified market and multi-sided market. The BMC's focus on mass market does not separate the customers, but treats them as one group, while the BMC in niche markets tailors the building blocks such as value propositions, distribution channels and customer relationships to specific requirements (based on unique selling propositions). Segmentation is about dividing the market into groups, often based on needs or attitudes, which are similar inside the segment but different from other segments. A diversified BMC is about a situation where a firm serves two or more unrelated customer segments.

## The case: a rock carving museum in Alta, Norway

The rock carving museum in Alta, Norway, is situated in the High North, above the Arctic Circle at 70°N. The rock carvings at Alta date from *c*. 4200 BC to 500 BC and are on the UNESCO list of World Heritage Sites (Alta Museum, 2016). Altogether, around 6,000 depictions that are up to 7,000 years old are found all around the Altafjord: fishing scenes, bear hunts, animals, geometric figures and portraits of people. The rock carvings in Alta are part of the world heritage and provide us with access to the imaginative world of the Stone Age (Visit Northern Norway, 2016). The carvings include reindeer and elk swimming with their heads sticking up above the water, and people in boats with fishing lines and large halibut swimming in the depths. Bear hunting, tools, animal life, geometric patterns and people are all portrayed. The motifs of the Alta rock carvings provide a unique insight into the thoughts and everyday life of people thousands of years ago.

Alta Museum is located in Hjemmeluft, Alta, near the biggest concentration of rock carvings. At this site, more than 3,000 figures exist on 85 panels. A 2.9 kilometre network of paths and ramps leads to a representative selection of the carvings, and guided tours of the rock carvings are organized in the summer months. In the winter, the area is covered in snow so it is only possible to see the exhibitions inside the museum. Other carvings around the Altafjord have not been marked or highlighted. In 1985, the rock carvings were inscribed on the UNESCO World Heritage list. Alta Museum also has exhibitions about research.

The rock carvings were made over a period of thousands of years. During the Ice Age 15–20,000 years ago, the land was pressed down by the mass of ice. When the ice began to melt around 17,000 years ago, the land gradually started to rise again. A Stone Age find high up on the hillside is thus older than one discovered closer to the water, because the people of Northern Norway have always settled as close to the sea as they could.

The homepage of Alta Museum (2016) presents detailed information on what to see at the site. The homepage also provides information regarding opening hours and so forth. The museum offers the patrons guided tours (an option) to learn in more detail about the rock carvings. The museum is open all year round, but the rock carvings are only accessible to visitors during the snow-free season, normally from May to the beginning of October. In the winter season, the carvings are covered with snow. Three small stones with rock carvings are exhibited inside the museum. The exhibitions include temporary exhibitions in addition to a permanent exhibition.

The total number of visitors was 45,000 in 2014. In 2013 and 2012, the visitor numbers were 41,000 and 40,000 respectively, revealing an increase in visitors from 2012 to 2014 of almost 9% (Museumsforbundet, 2016).

Alta Museum is part of a network. The Norwegian rock art network is one of 24 museum networks for different topics, created as a part of the national museum reform (2001–2008). It was established in 2007 in cooperation with the Norwegian Archives Library and the Museum Authority, which is now integrated into the responsibilities of the Arts Council Norway.

The museum opened in 1991 and includes an indoor exhibition, access to the rock carvings (outside), a café selling cold and hot drinks as well as waffles and cakes, and a store offering, among other things, books and magazines, T-shirts, mugs and jewellery. The museum store and café have the same opening hours as the museum and admission is free.

Alta Museum has a digital rock art archive, which is available online. The archive is still under construction and will eventually contain extensive material documenting all the rock art at Alta. The archive will continuously expand as time goes by.

For those who wish to get as much out of the archive as possible, all the material in the archive is available for download. The museum has developed a user manual for the archive. The archive material is free to use for non-commercial purposes under the precondition that Alta Museum is referenced as the source and the photographer/creator is properly credited (Alta Museum, 2016).

The entrance fee (indoor museum and outside rock carvings) ranges from 20 to 30 NOK for children, 50 to 85 NOK for students and 70 to 105 NOK for adults, dependent on the season (low season is wintertime, when the carvings are covered with snow). A guided tour (for groups) costs 600 NOK in addition to the entrance fee and lasts approximately 45 minutes.

### Business model canvas for a rock carving museum

Visitors to the rock carving museum in Alta may be grouped by customer residence (local residents versus tourists), by nationality (tourists), by age, by interests and attitudes, by intention of repeat visitation (repeat buying), by purpose for visitation (for work, such as researchers or for leisure, and so forth. In order to exemplify the use of the BMC for different segments, here three different segments are chosen: (1) local residents: children (aged six to ten years); (2) international summer tourists; and (3) researchers/scholars within the fields of rock carvings/Stone Age.

### Value propositions for customer segments

#### Children

Children living in Alta visit the museum together with adults (teachers, parents, grandparents) and other children (siblings, schoolmates). Schools may use the museum as an arena for learning, building identity and creating interest for the youngsters. The museum needs to communicate/sell the museum through parents, grandparents, teachers and schools. In order to attract visitors, the museum may

*Table 6.1* Business canvas model of three Alta Museum segments

| Customer type | Needs | How it is sold/ communicated | Value chain role | Profit model | What is sold/ communicated |
|---|---|---|---|---|---|
| 1. Children (aged between six and ten) | Learning<br>Fun<br>Edutainment<br>Excitement | Parents<br>Grandparents<br>Teachers<br>(Schools) | Communicating<br>Creating interest through the variety of learning activities<br>Booking (whole package for those outside Alta) | Low price for packages<br>Fee for extras enhancing value for family and school classes | Value for children and for family (learning, stories, fun and rock carvings) |
| 2. International tourists (summer, by air/bus/boat/car) | Learning in depth about rock carvings and the Stone Age<br>Value for money, utility, physical engagement (outdoors walking)<br>Edutainment | Online<br>Through travel agency | Communicating<br>Creating interest<br>Volume<br>Motivating<br>Bookings | Medium/high price extras | Heritage<br>Special interest<br>Culture<br>Rock carvings |
| 3. Researchers (special interest) | A setting for in-depth studies<br>Archives<br>A meeting platform | Online, information<br>Groups<br>Special interest<br>Journals | Communicating<br>Creating interest through knowledge<br>Booking | Medium/high, dependent on extras | Value of experience (special interest)<br>Network<br>Knowledge platform |

tailor and facilitate exhibitions for kids. This group may be attracted to visit during the low season, in particular in May and September, when the carvings are exposed (snow-free) but the number of tourists is slowing down. In terms of pricing strategy, the museum provides reduced prices for kids, whole year tickets, and group and family tickets. A potential here is to include extras, such as drinks and fruit, to attract these visitors. To attract kids to visit, the museum needs to attract parents, grandparents and school teachers as well as the kids themselves. Producing materials and education packages, including books, movies and stories, not only attracts kids to learn, but helps adults to provide history and culture to the kids, and is likely to be interesting. Making the visit easy by providing transport could be an option for schools. The packages could be sold through the internet (some free of charge to attract/tease children to want to learn more, and others with a fee). As this type of material incurs costs, the museum should collaborate with other museums. They can even sell each other in a positive way. When this segment increases its interest, it will be more likely to visit museums in other places as tourists. The museum could also visit the local school to inform, motivate, engage and teach pupils about rock carvings and the museum.

*International tourists*

A number of international tourists from all over the world visit the museum. The summer season is the most attractive time to visit, due to traditional summer tourism in the area and the fact that the carvings are exposed during this season. Most tourists arrive by bus or by car. However, a new type of tourist that is arriving in the area by air or by boat (cruise) and hiring a car is increasing greatly. Nature, including the midnight sun, has been the major attraction to the area. Recently, tourists seem not only to gaze at nature, but are actively enjoying nature through activities such as hiking, fishing and camping. Tourist visits to the area during the winter season are increasing heavily. One of the major attractions is the Northern Lights. Additionally, many tourists want to enjoy outdoor activities during the winter season, such as skiing, riding snow scooters and dogsledding. The museum is currently collaborating with tourism offices. A homepage also provides some information. The homepage and social media can be developed and tailored to various tourist groups. Experience packages including a visit to the museum could be a potential attraction. In particular, a winter package including the Northern Lights and the history of Haldde (the first observatory for the Northern Lights) could be intriguing. The museum could ensure that a part of the outdoor carvings is exposed for winter tourists. Finally, motivating and engaging the tourist through online communication by creating stories linking or comparing their own history to the Stone Age could create curiosity and interest. By developing a homepage, the museum should seek collaboration with other cultural heritage institutions, as all are interested in increasing demand. A network of international museums, actively informing and promoting the cultural heritage, is a strategy that should help improve interest in the longer term. This network could also sell packages including, for instance, five museums.

*Researchers*

Researchers visit the museum often because they hold a special interest in the topic. The museum could develop this further by facilitating the setting for the researcher to study the rock carvings in depth. Furthermore, they could facilitate researchers in communicating and working together through their homepage. Collaborating with researchers to communicate and provide stories for other segments could be a potential for both parties. In addition, the museum could invite researchers and special interest tourists to meet and discuss ideas such as writing books or journal articles together. This could be performed as workshops or as conferences with high profile keynote speakers. Here, a potential of collaborating with the local university is possible. As researchers are concerned with studying, analysing and learning about a special topic, a starting point could be to invite some highly skilled researchers on a topic(s) to discuss how and why researchers should be attracted to collaborate.

It should be mentioned that researchers from other fields, such as tourism and leisure scholars, could be invited to work on plans for collaboration, including project and data collection. They should be invited to co-create value potentials together.

## Value co-creation potential for museums

The examples above suggest various value propositions for the three segments. The propositions partly overlap when it comes to system—that is, networks and communication tools. The content, however, varies due to the different needs of the segments.

*Network*

Communities of practice are defined as "groups of people informally bound together by shared expertise and passion for a joint enterprise" (Wenger & Snyder, 2000, p. 139). In line with scholars such as Filieri, McNally, O'Dwyer, and O'Malley (2014) calling for co-creation in collaborative innovation networks, the present work reveals that museums reside in a complex market and should shift from the creation of offerings in isolation to the co-creation of value in collaborative innovation networks. The major reason for this is, of course, the synergy effect of collaboration regarding the required expertise, knowledge and credibility to develop innovative solutions (Lusch, Vargo, & Tanniru, 2010). In these networks, diverse stakeholders are working together to co-create innovative value. Co-creation in a network creates new challenges in terms of changed processes and outcomes. Research (Corsten & Felde, 2005) demonstrates that supplier collaboration has a positive effect on buyer performance, both in terms of innovative capability and financial results. The study shows that trust and dependence play an important role in supplier relationships.

*Empowerment of customers*

New perspectives within marketing and management literature have explored the process by which firms integrate one type of external stakeholder into their innovation process. In particular, an emergent stream of research focuses on use of the latest technologies to assign contributions from empowered consumers (Prahalad & Ramaswamy, 2013).

*Internet and social media*

Social media has changed the way people communicate. Firms develop their own websites based on social networking sites so that they can have direct interaction and connection with consumers (Hajli, Sims, Featherman, & Love, 2014). This provides huge opportunities for museums in both B2C and B2B situations.

Social media are delineated as a group of Internet-based applications that build on the ideological and technological foundations of Web 2.0, and that allow the creation and exchange of user generated content (Kaplan & Haenlein, 2010). Constantinides and Fountain (2008) suggest classifying social media into five categories: (1) blogs; (2) social networking sites (for example, Facebook and Google+); (3) content communities (for example, YouTube and Wikipedia); (4) e-forums; and (5) content aggregators. Amongst these five categories of Internet-based applications in social media, social networking sites (SNSs) seem to be the most popular sites currently.

In a study of social networks, customer engagement was found to exert a direct and positive influence on customer value co-creation (Zhang, Guo, Hu, & Liu, 2016). The study further reveals that customer value creation mediates the relationship between customer engagement and staying on the website, confirming the importance of developing an effective value creation strategy through the Internet and social media.

## Conclusions

The present chapter's focus on museums as economic entities may utilize various tools in order to explore and develop new business models. The work exemplifies how three different segments at a museum may provide different business opportunities. By utilizing the business model canvas, the three segments are designated. The examples point to the vast importance of building strong networks, empowering customers and developing strong communication strategies and tactics through the Internet and social media.

Alta Museum would benefit from applying the business canvas model in its innovation work. The model would help define customer segments in detail; then the management could analyse different value propositions for the chosen segments. Based on this work, they can develop full business models for all segments. In today's world, where institutions experience increased competition and less public support, the museum needs to develop a sustainable business model.

# References

Alta Museum. (2016). *Alta museum*. Retrieved from http://www.alta.museum.no/sider/artikler.asp?hovedmeny=hovedmeny-engelsk&meny=forside-engelsk&forside=true&mal= forside (accessed 27 December 2016).

Chen, J., Prebensen, N. K., & Uysal, M. (2014). Dynamic Drivers of Tourist Experiences. In N. K. Prebensen, J. S. Chen and M. S. Uysal (Eds.), *Creating experience value in tourism* (pp. 11–22). Oxfordshire: CABI.

Chesbrough, H., & Rosenbloom, R. S. (2002). The role of the business model in capturing value from innovation: Evidence from Xerox Corporation's technology spin-off companies. *Industrial and Corporate Change, 11*(3), 529.

Constantinides, E., & Fountain, S. J. (2008). Web 2:0: Conceptual foundations and marketing issues. *Journal of Direct, Data and Digital Marketing, 9*(3), 231–244.

Corsten, D., & Felde, J. (2005). Exploring the performance effects of key-supplier collaboration: An empirical investigation into Swiss buyer-supplier relationships. *International Journal of Physical Distribution & Logistics Management, 35*(6), 445–461.

Dewar, R. D., & Dutton, J. D. (1986). The adoption of radical and incremental innovations: An empirical analysis. *Management Science, 32*(11), 1422–1433.

Feather, F. (2006). Managing the documentary heritage: Issues for the present and future. In G. E. Gorman & Sydney J. Shep (Eds.), *Preservation management for libraries, archives and museums* (pp. 1–18). London: Facet.

Filieri, R., McNally, R. C., O'Dwyer, M., & O'Malley, L. (2014). Structural social capital evolution and knowledge transfer: Evidence from an Irish pharmaceutical network. *Industrial Marketing Management, 43*(3), 429–440.

Frochot, I. (2004). An investigation into the influences of the benefits sought by visitors on their quality evaluation of historic houses' service provision, *Journal of Vacation Marketing, 10*(3), 223–237.

Garcia, R., & Calantone, R. (2002). A critical look at technological innovation typology and innovativeness terminology: A literature review. *Journal of Product Innovation Management, 19*(2), 110–132.

Grönroos, C., & Voima, P. (2013). Critical service logic: Making sense of value creation and co-creation. *Journal of the Academy of Marketing Science, 41*(2), 133–150.

Hajli, M. N., Sims, J., Featherman, M., & Love, P. E. (2014). Credibility of information in online communities. *Journal of Strategic Marketing, 23*(3), 238–253.

Hewison, R. (1987). *The heritage industry: Britain in a climate of decline*. London: Methuen.

Kaplan, A. M., & Haenlein, M. (2010). Users of the world, unite! The challenges and opportunities of social media. *Business horizons, 53*(1), 59–68.

Kotler, P., & Armstrong, G. (2010). *Principles of marketing*. Boston, MA: Pearson Education.

Larsen, S., & Mossberg, L. (2007). The diversity of tourist experiences. *Scandinavian Journal of Hospitality and Tourism, 7*(1), 1–6.

Lusch, R. F., & Nambisan, S. (2015). Service innovation: A service-dominant logic perspective. *MIS Quarterly, 39*(1), 155–175.

Lusch, R. F., Vargo, S. L., & Tanniru, M. (2010). Service, value networks and learning. *Journal of the Academy of Marketing Science, 38*(1), 19–31.

Museumsforbundet. (2016). *Statistics of visitors at museums in Norway 2012, 2013 and 2014*. Retrieved from http://museumsforbundet.no/?page_id=9333.

Österwalder, A., & Pigneur, Y. (2010). *Business model generation: A handbook for visionaries, game changers, and challengers*. New Jersey, NJ: John Wiley & Sons.

Prahalad, C. K., & Ramaswamy, V. (2004). Co-creating unique value with customers. *Strategy & leadership, 32*(3), 4–9.

Prahalad, C. K., & Ramaswamy, V. (2013). *The future of competition: Co-creating unique value with customers*. Boston, MA: Harvard Business Press.

Prebensen, N. K., & Foss, L. (2011). Coping and co-creating in tourist experiences. *International Journal of Tourism Research, 13*(1), 54–67.

Prebensen, N. K., Vittersø, J., & Dahl, T. (2013). Value co-creation: Significance of tourist resources. *Annals of Tourism Research, 42*(July), 240–261.

Prebensen, N. K., Woo, E., Chen, J., & Uysal, M. (2014). Motivation and involvement as antecedents of the perceived value of the destination experience. *Journal of Travel Research, 5*(2), 253–264.

Prebensen, N. K., Woo, E., & Uysal, M. (2014). Experience value: Antecedents and consequences. *Current Issues in Tourism, 17*(10), 910–928.

Porter, M. E. (1990). The competitive advantage of notions. *Harvard Business Review, 68*(2), 73–93.

Ryan, C., & Hsu, S. Y. (2011). Why do visitors go to museums? The case of 921 earthquake museum, Wufong, Taichung. *Asia Pacific Journal of Tourism Research, 16*(2), 209–228.

Sfandla, C., & Björk, P. (2013). Tourism experience network: Co-creation of experiences in interactive processes. *International Journal of Tourism Research, 15*, 495–506.

Vargo, S. L., & Lusch, R. F. (2004). Evolving to a new dominant logic for marketing. *Journal of Marketing, 68*(1), 1–17.

Visit Northern Norway. (2016). https://www.visitnorway.com/places-to-go/northern-norway/ (accessed 27 September 2016).

Wenger, E., & Snyder, M. (2000). Communities of practice: The organizational frontier. *Harvard Business Review* (January–February), 139–145.

Zhang, M., Guo, L., Hu, M., & Liu, W. (2016). Influence of customer engagement with company social networks on stickiness: Mediating effect of customer value creation. *International Journal of Information Management*. http://www.sciencedirect.com/science/article/pii/S0268401216302195 (accessed 27 September 2016).

# 7 Value co-creation in geothermal tourism

The case of the 'ryokan' industry in Japan

*Timothy Lee*

## Introduction

The 'ryokan' (traditional Japanese-style inn) is a particular form of accommodation in Japan and it not only provides shelter but also a place displaying Japanese identity. There are predictions that ryokan can transform into spa facilities as the demand for health-related tourism is increasing. Japan is proud of its hospitality such as ryokan facilities and its great hot spring resources. Some scholars including international scholars, have researched the development of ryokan, however it has limitations. As one important element in ryokan is bathing, ryokan is closely associated with hot springs. When it comes to hot springs in Japan, it would be a mistake to not mention Beppu, a city blessed with a large number of hot springs. Unlike other famous destinations such as Atami, Hakone and so on, Beppu is not a close neighbor to a large city. However, it can develop its strengths, and promote its tourism and its lodging industry including ryokan.

Beppu ryokan is one of the typical examples of co-creation of values in the hospitality industry in Japan including the accommodation, spa, and local cuisine. The proactive and expanding involvement in the health tourism attractions and positive word-of-mouth of tourists of Beppu creates constant synergy effect for the city of Beppu as one of the most successful health and wellness tourism destinations in Japan. The co-creation is understood as involving a high level of customer participation in customizing the product or service, which requires 'collaboration with customers for the purpose of innovation' (Kristensson, Matthing, & Johansson, 2008, p. 475). The co-creation process moves away from a company-oriented view of customer orientation while emphasizing customer interaction. The contact between the customer and the company is managed in such a way as to encourage companies to co-create value with customers while addressing customer-oriented idiosyncratic needs (Chathoth, Altinay, Harrington, Okumus, & Chan, 2013). This study first reviews the literature on ryokan development along with the challenges and opportunities raised by different scholars. Then it conducts a case study to increase understanding using Beppu ryokan. Ryokan display Japanese culture in their unique lodging facilities, but they are businesses and must function and succeed as businesses. Moreover, in order to survive, change is necessary (Guichard-Anguis, 2007), but maintenance of their unique identity is essential. Currently, the lodging industry in Japan is attempting to attract foreign guests due to domestic market problems such as an aging society (Takeuchi, 2010, p. 12).

This chapter has three objectives: (a) to provide understanding of ryokan in general and ryokan in Beppu; (b) to identify the challenges and opportunities that ryokan businesses face; and (c) to suggest recommendations for the development of ryokan businesses to provide sustainable co-creation values in the hospitality industry. The case study of Beppu ryokan will ensure this study reveals deeper insights into the ryokan business. The aim is that the findings and suggestions will contribute to the future prospects of ryokan, a competitive and sustainable accommodation facility type of Japan.

## Background: traditional Japanese-style inn – ryokan

### *History*

The roots of ryokan trace back a long time as Japan has a long history of tourism travel. For many years, the main motive to travel was religious to study shrines and temples (Carlile, 2010, p. 278). According to Japan Ryokan Association (JRA), lodging facilities, so-called 'fuseya' in Nara and Heian periods (710–1191), are thought to be the oldest provided for travelers in Japan. Monks who wanted to assist travelers ran the earliest establishments. The number of fuseya increased along with the development of transportation facilities such as roads and bridges. In the Heian period, temples and shrines started to provide accommodations, mostly concentrated in the religious destinations. Those opened specifically for devotees and worshipers were called 'shukubo' ('lodging' and 'monk').

Japanese people have a long history of bathing in hot springs and it is claimed that the oldest hot spring formed over 1,500 years ago. The meaning and use of hot springs have changed over time. Traveling to hot springs was similar to a 'spiritual journey' in the Edo period (1603–1868), then became 'institutionalized events' in the Meiji era (1868–1912) and a 'recreation-oriented' trip in the latter part of the 20th century. Recently, medical purposes have become important for elderly travelers (Ratz, 2011, p. 3). When it comes to the relationship between ryokan and hot springs, the preference for hot water bathing among the Japanese plays an important role in the development of ryokan. Guichard-Anguis (2007, p. 20) confirms that the history of ryokan is closely related to hot springs. The demand for purification by monks and therapeutic baths by others in the past are important reasons. However, although the image of ryokan nowadays usually includes warm baths in natural surroundings, the so-called 'hot spring ryokan' had not been shaped in the Meiji period. At that time, the involvement of hot springs in lodging facilities had not yet become popular (Ikeda, 1987, p. 4). From these findings, it can be said that the extremely close connection between hot springs and ryokan has developed since the Meiji period.

The addition of hot springs or waterfalls and rustic beauty started with some ryokan near big cities towards the end of the Meiji period. Ikeda (1987) argues that near urban destinations, guest room facilities were designed with hot springs, including building such things as artificial mountains, pumped waterfalls and springs. Commodification in summer occurred with seating to enjoy the waterfall, renting yukata, serving light meals and selling the refreshing ambience (Ikeda, 1987, p. 5, 6). Customers from urban areas require not only the lodging facility with bathing but also the enjoyment of surroundings and communing with nature. That is similar to the modern attractive components of hot spring experiences, which Ratz (2011, p. 2) claims include 'nutrition, sightseeing, exercise and relaxation in natural surroundings'. Hot springs and rustic beauty play a very important part in serving guests in ryokan.

However, the term ryokan had not generally emerged in the Taisho period but there were several up-market lodging facilities available. In addition, the Taisho period witnessed the first vote for best sites and a large number of tourists from other places came to famous destinations. Importantly, from the Taisho period, foreign guests came to stay in ryokan. Compared to the Meiji period, the scale and business perspective of ryokan changed with these macroeconomic features. The term hotel was even interpreted as 'big ryokan' or 'western style ryokan' at this time. Accommodation offered is closely related to motives of travelers and what they want. Ryokan has gradually changed, influenced by tourism orientation. Therefore, understanding of trends is essential to improve the facilities provided for target travelers. In the time of aging populations and many changes in society itself and the global situation, Japanese inns should consider carefully their future development.

## Current situation of Japanese ryokan

Lee and Lim (2013) emphasize that 'ryokan is a unique accommodation system that exists only in Japan' (p. 74). Currently, ryokan is generally admitted as containing three basic elements, which are tatami (Japanese floor mat), hot springs, and dining in Japanese costumes. These correspond to the three main functions that ryokan provide, bathing, eating, and sleeping, regardless of different architectural styles (Guichard-Anguis, 2007, p. 21). Interestingly, ryokan goes beyond the function as a type of accommodation. Ryokan tries to transmit quietness, the passing of the seasons and Japanese hospitality. Guests not only get a place to stay but also enjoy nature, local history and Japanese culture as well. Moreover, ryokan offers a compact system of scheduled times such as breakfast, dining, bathing, check-in and -out time, which are distinct in comparison with other lodging facilities (Guichard-Anguis, 2007, p. 22).

Although a unique lodging facility, ryokan has its limitations and it struggles in the current situation. The ryokan business throughout Japan faces both internal and external issues. Many ryokan struggle and even close down. Lee and Lim (2013, p. 72) depict the three main problems of ryokan business: inconvenience due to cultural and language barriers, relatively poor accessibility if near nature or hot spring destinations, and family ownership with some management or financial issues. In addition, the global economic conditions in recent years have influenced tourism as well as the hospitality industry. The ryokan business in Japan has undergone a decline in numbers from 1991 to 2003, 'more than half of the business owners operating ryokan have closed their business' (Lee & Lim, 2013, p. 71). The situation of the economy also influenced overnight tourism trips as spending cuts in families and companies seem to go first as the economic environment turns unfavorable (Takeuchi, 2010, pp. 5–7).

Furthermore, threats from other lodging facilities are significant to ryokan business. Since 2000, many global luxury hotel brands have entered Japan market (Takeuchi, 2010, p. 1). Ryokan has to compete with not only the modern hotels but also new types of lodgings such as capsule hotels. Ryokan business has been decreasing significantly in terms of facilities, rooms and market size. While the number of hotel facilities and rooms increased from 1990 to 2008, the number of ryokan and rooms decreased around 33% and 20% respectively in the same period. In addition, there are plans to create a large supply of new hotels and expansion in the coming years (Takeuchi, 2010, pp. 4–5). Facing the hard competition from other lodging facilities, some ryokan have adapted. Furthermore, different types of room are available, Japanese; half Japanese half Western or Western. The association with famous features of locals, 'geigi', and their dances in the case of Atami, is also included. For some smaller ryokan, keeping the traditional and becoming places of Japanese identity can be a strategy promoted using the Internet or by international staff (Guichard-Anguis, 2007, pp. 24–25).

Many foreign scholars introduce the modern role of a ryokan as a spa. Ratz (2011, pp. 6–7) also suggests that ryokan can play the role of the finest spa in the world. Hot spring ryokan can serve tourists not only hot springs and beautiful natural surroundings but also high quality food, applying the 'slow food' concept. Ryokan constructed with mostly natural materials also creates an environment to respect Japanese traditional practices. Visiting ryokan is a chance to be exposed to Japanese identity, especially to foreign visitors. Lee and Lim (2013, p. 74) suggest if it is possible to overcome the issues of languages and managerial professionalism, ryokan can be a 'premier tourism product'.

## Tourism industry in Beppu, Japan

Beppu is a city located in the central part of Oita prefecture, lying between Mount Tsurumi and the sea. The city enjoys relatively favorable weather with four seasons. Beppu, blessed with rich sources of hot springs, has legendary healing powers. Beppu attracts not only a significant number of domestic tourists but also an impressive number of foreign visitors. From tourism professional perspectives, Beppu is a typical case of hot spring tourism in Japan. This section will identify challenges and opportunities of Beppu city in general. The challenge is to build a more competitive brand image as well as encourage better investment and cooperation in the tourism sector. Opportunities exist with the current high demand for relaxing hot spring tourism from local residents and foreign tourists.

Beppu is thought to be the most famous destination for hot springs in Japan, with the so-called 'hot spring heaven' reputation. Travelers can access Beppu using all means of transportation, including train, air, ferry and highway.

The most famous attraction of Beppu is Beppu Hatto, the main eight hot spring areas. Some places are not for bathing but highlight the unique volcanic features of Beppu, called 'jigoku' (which means 'hell'). According to Cooper and Cooper (2009, p. 19), the jigoku attracts tourists due its geothermal features. These 'hells' usually have small shrines for prayers and offer warm footbaths, hand spas, and hot spring cooked food as well. The population of Beppu peaked in 1980 around 136,000 then stabilized around 120,000. It is noticeable that a high percentage of employment is from tourism-related sectors such as lodgings, restaurants, transportation and services. Recent impacts from the economic situation have negatively influenced the job market in Beppu (Han & Yotsumoto, p. 68).

Tourism is one of the most important industries for the city. The population was 120,000 in 2014, and in the same year, the number of overnight guests was 2.5 million (City.beppu.oita.jp). Beppu tourism experienced its golden age in the 1980s, before the period of 'the bubble economy' in Japan, witnessing the peak number of tourists. The profile of tourists has also changed with the number of visitors staying declining while day-trip numbers have increased. Beppu tourism mainly relies on group tourists and overnight-banquet tourists (Cooper & Cooper, 2009, p. 19).

In recent years, an increasing number of not only Japanese but also people from other countries such as China is demanding the experience of hot spring tourism, so Beppu can make use of its strengths to improve its tourism sector. Beppu ranks twentieth in the top 20 Japanese locations that foreign tourists want to recommend to friends due to attractive hot springs (Han & Yotsumoto, 2009, p. 67).

## The strength and contribution of hot spring tourism in Japan and Beppu

The revenue from the tourism industry of Japan in 2012 mostly came from domestic travel, and 59.1% of the whole benefit was generated from stay-overnight travel (15.1 trillion Japanese yen) (Japan Association of Travel Agency, 2014). Survey results of desired travel categories among Japanese people reveal that hot spring ranks top, followed by nature, culinary, culture and history, and theme park. Moreover, the percentage of hot spring travel rose from 12.7% in 2009 to 15.6% in 2011. Interestingly, although Japan is surrounded by sea, hot spring visits definitely surpass enjoying bathing in the sea. It can be said that to Japanese people, the relaxation of hot springs is very important, and it is a strong motive for them to travel. Travel to enjoy hot springs normally generates longer stays and more benefits. The demand for hot spring tourism among the Japanese has been answered by various hot spring destinations throughout Japan. The Japan Association of Travel Agency (2014) illustrates the ranking of hot spring destinations in Japan. Hokkaido and Nagano prefectures rank first and second, followed by Tokyo with famous names such as Hakone destination. However, Oita prefecture, where Beppu city is located, ranks fifteenth although it calls itself the 'hot spring prefecture' in tourism promotions.

Foreign tourists coming to the city is not a new phenomenon. According to Cooper and Cooper (2009, p. 130), from the Taisho era, Beppu welcomed not only government and military officials with its resorts and meeting facilities but also received tourists from Germany and Italy for hot springs. Suzuki (2013, p. 81) mentions the term for Beppu tourism is 'earn the money from foreigners!' after World War I. Many foreign visitors came to Beppu by ships and stayed in the port. Among foreign visitors, there were also famous names such as Charlie Chaplin, Bernard Shaw, Helen Keller and so forth. The number of foreign tourists to Beppu is among the top in Japan. In 2012, the city received around 186,000 foreign guests, spending around 4 billion yen, mostly from Korea, China and Taiwan. When it comes to the contribution of the most internationalized university located in Beppu (the Ritsumeikan Asia Pacific University, APU), the university takes a role as a research institution and its students can be the labor force helping the aging population in the city. From 2008, collaboration between Beppu Foreign Tourist Welcoming Committee and the university officially established statistics gathering of foreign tourists (Han & Yotsumoto, 2009, p. 69). Currently, it is not strange to see APU students working part time in food and beverage or lodging facilities in Beppu city or as translators in other sectors.

## The development of Beppu ryokan

There has also been a very close relationship between tourism sectors and lodging businesses in Beppu. The significant investment after the war from the government to Beppu with several big projects such as African Safari Park, Kijima Theme Park, Beppu International Tourist Port and the Trans-Kyushu highway, was the push for accommodation facilities to modernize and/or extend. Tourist visits to Beppu reached a peak at 13 million in 1976 and many visitors stayed to enjoy the new attraction and accommodation facilities.

However, after the golden age in the 1980s, due to the decline of overnight stays, school trips and regular customers, the accommodation capacity decreased significantly. Accommodation facilities started to receive mainly overnight banquet tourists with a set pattern: arriving in the evening, enjoying the dinner and hot springs, then group party at night and leave the next day with or without visiting any attractions. In addition, during the 1980s the large hotels were established before access was improved through the highways, located far away from the old town, which directly competes with the lodging facilities located downtown. With the decrease in tourist numbers, and at the same time the attractions turned old, all the accommodation facilities in Beppu found it difficult to adapt to the changing situation (Cooper & Cooper, 2009, pp. 130–133). The general information of ryokan, association with hot spring and the evolution of ryokan has been presented. In this part, the history and the recent situation of ryokan business in Beppu city is provided. The history of Beppu ryokan is not only associated with the hot springs in the city but also with the renowned families at that time. The changes in various aspects of ryokan in Beppu were influenced by the changes in social perspectives or orientations. More recently, ryokan businesses in Beppu have coped with diversified impact factors.

## Medical orientation to tourism orientation

In the past, the changes in orientation or motives of travelers to hot springs have influenced the changes in Beppu ryokan businesses. Although long-term stays had decreased while short-term (1–2 nights) stays had increased, possibly with the improvement of the transportation system, the change from medical orientation to tourism orientation contributed to the rise of ryokan (Matsuda & Oba, 2004, p. 151). After the golden age, the change in the profile of guest to Beppu led to the ryokan business struggling. The decrease in the number of large groups of tourists made the total number of stayers decline. The old part of the city of Beppu with its lack of proper entertainment attractions certainly finds it difficult to attract large tourist groups such as study field trips normally conducted in Japan.

This triggers the question: can some changes in motive help Beppu to create sources of visitors, especially stayers for its ryokan businesses? According to Ura (2006, p. 11), in the past people came to Beppu for medical purposes. Later the tourism orientation emerged and influenced changes in scale, location and other aspects as already mentioned. Ura (2006, p. 11) also raised the four phrases theory of Junji, illustrated in Figure 7.1. Following that theory, in the past, hot spring destinations were mainly for medical purposes in the first stage, then pamper and relax in the second stage. With the change in orientation, in stage 3, the destination serves the leisure travel mass tourism market and in the last stage, the destination focus changes to its hot spring resources as well as its medical benefits. Beppu is already at stage 4, a hot spring tourism city; however, it requires more effort to be successful. Other scholars also suggest Beppu should become a health tourism destination as the trend of health and wellness tourism worldwide grows. Some suggest adding competitive facilities such as a hot spring theme park (Cooper & Cooper, 2009, p. 135).

## Recent situation and influence factors of Beppu ryokan businesses

Beppu ryokan experienced its golden age then declined significantly. The numbers peaked in 1967 when African safari opened that offered around 13 million visitors and 6 million overnight stayers. However, the definition of ryokan is itself challenging, therefore, the number of ryokan in different sources of information offer different numbers. According to the data of the Beppu ryokan association, in 2012, there were around 107 ryokan in the city (Ura, 2013, p. 21).

On the other hand, in terms of concentration, the data from the study of Ura (2006, p. 11) show that in the period from 1885 to 2004, the ryokan were mostly concentrate in Beppu, Kanawa, and Hamawaki. However, as the number of ryokan declined the number in Beppu and Hamawaki decreased as well, but not in the Kanawa area. The reason could be the support of hot spring resources in Kanawa with various attractions already established. Beppu ryokan businesses are influenced by the number of tourists to Beppu. The peak of stayers in Beppu coincides with the peak number of ryokan in 1967. The bubble economy period

- Medical orientation

- Tourism orientation

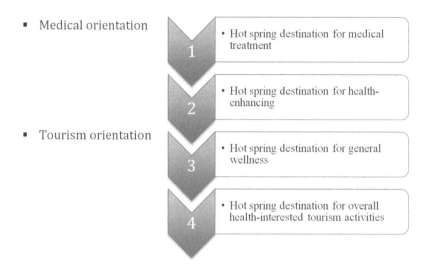

- 1 • Hot spring destination for medical treatment
- 2 • Hot spring destination for health-enhancing
- 3 • Hot spring destination for general wellness
- 4 • Hot spring destination for overall health-interested tourism activities

*Figure 7.1* Four stages of hot spring destination development (adapted from Ura, 2006)

across Japan created the peak of day trip visitors but these visitors might not actively contribute to Beppu ryokan businesses. Therefore, how to boost the ryokan business is really the way to increase the number of stayers, not visitors. Besides, the decline in large group tourist such as field trips to Beppu also had negative impacts on the ryokan businesses in the city.

Besides the influence of new attractions and the change in the profile of tourists, there are several other factors such as economic events, policies, and foreign affairs acting as catalysts. Economic events such as the oil shock overseas in 1973 or the bubble economy, followed by economic crisis in Japan either helped or made the tourism industry, as well as lodging businesses, suffer. Furthermore, since Beppu city also receives a significant number of foreign tourists, factors such as foreign affairs, currency and any catastrophe, earthquake, terrorism, epidemic and so on, influence the total number of guest. For example, when Avian Influence occurred, many tours were cancelled, which resulted in a huge loss for the tourism sectors, especially with lodging facilities. Likewise, in August, 2012, impacts were felt when a large-scale anti-Japan movement took place in China, which was followed by a significant decline in the number of tourists (Suzuki, 2013, p. 82).

## The adaption to the situation of Beppu ryokan

Ryokan in Beppu are either traditional or modern types. The following briefly describes these two types and discusses some adaptions made by them.

### Traditional types

Some ryokan face managerial and financial issues, as they are family owned. Such traditional ryokan may struggle to deal with the changes of time and generations. In order to adapt to new situations, there are adjustment or strategies taken by some ryokan that can be quite successful. Currently, traditional ryokan can use one of two strategies, high-end strategy or popular strategy (Ura, 2008).

Today, in Beppu, some traditional small-scale ryokan have adopted the high-end strategy. Although they already are close to natural hot spring resources, those ryokan continue to improve their bathing facilities such as providing outdoor hot springs, private hot springs, and hot springs for families (Ura, 2008, p. 6). The traditional small ryokan can improve their bathing facilities such as offering towels or improving the spa design. On the other hand, traditional ryokan can become destinations at which to enjoy the finest cuisine, with benefits such as genuine Japanese settings, local and seasonal materials, fresh ingredients from the sea, hand-made materials, and so on. Some offer lunch included in the stay and continue to serve delicate food to their guests.

Another sale point is the location of these ryokan as some originated from private resort houses with beautiful surroundings. These ryokan are far away from the crowded city, where guests can enjoy the quietness. Moreover, these ryokan become the destination of 'harmony' and 'Japanese hospitality' in all the elements: facility, cuisine, service and ambience (Ura, 2008, p. 7). These ryokan also become a very special cultural destination and their business contributes to

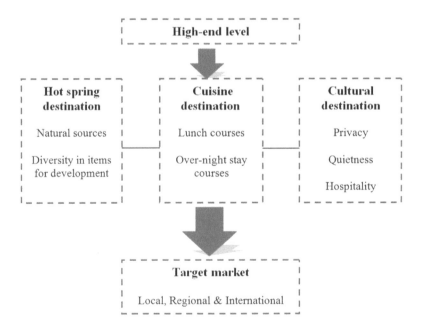

*Figure 7.2* Development model of traditional ryokan in Beppu (adapted from Ura, 2008)

local values. Currently, the main guests of such ryokan are guests from Fukuoka areas and group guests from companies.

## *Modern style*

It is not hard to find modern style ryokan in Beppu such as Shiragiku and Seikai. The two are members of the Japan Ryokan Association with the other four members in the Oita area. It can be confusing to understand why they are called ryokan and not hotels. Currently, Shiragiku located near Beppu station calls itself a Spa hotel; however, the local people keep calling it ryokan or ryokan hotel. Seikai calls itself an Onsen resort ryokan (onsen means hot spring) on its English site, however, people can also call it a hotel. The reason can be the combination of traditional style and modern style in its facilities.

## Conclusion

This study examined the co-created value of ryokan, a unique accommodation facility style in Japan, using a case study of ryokan in Beppu city. The case of Beppu contributes to the understanding of ryokan businesses and reveals the current challenges and opportunities. First, through the literature review of ryokan development, including relevant materials in both English and Japanese, the development process as well as the characteristics of ryokan was presented. From that it can be said that ryokan has various origins, a deep association with hot springs, displays continuous innovations, but also faces challenges. Modern ryokan is generated from the merger of various styles. Through time, ryokan has continuously adjusted to changes; however, the close relationship with hot springs remains extremely strong. Important influences on the innovation of ryokan in the past were the change of orientation from a medical focus to a general tourism one. That change made the ryokan adjust its scale, structure and service system, especially during the Taisho period. Ryokan is a unique kind of accommodation because it not only has distinct characteristics of facilities and systems but also offers the ambience to respect tradition, local culture and nature. Ryokan is believed to have the strong potential to become the spa and health-related destination in the future.

However, ryokan currently face several issues internally: competition from other lodging facilities and new trends in tourism, society and economy, both domestic and overseas. Management problems and severe competition in the lodging industry led to a decline in the number of ryokan. Closely related to the tourism sectors, external factors influencing the number of guests are similar to that of the tourist market more generally. To deal with the difficulties, modern ryokan adapt such as introducing new amenities, services and management systems. Some ryokan and ryokan destinations also aim to be spa facilities or spa and wellness towns. At the same time, ryokan businesses also try to appeal to new fans overseas, as ryokan is the bastion of Japanese culture. Such steps are important for ryokan business to survive and continue to develop in the future.

This study can contribute to the understanding about ryokan businesses in general. Beppu ryokan is a specific example to show that ryokan can make adjustments in term of location, ownership, scale and structure. Due to transportation improvement and changes in motives to visit hot springs, from medication to relaxation and leisure, ryokan can change and increase visit numbers significantly. However, not all ryokan can survive, such as Hatago, and some have declined and nearly disappeared. Ownership has also expanded from individual families to the newly emerged businessperson. Large-scale ryokan have increased in number and changed the structure and the system to serve more tourists. The modern ryokan business is very sensitive to the policy of government, the local economy and other events. The introduction of local attractions and a favorable economy, and the investment of government were an important push for the ryokan business. In recent years, factors such as the economic crisis, currency policy, foreign affairs and other events such as natural disasters, terrorism events, and epidemics can influence the number of guests to ryokan businesses. Understanding the appropriate response to the changing situation, and knowledge of risk management is important in the time of globalization.

The change in the profile of guests triggers the need to continuing to improve and find new tourist targets. The new sources of potential stayers and group tourists can boost the ryokan businesses in Beppu and ryokan businesses in Japan in general. However, understanding the preferences of new sources of tourists is necessary and research is important. One of the new sources of guests can be international travelers who want to enjoy hot springs, relax and are interest in Japanese culture. The strategies of some ryokan in Beppu are presented. Traditional style ryokan can either become high-end or popular accommodation. Modern style ryokan can improve management and facilities to serve more segmentation of guests. In order to serve foreign guests, some ryokan have adjusted promotion and management such as using Internet sites, having instructions in English and other languages, offering reasonable price for backpackers and so on.

Beppu has its own unique features and strengths to deal with its problems and continue to develop. Nature, hot springs and additional values will never fail to be attractive features of ryokan. Beppu is blessed with rich nature and culture, a good location and nice climate, and a great source of hot springs. Beppu and the city already have a significant number of foreign residents as it has an international university, APU. The increasing demand for hot spring tourism and health-related tourism in Japan and in other part of the world presents a great opportunity for ryokan businesses. The development of transportation such as LCC and cruise ships can help to bring new tourists to the city; the advance of technology can help in promotion and management. Nevertheless, how to make these elements contribute to the development of Ryokan are the current challenges for ryokan businesses in Beppu.

## References

Carlile, L. E. (2010). Japanese tourism and travel culture. *Annals of Tourism Research,* *1*(37), 278–280.

Chathoth, P., Altinay, L., Harrington, R. J., Okumus, F., & Chan, E. S.W. (2013). Co-production versus co-creation: A process based continuum in the hotel service context. *International Journal of Hospitality* Management, 32, 11–20.

City.beppu.oita.jp (2016). Beppu tourism report. Retrieved from https://www.city.beppu.oita.jp/02kankou/toukei/index.html (accessed 9 January 2017).

Cooper, M., & Cooper, P. (2009). Beppu reconstruction: A domestic hot spring destination in search of a 21st century global role. *Geographical Sciences, 64*(3), 127–139.

Guichard-Anguis, S. (2007). Japanese inns (ryokan) in Atami (Japan) and the shaping of coming. *Tourism Review International, 11*(1), 19–31.

Han, J., & Yotsumoto, Y. (2009). The trends regarding foreign tourists to Beppu, Oita prefecture in Japan. *Ritsumekan Journal of Asia Pacific Studies, 2*(6), 61–72. Retrieved from http://www.ritsumei.ac.jp/acd/re/k-rsc/hss/book/pdf/vol02_06.pdf.

Ikeda, T. (1987). A study of Japanese style inn after Meiji era. *Memoirs of the Fukui Institute of Technology, 17*, 155–164.

Japan Association of Travel Agency (JATA). (2014). Statistics of travel industry in Japan. Retrieved from http://www.jata-net.or.jp/data/stats/2013/pdf/2013_sujryoko.pdf.

Japan Ryokan Association. (JRA). Origin and history of the Japanese ryokan. Retrieved from http://www.ryokan.or.jp/past/english/what/index.html (accessed 1 November 2016).

Kristensson, P., Matthing, J., & Johansson, N. (2008). Key strategies for the successful involvement of customers in the co-creation of new technology-based services. *International Journal of Service Industry Management, 19*(4), 474–491.

Lee, T. J., & Lim, B. (2013). Ryokan facilities in Japan compared with spa hotels in Australia. In V. Joukes, L. Lourenço-Gomes & A. Marta-Costa (Eds.), *Sustainable medical and wellness destinations* (pp. 71–79). Proceedings of the International Conference Held in Chaves (Portugal), 13–15/10/2011. CIDESD-Centro de Invest. em Desporto, Saúde e Desenv. Humano.

Matsuda, N., & Oba, O. (2004). The formation process of the modern spa town, and various aspects of the large-scale ryokan: The case study of the Beppu spa, Oita. *Journal of Architecture and Planning,* (582), 145–152.

Matsuda, N., & Oba, O. (2003). The location tendency and its changes process of the 'ryokan' in Beppu hot spring: One consideration about the formation process of the 'ryokan' town in modern hot spring town. 日本建築学会近畿支部研究報告集. 計画系, (43), 961–964.

Ratz, T. (2011). Spa tourism in Japan and Hungary: A comparative analysis of perceptions and potential. *International Journal of Agricultural Travel and Tourism, 2*, 94–105.

Suzuki, S. (2013). Study on the international tourism in Beppu. *Bulletin of Beppu University Junior College, 32*, 75–83

Takeuchi, K. (2010). Overview of the Japan hotel market. Real Estate Analysis Report. NLI Research Institute, May, 1–13.

Ura, T. (2006). The cycle of hot spring destination: Beppu hatto and future prospects, (19), 11–20.

Ura, T. (2008). Current business trends of small sized ryokan in Beppu spa, Oita prefecture. *Journal of Osaka University of Tourism, 8*, 1–8.

Ura, T. (2013). Current business trends of well-established ryokan with hot spring facility in Beppu city, Oita prefecture. *Journal of Osaka University of Tourism, 13*, 21–27.

# 8 Value creation through heritage and identity

*Ruhet Genc*

## Introduction

Building a strong experience value has become the backbone of increasingly sophisticated tourism. One of the most significant methods for creating this experience value is through identity and heritage. The terms "identity" and "heritage" considered here are not only those that belong to the physical tourism facility but also those of the targeted tourist groups. Careful analysis of tourist expectations and efficient utilization of identity and heritage would lead to a strong experience value.

In this chapter, we will focus on how the aspects of identity and heritage are used to build experience value and what the possible outcomes would be for such utilization. As the experience value is created by individual tourists, group of tourists and their interactions with each other along with the location (i.e. a whole area of a country or a single hotel), all of these aspects will be considered as parts of the equation for optimal experience value.

This chapter aims to put factors of consumer behavior together with major and minor psychological and physical perspectives in a broad framework. The framework will be established on a timeline of pre-arrival, immediate and after-departure satisfaction which together assemble the concept of experience value as a whole. The theoretical background will be combined with practical knowledge for readers from different standpoints in tourism.

Starting with the theoretical framework of value, we will highlight the concept of experience value in the process of value creation. Next, we will present the two main elements of our hypothesis, heritage and identity, and we will discuss their contribution to the creation of experience value. Finally, we will roughly model this interaction in order to depict the mathematical aspects of the value-creation process, which would allow further investigation for the analysis of value creation in a quantitative sense.

## Theoretical perspectives

### What is value?

Attributing a universal definition to the concept of "value" is a hard task, as value is an ambiguous term, the definition of which includes objective elements as well as subjective judgments. Due to this complexity, we initially put forward the operational definition of value in order to overcome the possible misconceptual-izations. Next, we will list and shortly explain the dimensions of value so that we would present a clear picture of in what sense we depict the relationship between value creation and the interaction of identity and heritage.

In this chapter, value will be considered as a multidimensional concept, including a range of meanings since value may be attributed to rank, significance, material or monetary worth, power, usefulness or one's judgment for the importance in life, as argued by Sanders and Simons (2009). Through the collective creativity of peo-ple, value is produced as a form of value co-creation (Sanders & Simons, 2009). Considering the types of value in co-creative activities and interactions, we may list three main types of value: monetary value, use/experience value, and social value (Sanders & Simons, 2009). A summary of types of value defined on the basis of five properties such that objectives, mindset, how people are seen, deliverables and the time frame, can be found in Table 8.1.

Starting with the monetary value of co-creation, we may define the source of value as the desire for making money in new ways, more effective ways or in ways which are capable of providing sustainable, long-term revenues (Sanders & Simons, 2009). Therefore, monetary value receives the most attention in business cycles although it does not require direct contact between the company and cus-tomers, since the tools of information and communication are successful in terms of delivering conversation between those agents (Sanders & Simons, 2009).

Second, as Prahalad and Ramaswamy (2004) argue, the meaning of value as well as the creation of value shift from a product- and firm-centric perspective to a more personalized level where customer experiences matter. Hence, the expe-rience value stems from desires of the companies for transforming consumers into users where the products and services they supply will be better in terms of meeting the needs and wants of the individuals in the market (Sanders & Simons, 2009). Furthermore, the experience value of co-creation can be applicable to brands and branded environments, since, in today's world, brand stands as an emotional aspect which is based on trust of customers to a specific brand (Sanders & Simons, 2009). In short, participation of individuals in the value-creation process is an integral element of experience value, as it maximizes the satisfaction of customers with respect to their demands.

Last but not least, social value of co-creation is distinguished from monetary and experience value by targeting long-term aspirations, and suggesting human-istic and more sustainable alternatives for living (Sanders & Simons, 2009). In this respect, co-creation of social value requires an integration of ordinary people and experts working together where various perspectives are expressed and discussed by the means of direct personal involvement and empathy, which, in turn, enhance the collective creativity (Sanders & Simons, 2009). We need to underline the importance of personal interactions and conversations in the process of co-creation of social value, despite the useful role of social networks in terms of identification and placement of the participants (Sanders & Simons, 2009).

Although each of these terms have great importance in value creation, we will focus on the concept of experience value in our study as we want to

Table 8.1 Comparison of three types of value co-creation

| Co-creation of value | Objectives | Mindset | Perception of people | Deliverables | Time frame |
|---|---|---|---|---|---|
| **Monetary** | Production<br>Consumption<br>Maximization of shareholder wealth | Business<br>Commercial<br>Economic | Customers<br>Consumers | Marketplace results<br>Business advancement<br>Products that sell | Short-term |
| **Experiental** | Positive Experiences<br>Personalization<br>Customization | Experience-driven<br>Service orientation | End-users<br>Empowered consumers | Products and services that people need and want | From life-stage to lifetime<br>Long-term |
| **Societal** | Human-centered<br>Ecological | Partners<br>Participants<br>Owners | Transformation<br>Ownership<br>Learning<br>Behavior change<br>Happiness<br>Survival | Over many generations<br>Longer-term | Improve quality of life<br>Sustainability |

explain the impact of heritage and identity on personalized aspects in value creation.

Now, we will shift our attention to the two main concepts that we want to analyze their impact in the value creation process. These are (cultural) heritage and (cultural) identity.

## *Cultural heritage and identity*

Heritage is defined as physical objects and places which have been passed on from one generation to another and it incorporates divergent practices and intangible properties such as language and cultural behavior (Tengberg et al., 2012). Moreover, heritage incorporates the means for conserving things and choices that we are making about what to remember and what to forget, most of the time under a potential threat with respect to future generations (Harrison, 2010). Therefore, (cultural) heritage is not restricted to its creation by former generations but also it includes the way it is interpreted, valued and managed by the next generations (Tengberg et al., 2012) such as public/private sector, official/non-official elements and insider/outsider impacts, where each of these stakeholders has varied and there are multiple objectives in the creation and management of heritage (Ashworth & Graham, 2005). In short, heritage is not a static term, but rather it refers to a constantly changing concept which can be re-evaluated and interpreted by different actors and in many ways during the course of history (Tengberg et al., 2012).

On the other hand, cultural identity refers to the current cultural linkage between individuals and their environment (Hassan, Scholes, & Ash, 2005). Furthermore, contemporary psychology defines cultural identity as the individual's sense of self with respect to a range of social and interpersonal links and roles (Tengberg et al., 2012). Triandis (1994) argues that culture is to society what memory is to individuals, since culture includes traditions by which individuals acknowledge what has worked properly in the past meanwhile encompassing the way individuals perceive their environment and themselves based on the linkage between individuals and their landscape (Tengberg et al., 2012).

Combining these two, presence of cultural heritage leads individuals obtain some non-material benefits such as spiritual enrichment, cognitive, emotional and social development, reflection, recreation and aesthetic experiences (Hassan, Scholes, & Ash, 2005) which, in turn, play a role in the construction as well as the expression of the identity. Heritage values such as special or historical properties within a landscape provide a sense of continuity and understanding of place in the natural and cultural environment by reminding individuals of their collective and individual roots (Tengberg et al., 2012).

## *Value creation through heritage and identity*

Initially, we may focus on the objective of experience value when considering its creation process. The main objectives of experience value are positive experiences and personalization as shown in Table 8.1. In order to enhance the amount of positive experiences, one's interaction with the cultural environment which has been structured, shaped and transmitted through generations, is of great importance. Meanwhile, these positive experiences become a part of individuals' identities through memorization. Therefore, presence of an interplay between cultural heritage and cultural identity in the creation of positive experience can be argued. Considering the example of CHESS (Cultural Heritage Experiences through Socio-personal interactions and Storytelling) Project, which is a project co-founded by European Commission and aims to "research, implement and evaluate . . . the experiencing of personalized interactive stories for visitors" via personalization, adaptivity, digital storytelling, interaction methodologies, and narrative-oriented mobile and mixed reality technologies (CHESS, 2011), the linkage between cultural heritage and personal aspects of social interactions in the emergence and proliferation of such experiences may be found.

Next, the mindset behind the creation of experience value is experience-driven as Sanders and Simons argue (2009). Promoting experience for the creation as well as the maintenance and the transformation through generations of such values would be a coherent argument in the part of cultural heritage. On the other hand, experience-driven construction of identity, specifically by emotional and cognitive aspects of personality development would be, in turn, the main contributor for the creation of experience values. Hence, the interplay between cultural heritage and identity resembles a cycle at that level, in which experiences with the cultural heritage contribute to the construction of identity via personal development on the basis of these experiences. In the end, these identities shape and transform the cultural heritage to the next generations, where the new generations will interact with them and construct their identities with respect to their experience values.

In the creation of experience value, people are seen as end-users and empowered consumers according to the Table 8.1. Since the whole value-creation process emphasizes the personal aspect of subjective experience, individuals stand as the key point of such process and their needs and wants regarding products and services play a crucial part in the creation of value. The interplay between cultural heritage and identity at this point can be explained by the motivation behind the attribution of people as end-users or empowered agents who shape the quality of products and services with their needs and wants. It can be argued that cultural heritage depicts the physical environment where individuals' needs and wants are formed by an impact of external factors. Furthermore, internal factors which are responsible for the emergence of these needs and wants can be considered within the scope of cultural identity. Thus, the factors which flourish experience value have a two-fold structure; in one part, external factors framed by the cultural heritage play a role in determining the extent of these needs and wants, in the other, cultural identity inherently determines the needs and wants of the individuals as an internal factor. Nevertheless, it is hard to argue that one of these factors is more powerful at the final decision of individuals, however, they both take part in the embodiment of these needs and wants by making the individuals end-users or empowered agents in the creation of experience value.

The last point that can be considered under the creation of experience value is the time frame of such value creation. As Sanders and Simons (2009) argue, the time frame for the creation of experience value is long-term and from life-stage to life-time. Again, it is highly consistent with our argumentation on the interplay between cultural heritage and identity, since neither cultural heritage nor cultural identity is the result of short-term, daily interactions, and creation of which, require long periods. Therefore we can claim that incorporation of experiences into the creation of heritage and identity takes a long time and we expect a longer time frame for the involvement of cultural heritage and identity, which have been shaped by the previous experiences, in the process of experience value creation.

To recap, the creation of experience value through heritage and identity can be consistently explained under the five features of experience value, which are its objectives, mindset, perception of people, deliverables, and time frame, as argued by Sanders and Simons (2009).

## Constructing a simple model

Having argued the main characteristics of experience value creation through cultural heritage and identity, we now shift our attention to the construction of a simple model. The reason why we want to model this interplay is quite straightforward: we need to reassure ourselves that our investigation regarding to theoretical and qualitative concepts lead to sound results as scientific as possible. Hence we suggest a model for the interplay between cultural heritage and cultural identity in the creation of experience value as following:

$$EV = \beta 0 + \beta 1.CH + \beta 2.CI + \varepsilon$$

where,

EV implies experience value, the amount of value created in this process.

CH implies cultural heritage, the extent of cultural entities that are subject to transfer from one generation to the other.

CI implies cultural identity referring to the level of engagement of one individual with her cultural environment

$\beta 0$, $\beta 1$ and $\beta 2$ imply coefficients, and

$\varepsilon$ implies residual (i.e. the effect of other variables).

The main obstacle for the construction of such modeling is the transformation of qualitative elements (cultural heritage and identity) into quantitatively measurable forms. Yet, further studies may overcome this problem by providing the operational definitions for the concepts with respect to the study of interest and measure the effect of interaction between cultural heritage and cultural identity on a quantitative basis.

## Conclusion

In this chapter, we have suggested a new model consisting of two main aspects, heritage and identity, in order to explain their impact in the creation of experience value. We have started with the operational definition of value by presenting three different types of value creation, and then we have selected and focused on the concept of experience value, since it has more importance in the context of tourism industry. Next, we have broadly discussed the concepts of cultural heritage and identity, and analyzed their impact on the creation of experience value in more detail. After completing the discussion, we have presented a mathematical model explaining the effect of heritage and identity on value creation.

Although the scope of this chapter is limited to theoretical discussion, we believe that it will provide an intuition for further studies. Moreover, in the light of scientific analysis of the interplay between heritage and identity for the creation of experience value that we have presented in this chapter, more substantial results will be obtained and these results can be used in the practical domain of tourism industry as well as contributing to the theoretical framework of academic investigation. All in all, heritage and identity appear as two inseparable aspects of experience value creation but theoretical argument will be insufficient to clarify the significance of such interaction and we need a quantitative analysis in order to reveal this effect in a falsifiable manner.

## References

Ashworth, G. J., & Graham, B. (eds) (2005). *Senses of place: Senses of time.* Aldershot: Ashgate.

CHESS. (2011–2016). *The main page of Cultural Heritage Experiences through Socio-personal interactions and Storytelling webpage.* Retrieved from http://www.chess experience.eu/ (June 5, 2016).

Fowler, P., & Boniface, P. (1993). *Heritage and tourism in "the global village".* New York, NY: Routledge.

Harrison, R. (2010). *Understanding the politics of heritage.* Manchester: Manchester University Press.

Hassan., R., Scholes, R., & Ash, N. (2005). *The Millennium Ecosystem Assessment (MA) Ecosystems and human well-being: current state and trends – Findings of the conditions and trends working group.* Washington, DC: Island Press.

Prahalad, C. K., & Ramaswamy, V. (2004). The future of competition: Co-creating unique value with customers. *Journal of Interactive Marketing Volume, 18*(3). DOI: 10.1002/dir.20015.

Sanders, L., & Simons, G. (2009). A social vision for value co-creation in design. *Technology Innovation Management Review.* Retrieved from http://timreview.ca/article/310 (June 1, 2016).

Tengberg, A., Fredholm, S., Eliasson, I., Knez, I., Saltzman, K., & Wetterberg O. (2012). Cultural ecosystem services provided by landscapes: Assessment of heritage values and identity. In H. C. Triandis (Ed.), *Culture and social behavior.* McGraw-Hill, NY: Ecosystem.

Triandis, H. C. (1994). *Culture and Social behaviour.* New York, NY: Praeger.

# 9    Gastronomy in a co-creation context

*Ruhet Genc*

## Introduction

Eating is one of our fundamental behaviors in order to maintain our bodily functions properly, and to survive. However, this is not the end of story as we have formed a special relationship with food through the course of history. Human beings have developed numerous eating practices, cuisines and cultures around the food they eat. The proliferation and diversification of such eating habits can be considered as a claim that food is not only a necessity for survival but also a way of entertainment.

In addition to the fact that food constitutes a fundamental requirement of the human body, it could also be associated with the basic elements of social and national values. Thus, the social impact assisting the evolution and transformation processes of food could not only be claimed to create traditions but also to result in artistic representation of the food.

Besides being a significant component of daily life and having an essential position as a social and artistic element, an increasing number of travelers consider food as a central decision-making factor while deciding their travel destinations. Changing conditions also have an impact on the restaurants and cafes; in the current situation, offering a high quality of gastronomic experience to customers is not sufficient, but it also constitutes an important factor of competition with other tourism destinations.

Food, as an essential element of the tourist experience, has just started to be taken into consideration as a subject of study in recent years. This fact could appear to be surprising at first glance. However, it could be claimed that the acceptance of food as a fundamental component of everyday life resulted in underestimation of food for being taken as an area of serious study (Boyne & Hall, 2003).

In this chapter, our intention is to explore and analyze the food experience extensively. First, we will look at the history of food and its evolution throughout centuries. This will provide an understanding about the stages that the food service sector has been passing through and it will reveal the major shifts within the area of gastronomy. Then we will move to the concept of co-creation and the importance of co-creative values in creating gastronomy as an essential part of the tourism sector. The discussion of the value of co-creation will include the representation of co-creation on the basis of tourist satisfaction in a naïve model. Finally, the chapter will argue the influence of postmodernism on culinary consumption in order to provide a coherent picture of the position of gastronomy within touristic activities through the course of history.

## The course of food in history

Historically, the first remarkable change in food occurred with the discovery of fire. Before this, humans were consuming what they gathered in a raw, cold form. However, the discovery of fire brought about the activity of cooking. With the involvement of cooking in the food consumption process, the perception of food, which used to be a fuel for the human body, has changed. Following the subsequent change in the perception of food, transformation of food into a social phenomenon has occurred, including the rituals of preparing and servicing the food. As time passed, humans have reached the step of domestication of animals, such as cattle and sheep which provide a variety of food like dairy products, beef and giblets. At the same time, agricultural activities have started, transforming humans from mere consumers as hunters and gatherers into farmers who produce food by the effective use of land. Switching the life-style from nomadic type to settlements, food becomes the mark of social differentiation, since some people have more access to food and stock higher amounts than the others who barely find food and are dependent on people who have stock in order to maintain their lives.

Placement of food, for instance, in the Antique Age, Egyptian, Chinese, Indian and Greek figures and written archives allow us to be informed about how people maintained a culture shaped around food and how this culture reflected on their social interactions.

In the enormous geography that they took under their control, the Romans derived the food culture of different lands and created a mixture of East and West for a new, enriched cuisine culture. Feasts were the characteristic activity of the Roman Empire where they served an abundance of meals and wine. In this sense, feasts can be considered as today's "all-inclusive" holiday options, co-created with gastronomic entity: food. Furthermore, taverns were also indigenous to Roman culture, referring to the small restaurant-like units for food and wine service.

The tradition of eating outside in the form of feasts lost its prominence following the collapse of the Roman Empire. The only places which could maintain their work were the inns, placed on the safe and busy routes. Similar to the case of China, trade as a form of social interaction made the continuation of food servicing possible. Additionally, priests and monks were the main characters who continued the tradition of mass feeding in monasteries. Two important aspects of the Middle Ages, famine and epidemics, played a crucial role in the church's domination on feeding, declaring gluttony as the biggest sin and putting in some measures in order to cope with it.

The methods were well-developed for cooking, baking, wine- and beer-making in the monasteries. Initiatives of food service units later learned the art of food and formed guilds for carrying out the food production services. Most of the standards and traditions in kitchens come from the professional kitchen teams formed in the guilds of the Middle Ages.

A different period in the history of food was started by the development of transportation. Local foods as well as their seeds have been transported to different parts of the world and become cultivated. The discovery of America also helped this worldwide circulation of food process. For instance, tomatoes and potatoes came from the Andes (Chile) region, and oranges were brought from North China, enriching the variety of food for people.

The development in the perspective of art and aesthetics reflected on the advancement in cuisine culture in the Renaissance period. As upper classes became richer, they could afford more expensive and various goods such as almonds, raisins and spices coming from China or India, which in return increased the possibility of cooks to enrich the cuisine with new recipes. Step by step, soon after the beginning of the Renaissance of food in Italy, it spread to France and flourished there. The Renaissance of food continued to grow in Continental Europe (Germany, Austria, Spain, etc.) as well as England and Ireland.

Based on the aesthetic tendencies of the Renaissance Era combined with the techniques of cooking and food decoration learnt from the Chinese, Europe appeared as the centre of food and cuisine with various flavour.

Pursuing this further, the industrial revolution in the midst of the 19th century contributed to a substantial amount of change in food. Parallel to the advancements in mass production, food products have also become industrialized. In other terms, food is collected and packaged in larger factories for being distributed to supermarkets. Moreover, service of food as well as beverages has turned into a new industry, in accordance with the newly emerged tourism industry as a result of leisure-time necessity of labour.

Before it received its meaning that we are familiar with today, the word "restaurant" meant "healing broth". The first modern restaurant was created in Paris, in the 1700s, by a man named Boulanger (Morgan, 2006). The opening of the first restaurants which could be described as both an interesting cookery enterprise and a scientific innovation was a quest for health as much as an attraction of the 18th-century distinguished culture of food (Spang, 2000).

Finally, the globalization process, especially after the 1970s, resulted in the global standardization movement where market- and restaurant-chains provide the same quality of food to people both locally and internationally. For instance, the standards (ingredients, taste etc.) of a BigMac are more or less the same across the world; there are only minimal variations due to cultural difference, such as the use of beef instead of pork in countries where the majority of people are Muslim or the amount of salt used as an ingredient. Nevertheless, McDonalds provides people a standardized set of choices which can be found in every part of the world.

We have briefly covered the history of food and the transformation of food gastronomy into different types of art form in addition to the typical industrialization. It is important to understand the history of techniques, traditions and ingredients to understand the gastronomic scene of the present time and improve it with better knowledge. Today, food experience is a significant part of tourism and it is creating its own field. In the next section, we will explore food experience value in tourism in detail and discuss how we could create value in consumption.

## Basics of food experience

Human beings cannot survive without food and wherever we travel, we need to eat. Food is also "a common language and, above all, a universal right. As any language, it is spoken to communicate, to share emotions, feelings, and sensations" (Buiatti, 2011). Therefore, the food experience is not only about taste but it is also a social link between people.

When people share their food, they take pleasure sitting at a table together and contemplating their pleasures related to the food and the service; hence a good food experience is closely related to the hospitality. The word *hospes* has two meanings in languages deriving from Latin; it means both the person who welcomes and the one who is welcomed (Buiatti, 2011). The host and guest relationship is a significant part of the gastronomic experience that this chapter is built on and the best way to explore it is to focus on "slow food experience". That is not to say that fast food does not require good hospitality; however, its practices are very different and do not reflect the kind of experience we would like to delve in to as it lacks important dimensions.

Food experience has always been an essential part of the tourist experience, as wherever they travel, people need to eat, and their expectations change according to the itinerary they planned. The tourism industry creates value in an essential service such as food by "making experiences memorable". The experiences are designed to take into account tourist's means, time and space. Pleasure and convenience are merged together. On the other hand, culinary tourism is a relatively new field. In culinary tourism, the food is in the spotlight. People focus on food when they make their plans. This might be as simple as making a reservation in a restaurant or travelling long distances and organizing their itineraries around wineries, restaurants, cooking schools, local farms, food festivals, and so on (Kirshenblatt-Gimblett, 2004). When people focus on food experiences, it becomes even more crucial for those who work in tourism to provide an immaculate service and create higher value together with the customer in the food experience.

From the beginning of this chapter, we have investigated the position of gastronomy in the tourism sector. Now we will take one step further and try to insert the effect of co-creation with respect to gastronomy as an irreplaceable part of the tourism industry. First, we start with identifying the concept of co-creation in a detailed way. Then we put forward our research question on how co-creation in gastronomy affects the scope of tourism industry. Following the argument for immeasurability of the effect of co-creation, we will offer a model where tourist satisfaction stands as the dependent variable, consistent with the findings in co-creation literature. Finally, we will consider the Cittaslow movement as a successful example of co-creation in gastronomy with respect to tourism industry and the reflection of the Cittaslow movement in Turkey as in the case of Seferihisar.

# Co-creation

The concept of co-creation is defined as "the joint creation of value by the company and the customer; allowing the customer to co-construct the service experience to suit their context" (Prahalad & Ramaswamy, 2004, p. 8). Leaving behind the traditional, company-centric concept of market, where the producers determine the quality of goods and services, and supply them into the market as values, co-creation focuses on the reciprocal relationship between producers and consumers by emphasizing the role of consumers' experiences in value creation.

As the interaction between company and consumers becomes the main source of value creation, we need a better understanding of the process of co-creation through its four major building blocks: dialogue, access, risk assessment, and transparency, which constitute the DART model of value co-creation as Prahalad and Ramaswamy (2004, p. 9) introduce.

# Examples of co-creation experience in tourism

The 'new tourist' wants to be in charge and this can be observed more and more as the number of people responding to their own travel requirements by consulting and booking through the Internet increases, as Poon (1993) has argued. Moreover, virtual tourism communities such as forums, Wikis and blogs, where experiences are compared, evaluated, defined and exchanged are increasing as well (Binkhorst & Den Dekker, 2009). Websites for house or bed sharing and coach surfing can be considered as some examples. For instance, Audio snacks is an example of a virtual space to find, purchase, download, listen to, and enjoy user-generated pod tours which people themselves have created to share (Binkhorst & Den Dekker, 2009). It is a virtual space where everyone interact with others (www.audio snacks.com). These are all examples of co-creation between potential tourists.

Another type of co-creation can be named as co-creation between visitors and locals while at the destination, possibly starting before taking off and continuing after travels. For example, "Like-a-local", is a Dutch organization which allows visitors to step into the daily life of a local, to taste the local food, see and experience the local culture. In particular, a wide range of local experiences are available in Amsterdam, Rotterdam, Barcelona, Lisbon, Madrid and Stockholm. Tourists may create their own touristic experience, ranging from one single activity to a complete holiday, and make reservations through the website (www.like-a-local.com). Likewise "Like-a-local", the organization named "Dine with the Dutch" allows tourists to join local people for a typical Dutch dinner in a private home setting so that tourists may enjoy local gastronomic experiences in a more intense way (www.dinewiththedutch.nl). Moreover, interactive workshops of all sorts offered by local experts to teach visitors about local specialties such as gastronomy, art, pottery, painting, dancing, learning the language, and so on have become more popular in more and more destinations (Binkhorst & Den Dekker, 2009). These examples of various forms of co-creation in tourism underline the requirement of change in the perspective on tourism.

## Gastronomy and experience value

As we have discussed in the first section, food is not only an element for meeting basic human needs, but it also creates a social dimension through human inter-action and cultural practices. In this context, food has more than a maintenance function; it allows individuals (in particular tourists, parallel to aim of this chapter) to maximize their satisfaction via diverse activities and experiences regarding to food consumption.

Gastronomy is the fundamental part of touristic experience, since there is no way to maintain a touristic activity without providing food. However, touristic companies take the advantage of food servicing by using it as a part of touristic experience. Providing a large variety of food with high quality can be a reason to be chosen instead of other touristic companies. Therefore, we ask to what extent co-creation is capable of changing the quality of gastronomic entity, which, in turn, affects the overall performance of touristic company in terms of tourist satisfaction.

Considering tourist satisfaction as the basis of our analysis, this study will inves-tigate the relationship between tourist satisfaction and the effect of co-creation. Tourist perceptions are the key elements of successful destination marketing since they affect the choice of a destination (Ahmed, 1991), the consumption of goods and services during holiday, and the decision to return (Stevens, 1992). According to Laws (1995), there are many tourists who have experiences in other destinations, and their perceptions of these destinations are affected by comparisons among facilities, attractions and service standards. The literature on tourist satisfaction has indicated that when measuring tourist satisfaction, different decisions have been made such that comparing pre-holiday expectations and post-holiday perceptions (Duke & Persia, 1996; Pizam & Milman, 1993), monitoring during the holiday time (Gyte & Phelps, 1989), completing the overall tour experience (Loundsbury & Hoopes, 1985; Pearce, 1980), and just before completing the holiday (Goodrich, 1978; Vogt & Fesenmaier, 1995).

## Modelling value co-creation

The main consumers of the tourism industry are the consumers who enjoy the services provided by the tourism companies, that is, tourists. Therefore, a model of the co-creation in the tourism sector should include the tourist's perception of the experience comprising his or her own participation in creating the experience. Evaluation such as tourist satisfaction would then be the dependent variable.

Benefits derived from the creation of other types of activities can be added into the model. Considering the positive effect of gastronomy in the tourism sector in terms of enriching the options and increasing the satisfaction may also lead spor-tive facilities to be established as an inseparable part of touristic companies in order to prevent people from gaining weight due to the gastronomic quality of the facility. Another variable can be considered as the satisfaction of the host com-munities. Since co-creation has a two-fold effect, it is very likely that it can lead to an increase in the quality of life of those who serve.

Hence our model can be considered as:

(1)  $CE = \beta_0 + \beta_1.TS + \varepsilon$

where,

CE implies the *effect of co-creation*

TS implies *tourist satisfaction*

$\beta_0$ and $\beta_1$ imply coefficients, and

$\varepsilon$ implies residual (i.e. the effect of other variables).

In order to avoid an omitted variable bias, we may extend our model by adding other variables that we have explained above, such that:

(2)  $CE = \beta_0 + \beta_1.TS + \beta_2.OB + \beta_3.HS + \varepsilon$

where, additional to (1),

OB implies *other benefits* derived from the creation of other types of activities,

HS implies *host satisfaction* related to the establishment of co-creation activity, and

$\beta_2$ and $\beta_3$ imply coefficients.

By using model (1) above, we claim that any measurable outcome of tourist satisfaction can lead to finding the effect of co-creation. Additionally, a more reliable outcome can be achieved by extending the model into (2), that is, including the effects of other benefits and host satisfaction, since it increases the variance explained by the model.

Conceptually, the model replaces the *homo-economicus* figure, that is making choices on the principles of bounded rationality, with *homo-satisfaciendus*, who are unable to maximize their utility function but only meet their needs in a satisfactory manner, parallel to the argument of H. A. Simona (Przybyla, 2010). Therefore the aim of our model is not providing the ultimate tourist satisfaction for tourists who rationally seek to maximize their utility, but rather understanding the concept of satisfaction as the ultimate goal and organizing services and activities accordingly. With this replacement, the abstract nature of measuring such benefits on a scale of mathematical calculations with respect to assumptional rationality gives way to scientifically sound measurement, which uses the means and findings of modern psychology.

A related example can be seen in the study of Björk and Kauppinen-Räisänen (2014) on food sourcing. The results of the Björk and Kauppinen-Räisänen (2014) study shows that the top two searches for the food information are about "Recommended food places" and "Local food specialties" rather than, for instance, "Price level of local food" or "The safety of local food" (p. 66). Furthermore, the top answer given to the reason for collecting food information when travelling is

"I am interested in food" (p. 66). These two findings reflect that tourists are also looking for satisfaction through gastronomic activities.

San Sebastian can be considered as a living example of gastronomy-centred touristic activity. Currently, San Sebastian has more restaurants with Michelin Stars per square metre than any other city in the world, hence it is known as one of the major culinary capitals (eitb, 2013). When the global economic crisis hit Spain, as well as other countries in the world, San Sebastian kept attracting tourists and enjoyed economic revenues from touristic activity. The reason why San Sebastian continued to profit whereas other industries in other parts of Spain, including tourism, were experiencing the adverse effects of economic crisis, is that San Sebastian offers a differentiated touristic experience characterized by the co-creational aspects of gastronomy. Along with the suitable environment for summer tourism, San Sebastian makes use of its culinary potential, leading to the emergence of other activities regarding to tourism, and hence attracts tourists even in the worse periods for economic activities. Addressing the satisfaction of tourists with a distinctive feature, San Sebastian stands as a major touristic capital on a global scale.

## Creating value in food experience and the role of consumer behaviour

In order to come up with ways to add value to the food experience, we need to understand the construction of value. Value is an abstract concept and it is related to many aspects of consumer behaviour such as motivations, perceptions and perspectives (Zins, 2000). There are different views among academics about the definition of value, as Zins (2000, p. 121) set out to summarize:

- "a relation or trade-off between all advantages received and disadvantages taken into account (e.g. Monroe and Krishnan, 1985) or similar;
- a weighted comparison between give- and get-characteristics (Sawyer & Dickson, 1984);
- "the consumer's overall assessment of the utility of a product based on perceptions of what is received and what is given" (Zeithaml, 1988); or
- "value is not to be reduced to its functional aspects but spans to social, emotional and epistemic components" (Sheth, Newman & Gross,1991).

The examples above set out the scene of today's tourism where customers are entitled to demand the experience they want, or even the ones that they cannot imagine.

## Postmodernism and its influence on culinary consumption

Postmodernism came along with a major transformation in consumer behaviour. Setting forth one of the first expansive theoretical frameworks by Jameson (1991), postmodernism has been characterized by "a transnational and global capital that valorises difference, multiplicity, eclecticism, populism, and intensified consumerism in a new information/entertainment society" (Kellner, 1999). Perhaps not the remaining part of the world per se, but the developed world consists of consumer societies. When we say "consumer", it does not only refer to customers buying tangible products from retail outlets anymore. In consumer societies, "any form of service, whether in the commercial or public sectors, should adopt an explicit 'customer orientation'", because the scope of the term consumer has widely expanded (Sloan, 2004).

In this context, it is not a surprise that culinary tourism is flourishing as a separate field, ascending from its position as a part of the general tourism. In the postmodern society, individuals are forming their own self-identities through consumption (Sloan, 2004). How people consume demonstrates which group or groups they belong to in the society. It defines their socio-economic class, the trends and social conventions they follow and what method they use to seek social acceptance. Culinary taste might seem to be an individual preference, but it is more about social acceptance (Sloan, 2004). Hence, providers of food service should take social context and profiles of their customers into account in order to excel in the food experience they provide. What customers prefer might sometimes be different from their taste.

Food is a way to live the experience of visiting somewhere, without necessarily being there. In order to achieve this experience, a restaurant should be true to the food and wrap it with the right atmosphere. It is a stark opposition to how the global food chains like McDonalds, Burger King and so on, operate. Gourmet travellers are seeking respect to the original. In a way, these modern tourists are searching the purity of the past, a time before market forces contaminated the gastronomic scene (Scarpato & Daniele, 2003).

## Motivations

Although the main motivation of being in a food service facility might seem to be eating, customers actually come with plenty of different motivations, including a utilitarian motivation such as eating to be full or a more hedonic motivation such as enjoying the taste of the food or socializing. It is important for a business to observe and analyse these motivations to create value in the experience.

Rather than conceptualizing motivations on entertainment along a single dimension of pleasure-seeking, there is another dimension of motivation including meaningfulness-seeking that we name eudaimonic motivations (Oliver & Raney, 2011). Eudaimonic motivations can be considered as an impetus in creating a sustainable co-creative value in gastronomy, since motivations including learning, participation and so on, is more effective than pleasure-seeking activities in terms of co-creation. When meaningfulness-seeking as a higher-order need become the target, as Tamborini et. al. (2010) argue, people will be more encouraged to participate in co-creative activities. Because, if people directly participate in the gastronomical experience rather than enjoying the ready-made/fast-food culture on the basis of pleasure-seeking, they will be more satisfied at the end of the experience.

## Memory

Customers' memories, meaning their recollections about their past experiences are highly important for creating value in food experience. Memory of an experience is in fact more important than the experience itself, as what will bring the customers back is their memories (Wright, 2010).

In their detailed analysis, Kim, Ritchie and McCormick (2012) have developed a 24-item memorable tourism experience scale that can be applicable to most destination areas. The scale comprises seven domains, including hedonism, refreshment, local culture, meaningfulness, knowledge, involvement, and novelty. Their data support this dimensional structure of the memorable tourism experience along with its internal consistency and validity (such as content, construct, convergent, and discriminant validity). Although their analysis does not include food experiences, we may consider the memorable experience with food for tourists with respect to the results of this study.

In order to work with memory, food service businesses must appeal to the sensory system of the customers. It is obvious that a restaurant should offer delicious meals to appeal to the palate of their customers. However, they should not forget the fact that the sensory system includes visuality, sense of touch, hearing and the sense of smell. Ideally, a gastronomic experience should include all of these senses in a positive way to achieve an unforgettable and cherished memory. Therefore, businesses must organize their work in a way to appeal to as many of these senses as possible. Gibbs and Ritchie (2010) propose that considering the restaurant a theatre stage where every detail and move is to be integrated in harmony will help the business to excel in providing a valuable and memorable food experience.

## A case: Cittaslow movement and the example of Seferihisar

In the following section, we will investigate the Cittaslow movement as a significant example of co-creation, underlining the example of Seferihisar in Turkey.

The Cittaslow (Slow City) movement started in Italy in 1999 and currently it has over 120 member towns globally. Pink (2008, pp. 163–164) describe the Cittaslow movement within the framework of an indirect activism rather than involving direct confrontation in society and define the wave to include "a local distinctiveness and sustainability and seeks to improve local 'quality of life' in a context of what its leaders see as a homogenising globalisation process".

As the main source of the Cittaslow movement, Slow Food has gained a great deal of attention as a social movement which claims to counterpart enlarging globalization in terms of eating habits and the international food production. The network of towns, namely Cittaslow, is working together with the local urban development, aiming at high quality on the basis of similar principles as Slow Food (Nilsson, Widarsson & Wirell, 2011).

Integrating the past traditions with the contemporary lifestyles, the Cittaslow movement envelops progress and change based on sustainability. When we investigate the local applications of the Cittaslow movement, Seferihisar would be the best case to take into consideration among 11 Cittaslow cities in Turkey. The reason why we select Seferihisar is that it is one of the recent Cittaslow cities globally where changes brought by the Cittaslow movement can be easily observable. Second, the Mayor of Seferihisar, Tunç Soyer, is currently the Vice-President of the global Cittaslow movement, which brings particular attention to the case of Seferihisar as it rapidly integrated into the movement such that the representative of Seferihisar is positioned on the board of directors. Generally, Seferihisar enhances sharing local crafts, tastes and arts with next generations and guests in order to prevent them from becoming memos which belong to older generations. Furthermore, the use of clean and renewable energy sources which do not cause harm either to the environment or the local people and their culture and history has been encouraged in Seferihisar, likewise all the member countries of the Cittaslow association. The concept of Cittaslow has been accepted as a guideline for the Seferihisar local government and lead to an initiation for the protection of the future of Seferihisar. The Cittaslow concept prevents local people from obliterating their cultural heritage, traditions and customs for the sake of rapid and modern urbanization, becoming a part of global capitalism where the concepts of money and globalization are the only significant values (www.cittaslowseferi hisar.org). This movement particularly reflects on the food experience of tourists by encouraging investors to engage in opening restaurants or advertisement for local tastes such as mandarin jam (http://seferihisar.bel.tr/istanbul-slowfood/).

In general, like all small towns of the Cittaslow Movement, Seferihisar protects its characteristics and its unique identity and features since the Cittaslow Movement inherently aims to prevent local characteristics and properties, the standards and life styles of the local area, and the general city texture which differs the area from other cities from disappearing. All in all, Seferihisar tries to propose various strategies in order to conserve its own values as the people of Seferihisar do not want to lose their own values, which provide them a substantial amount of diversity and protect them from the destructive and assimilating effects of globalization that may cause them to vanish in the aforementioned process.

## Conclusions

In this chapter, we set out to explore the creation of value in food experience in a historic perspective, in particular the slow food service industry. The field of gastronomy has a long history dating back to ancient times, with Ancient Greeks and Romans considered to be the pioneers. The evolution of gastronomic experiences has been astonishing and in the 1700s, the French established the grounds for the "restaurant" that spread around the world and became a staple of our society today. At the present, we are in an era where customized experiences are highly valued in a world of competitive alternatives. Therefore, culinary tourism has flourished as an area of its own.

Food services need to add value to the experiences they provide to their customers, in order to have their place in the competition. This could only be achieved by creating a multi-faceted business taking all the dimensions of consumer behaviour and integrating it with quality service. A restaurant should pay close attention to staff organization, safety and hygiene in the workplace as a rule of thumb.

Furthermore, the chapter initiates modelling the effect of co-creation on the basis of tourist satisfaction, as well as other variables such as benefits derived from the activity of co-creation experience value. In doing so, we have proposed a new way of investigation, since quantitative analysis would be the best possible way for obtaining significant results.

The future has prospects for those who in particular understand the sophisticated nature of food experience, follow the local and global innovations closely and raise the value through the right means.

## References

Ahmed, Z. U. (1991). The influence of the components of a state's tourist image on product positioning strategy. *Tourism Management, 12*(4), 331–340.

AudioSnacks. Retrieved from www.audiosnacks.com (September 2016).

Binkhorst, E., & Den Dekker, T. (2009). Agenda for co-creation tourism experience research. *Journal of Hospitality Marketing & Management, 18*(2–3), 311–327.

Bjork, P., & Kauppinen-Räisänen, H. (2014). Culinary-gastronomic tourism: A search for local food experiences. *Nutrition & Food Science, 44*(4), 294–309.

Boyne, S., & Hall, D. (2003). Managing Food and tourism developments: Issues for planning and opportunities to add value. In C. M. Hall, L. Sharples, R. Mitchell, N. Macionis, & B. Cambourne (Eds.), *Food tourism around the world* (pp. 285–295). Oxford: Routledge.

Buiatti, S. (2011). Food and Tourism: The role of the "Slow Food" association. In K. L. Sidali, A. Spiller, B. Schulze (Eds.), *Food, agriculture and tourism* (pp. 92–101). New York, NY: Springer.

Cittaslow. Retrieved from http://cittaslowturkiye.org/cittaslow-seferihisar/ (January 2017).

Dine with the Dutch. Retrieved from www.dinewiththedutch.nl (September 2016).

Duke, C. R., & Persia, M. A. (1996). Performance-importance analysis of escorted tour evaluations. *Journal of Travel & Tourism Marketing, 5*(3), 207–223.

eitb.eus. (2013). Retrieved from http://www.eitb.eus/en/news/life/detail/1239682/san-sebastian-gastronomy--san-sebastian-mecca-food-lovers/ (December 12, 2016).

Seferihisar Belediyesi. Retrieved from http://seferihisar.bel.tr/istanbul-slowfood/ (December 12, 2016).

Gibbs, D., & Ritchie, C. (2010). Theatre in restaurants: Constructing the experience. In M. Morgan, P. Lugosi & J. R. Brent Ritchie (Eds.), *The tourism and leisure experience: Consumer and managerial perspectives* (pp. 182–201). Bristol: Channel View Publications.

Goodrich, J. N. (1978). The relationship between preferences for and perceptions of vacation destinations: Application of a choice model. *Journal of Travel Research, 17*(2), 8–13.

Gyte, D. M., & Phelps, A. (1989). Patterns of destination repeat business: British tourists in Mallorca, Spain. *Journal of Travel Research, 28*(1), 24–28.

Jameson, F. (1991). *Postmodernism, or, the cultural logic of late capitalism*. London: Duke University Press.

Kellner, D. (1999). The Frankfurt school and British cultural studies: The missed articulation. Retrieved from http://www.philosophyofculture.org/The%20Frankfurt%20School%20and%20British%20Cultural%20Studies_%20The%20Missed%20Articulation.pdf (September 8, 2007).

Kim J. H, Ritchie J. R. B., & McCormick, B. (2012). Development of a scale to measure memorable tourism experiences. *Journal of Travel Research, 51*(1), 12–25.

Kirshenblatt-Gimblett, B. (2004). Foreword. In L. M. Long (Ed.), *Culinary Tourism* (pp. xi–xiv). Kentucky: University Press of Kentucky.

Laws, E. (1995). *Tourist destination management: issues, analysis and policies.* Abingdon: Routledge.

Like a Local. Retrieved from www.like-a-local.com (September 2016).

Lounsbury, J. W., & Hoopes, L. L. (1985). An investigation of factors associated with vacation satisfaction. *Journal of Leisure Research, 17*(1), 1–13.

Monroe, K. B. & Krishnan, R. (1985). The effect of price on subjective product evaluations. In J. Jacoby & L. Olson (Eds.), *Perceived quality: How consumer view stores and merchandise* (pp. 209–232). Lexington, KY: Lexington Books.

Morgan, J. L. (2006). *Culinary creation: An introduction to foodservice and world cuisine.* New York, NY: Routledge.

Nilsson, J., Widarsson, A. S., & Wirell, T. (2011). Cittáslow' ecogastronomic heritage as a tool for destination development. *Current Issues in Tourism, 14*(4), 373–386.

Oliver, M. B., & Raney, A. A. (2011). Entertainment as pleasurable and meaningful: Identifying hedonic and eudaimonic motivations for entertainment consumption. *Journal of Communication, 61*(5), 984–1004.

Pearce, P. L. (1980). A favorability-satisfaction model of tourists' evaluations. *Journal of Travel Research, 19*(1), 13–17.

Pink, S. (2008). Re-thinking contemporary activism: From community to emplaced sociality. *Ethnos, 73*(2), 163–188.

Pizam, A., & Milman, A. (1993). Predicting satisfaction among first-time visitors to a destination by using the expectancy disconfirmation theory. *International Journal of Hospitality Management, 12*(2), 197–209.

Poon, A. (1993). *Tourism, technology and competitive strategies.* Wallingford,: CAB International.

Prahalad, C. K., & Ramaswamy, V. (2004). *The future of competition.* Boston, MA: Harvard Business School Press.

Przybyła, H. (2010) Wybór filozofii gospodarczej jako podstawa ekonomii. W: Dokonania współczesnej myśli ekonomicznej – znaczenie kategorii wyboru w teoriach ekonomicznych i praktyce gospodarczej. Red. U. Zagóra-Jonszta. UE, Katowice, p. 75

Sawyer, A. G., & Dickson, P. (1984). Psychological perspectives on consumer response to sales promotions. In C. Jocz (Ed.), *Research on sales promotion: Collected papers* (pp. 1–21). Cambridge: Marketing Science Institute.

Scarpato, R., & Daniele, R. (2003). New global cuisine: Tourism, authenticity and sense of place in postmodern gastronomy. In C. M. Hall, L. Sharples, R. Mitchell, N. Macionis, & B. Cambourne (Eds.), *Food tourism around the world* (pp. 296–313). Oxford: Routledge.

Sheth, J. N., Newman, B. I., & Gross, B. L. (1991). Why we buy what we buy: A theory of consumption values. *Journal of Business Research, 22*(2), 159–170.

Sloan, D. (2004). *Culinary taste: Consumer behaviour in the international restaurant sector.* Oxford: Routledge.

Spang, R. L. (2000). *The invention of the restaurant: Paris and modern gastronomic culture.* Cambridge, MA: Harvard University Press.

Stevens, B. F. (1992). Price value perceptions of travelers. *Journal of Travel Research, 31*(2), 44–48.

Tamborini, R., Bowman, N. D., Eden, A., Grizzard, M., & Organ, A. (2010). Defining media enjoyment as the satisfaction of intrinsic needs. *Journal of Communication, 60*(4), 758–777.

Vogt, C. A., & Fesenmaier, D. R. (1995). Tourists' and retailers' perceptions of services. *Annals of Tourism Research, 22*(4), 763–780.

Wright, R. K. (2010). "Been there, done that": Embracing our post-trip experiential recollections through the social construction and subjective consumption of personal narratives. In M. Morgan, P. Lugosi & J. R. Brent Ritchie (Eds.), *The tourism and leisure experience: Consumer and managerial perspectives* (pp. 117–136). Bristol: Channel View Publications.

Zeithaml, V. A. (1988). Consumer perceptions of price, quality, and value: A means-end model and synthesis of evidence. *The Journal of Marketing, 52*(3)2–22.

Zins, A. H. (2000). Two means to the same end: Hierarchical value maps in tourism – comparing the association pattern technique with direct importance ratings. In J. A. Mazanec, G. I. Crouch, J. R. Brent Ritchie, & A. G. Woodside (Eds.), *Consumer psychology of tourism, hospitality and leisure* (pp. 123–151). New York, NY: CABI Publishing.

# 10 Co-creating customer experience

## The role of employees in tourism and hospitality services

*Prakash K. Chathoth, Eric S. W. Chan,*
*Robert J. Harrington, Fevzi Okumus*
*and Zibin Song*

### Introduction

Co-creation is a "joint, collaborative . . . process of producing new value" (Galvagno & Dalli, 2014, p. 644). It involves active participation and interaction between stakeholders (e.g., service providers and customers), who are connected in different ways (e.g., emotional, cognitive, physical and social) (Campos, Mendes, Valle, & Scott, 2015), to create superior experiences (Grewal, Levy, & Kumar, 2009; Verhoef et al., 2009). To date, the role of a firm's stakeholders in co-creating value during the exchange mechanism in service transactions has been explored in both the mainstream literature (Prahalad & Ramaswamy, 2004a, 2004b; Vargo & Lusch, 2004, 2008) and, to some extent, in the hospitality and tourism literature (e.g., Campos et al., 2015; Chathoth, Altinay, Harrington, Okumus, & Chan, 2013; Chathoth, Ungson, Altinay, Chan, Harrington, & Okumus, 2014a; Chathoth, Ungson, Harrington, Altinay, Okumus, & Chan, 2014b; Chathoth, Ungson, Harrington, & Chan, 2016; Shaw, Bailey, & Williams, 2011). Past work has highlighted the transformation of inputs to outputs in service transactions and the specific role that employees play during this process (Ramaswamy & Guillart, 2010). From information processing to resource allocation and utilisation, employees, in conjunction with customers, are co-creators of value in the interchange between the firm and its stakeholders (Prahalad & Ramaswamy, 2004a, 2004b). Despite support in the literature that co-creation is an integral element of value creation in service transactions in the tourism and hospitality industry (e.g., Chathoth et al., 2013), an exploration of how employees actually add value in service transactions has not been fully documented in the literature.

The literature provides a basis for understanding co-creation as a value-based system. However, there is still a dearth of studies that clearly explicate the role of the service provider (Grönroos & Voima, 2013). In particular, the literature does not delve much into specific employee characteristics and orientation that facilitate co-creation-based transactions in the tourism and hospitality context. Notably, exemplars through case studies are lacking that clearly elucidate the role of employees in creating experiential value in service transactions. Here, experiential value is defined as the creation of value through an exchange among the co-creators of services, including customers, employees and other stakeholders in a particular context (Grönroos, 2008). The perceptions and involvement of customers will determine the value they derive in service interactions. In addition to the importance of customer participation, for the emergence of co-creation, it is imperative for creating positive employee experiences (Payne, Storbacka, & Frow, 2008). The employees' capabilities, perceived by customers during co-creation, are also of importance (Bandura, 2001).

This chapter evaluates the intrinsic and extrinsic factors that influence employees in the co-creation of customer experiences, and hence value, from a tourism and hospitality perspective. These factors are explored through a real-life case study. The primary objective of this chapter is to provide practitioners with a basis for understanding the significance of a co-creation-based approach in terms of managing their internal resources, and employees in particular. Emphasis is given to the use of customer/employee knowledge and skills as an operant resource in the co-creation of value. The chapter first examines the factors affecting the co-creation of customer experiences, including employee engagement and customer participation. It then uses a real-life case study to tease out the key characteristics that define the role of employees during the co-creation of services and their implications.

## Theoretical perspectives

### Factors affecting co-creation of customer experiences

According to Meyer and Schwager (2007) and Verhoef et al. (2009), a customer's co-creation experience is shaped by his or her individual and subjective response to any direct and indirect contact with the service provider(s). In turn, service providers and their services are influenced by multifarious factors in a business transaction. Mullins (2007) noted that situational, organisational and personal factors influence the way that employees interact with their customers, and vice versa. He further explained that situational factors are defined by the task at hand and are hence extrinsic. In contrast, personal factors are intrinsic and employee-specific as they are defined by the person and influenced by the individual's behaviour. Situational factors influence all employees in a particular service situation and are generic to that service transaction.

Conversely, employee-specific factors are person-specific resources that are part of the value-creation process. They include the skills, knowledge and level of motivation and commitment, influenced by the attitude and behaviour of the incumbent. Skills and knowledge influence the server/service efficiency of the incumbent/system and eventually increase customer satisfaction (Bitner, 1990). Note that motivation manifests in terms of the responsiveness of employees to specific situations. Service co-creation situations are dependent on how circumstances interact with the individual employee in question. Therefore, the response of the employee can vary from transaction to transaction.

Organisation-specific factors, in contrast, include the broader dynamics that influence all actors within a given service context. Chathoth et al. (2013, 2016) explain that these elements include the firm's overall orientation (mission, vision, goals and objectives) towards stakeholder-related collaborative mechanisms of value creation; the systems and resources available to all actors, including engagement platforms; and the operant resources, such as knowledge and skills, that influence the deployment of other resources (see also Alves, Ferreira, & Fernandes, 2016). In addition, the norms established to define, monitor and assess co-creation-related exchanges; employee-specific incentives and reward systems to motivate and induce a positive orientation/behaviour towards co-creation including empowerment; and the organisational structure and resource allocation system also play a role. Finally, the measurement and management of output, in addition to transparency, flexibility and efficacy to manage such transactions, can be considered as organisation-specific factors.

### Employee engagement and customer participation

Employee engagement can be initiated through internal branding that connects the firm's brand values, as perceived by external constituents, to that of internal stakeholders, the employees (Mitchell, 2002). Employee engagement is characterised by the emotional commitment, pride and support that the employee has towards the organisation (its mission, vision, goals and objectives) (Abraham, 2012; Kruse, 2012). The literature identifies three approaches to employee engagement which include a "set of motivating resources such as support and recognition from colleagues and supervisors, performance feedback, opportunities for learning and development, and opportunities for skill use" (Bakker & Schaufeli, 2008, p. 151). Extant research further identifies a positive relationship between employee engagement and firm performance at the business unit level in terms of metrics related to customer- and employee-related performance, particularly customer satisfaction and loyalty (Harter, Schmidt, & Hayes, 2002).

The second approach entails commitment and extra-role behaviour (Bakker & Schaufeli, 2008, p. 151), which, as the literature suggests, essentially require employees to be oriented towards the success of the company to the extent that they perform beyond what is required of the job. The third approach defines employee engagement as "a positive, fulfilling, affective-motivational state of work-related well-being that is the antipode of job burnout (Maslach, Schaufeli, & Leiter, 2001) . . . that consists of three interrelated dimensions: vigour, dedication, and absorption (Schaufeli, Bakker, & Salanova, 2006)" (Bakker & Schaufeli, 2008, p. 151).

The literature further identifies internal branding as an important element that gives employees direction in their work and makes them accept the company's efforts to fulfil the needs of both employees and customers alike (Mitchell, 2002; Punjaisri, Wilson, & Evanschitzky, 2009). Employee engagement is intensely connected to a firm's success through customer experience. It can eventually bring customer reliability and faithfulness, and ultimately the achievement of the firm's financial goals (Kumar & Swetha, 2011).

A higher level of customer participation affects employee motivation and engagement when self/other efficacy is at elevated levels. The practice of sharing data and taking into account customer recommendations can improve the firm's understanding of the customers' needs and desires, hence making their employment less demanding and the service more effective (Bitner, Faranda, Hubbert, & Zeithaml, 1997). This higher engagement should raise the employee 'emotional labour', such as happiness during the service process (Chandler & Lusch, 2015, p. 8). An employee's happiness (and well-being) in turn is likely to enhance customer disclosure, involvement and participation (Chandler & Lusch, 2015), leading to improved co-creative processes in service transactions (Payne et al., 2008).

According to Chathoth et al. (2016), employee engagement is a process variable that can be managed through input, throughput and output processes. In this framework, employees can play a significant role in each stage. During the input stage, they enhance the active participation of customers, while encouraging them to share information on idiosyncratic needs that relate to the service transaction. They also create greater customer awareness in terms of the latter's role in the value-creation process and enhance customer engagement through on-line and off-line (physical) mechanisms. These employees also act as mediators in the transformation of inputs to outputs because they enable the customer to access key resources (including value chain functions) in the co-creation of services. Moreover, the mediation is further established as employees act as an interface between the organisation's internal and external environments (Olsen, West, & Tse, 1998; Terglav, Ruzzier, & Kaše, 2016), and they are the medium through which an organisation can establish flexibility and transparency.

During the throughput phase, according to Chathoth et al. (2016), service employees play a key role in understanding the customer's idiosyncratic needs. This in turn enables the firm to customise/personalise each transaction to meet or exceed customer expectations. The use of customer information/knowledge/skills and the deployment of resources in conjunction with employee knowledge and skills are brought about through the involvement and engagement of employees during this phase. Note that repeated interactions with customers are further established through employee–customer interrelationships. These employees are agents who become the basis for the identification and resolution of barriers that can impede the co-creation of value (Chathoth et al., 2014a).

In the output phase, customer trust, satisfaction and delight are a function of the role of employees in creating experiential value (Chathoth et al., 2016). Notably, customer loyalty is a result of how customers derive value through their interactions with frontline and other service employees. The evolution of this relationship with customers will materialise only if employees act as a buffer in the relationship between the firm and the customer. In other words, the role of employees can either enhance or diminish the interaction between the customer and the firm, thereby affecting the evolution of such relationships (Chathoth, 2007).

## A case study: employees' role in co-creating customer value

The role of the co-creation of services in the creation of customer value is well established in the literature (Chandler & Lusch, 2015). However, as stated earlier, the role of employees in the creation of value has not yet received much attention. Even more limited is the lack of real-life case studies to elucidate the role of employees in the service value-creation process. This section uses a real-life case study to highlight the active role that employees play in the co-creation of customer value in service transactions. It primarily uses antecedent and transformational/metamorphic factors, including operant resources (i.e., customer/employee knowledge and skills), to highlight how value is created or diminished through repeated interactions with a service firm over a longitudinal service scenario, wherein the role of employees defines the essence of experiential value creation.

Consider the following real-life situation as an illustration: A customer, John (a fictitious name to maintain anonymity), made a booking with a well-reputed local travel agency for a business trip from City A in Continent X to City B in Continent Y. This was a six-hour journey in the latter half of 2015. The travel agency, which John uses for all his business trips, made the airline booking in addition to other bookings for the trip, such as train travel at the destination. The two-way economy ticket was booked with a global airline company that has been consistently rated as a leading airline and has won several global awards over the past two decades. While on board the flight, John realised that he did not request a special meal when purchasing the airline ticket as he does not consume meat products. For his medium- to long-haul trips, John usually orders the meal beforehand through the travel agency. The travel agency also overlooked the fact that John did not order food for the journey and did not consult John's client history to retrieve this information, which is a standard operating procedure, when confirming John's booking. John himself did not pay attention to the fact that meals for both the onward and return journeys were not pre-ordered.

During his onward journey, John noticed that the flight was not operating at full capacity. He called the flight attendant (stewardess) before the lunch service to address this situation. He particularly connected with a relatively young service staff member, hoping that she would assist him to find a solution. John has more than 25 years of global airline travel experience and he thought that the more experienced staff members would be more rigid, perhaps making it more difficult to find a solution.

In two previous circumstances, with two other leading global airline companies, John had not received a full meal. In those instances, the flight was full and the service staff served him a snack instead, as they did not have an extra seafood or vegetarian lunch/dinner meal. This experience and knowledge enabled John to approach the situation more prudently so that he could get the agent to address his service request. The staff member was very courteous to the extent that she arranged for a vegetarian meal in a timely manner. She went out of her way to ensure that all aspects of John's request were taken care of. John attributed the success of the service outcome to the service staff's attitude and behaviour (which influenced her enthusiasm/motivation and commitment) and the fact that the flight was not full (situational factor).

John stayed at the destination for three nights and was very busy attending seminars throughout the three days and dinners in the evening. He again overlooked the fact that for the return journey he would face a similar situation. As he arrived at the gate to board the return flight to City A, he realised that the flight was going to be full. This was confirmed when he boarded the flight and the effect was immediate as the staff were busy from the moment the passengers boarded the aircraft. John patiently waited for the service to begin once the aircraft was airborne. However, this time he had a steward to deal with as the others were busy with operations and he could not get the attention of anybody else other than the agent assigned to the section/aisle where he was seated. John made a request to the steward in a similar manner as for the onward journey. The steward was very polite and told John that he would look into the special request, but could not guarantee that it would be taken care of. John acknowledged this and waited for the agent to return with an answer.

In the meantime, the other passengers were being served their meals and the service was in full swing. The agents were busy walking up and down the aisle in a typical service operation running at full capacity. John was engrossed in watching a movie and did not realise that 20 minutes had gone by and there was no sign of the steward. John requested one of the other stewardesses passing by to look into the matter. She said that she would check with the steward who had originally agreed to assist John. John went back to the movie and got caught up not realising that the others had finished their meal and were waiting for clearance. Almost 45 to 50 minutes had gone by and there was still no news from the steward or the stewardess.

The clearance had begun and John spotted the flight attendant who took his request the second time. He got her attention as she approached his seat and asked her the status of his meal. She mentioned that her colleague, whom John had first approached, was looking into his request and would get back to him. John again waited for another 15 to 20 minutes before the steward finally informed him that he could not organise a vegetarian or seafood meal. He was about to leave, at which time John realised that he would have to go without a proper meal for the remaining 3 to 4 hours of the journey. He called out to the steward and requested him to serve him a standard meal tray with sides (salad, dessert, bread, crackers/cheese, etc.), but without the main course (this request was made by John using his previous experience in a similar situation with another airline company). The steward answered in the affirmative and brought John the tray with the sides. In essence, John was able to manage with the snacks and get by for the remainder of the flight.

The above two scenarios, involving the same customer and organisation, exemplify the co-creation of value. As per the original definition of co-creation proposed at the outset of this chapter, the joint/collaborative characteristics are evident in the case when the customer and flight attendants co-produce the product/service to create new value (Galvagno & Dalli, 2014). Moreover, the active participation and interaction among service provider and customer is also evident in the emotional, cognitive and physical engagements (Campos et al.,). Superior experiences (Grewal et al., 2009; Verhoef et al., 2009) are the end result in both scenarios, even though the first scenario led to better outcomes.

The use of operant resources is also exemplified by the deployment of the customer's/employees' knowledge, including information and skills. Finally, the joint creation of value is demonstrated by the fact that a solution to the customer's needs was found through co-creation in both scenarios, involving the same customer.

In the co-creation of value, it should be further noted that while the two scenarios involved the same airline, the service outcomes, including value creation, were influenced by the different organisational, situational and personal factors on the two flights with two different agents. In the first scenario, situational factors (the flight not being full) and personal factors (the employee's enthusiasm, willingness to process information and keenness to find a solution (i.e., commitment), were influential in creating a positive outcome for the customer. In contrast, in the second scenario, situational factors (the flight being full) and personal factors (the service agent's propensity to engage with the customer and his behavioural orientation, including motivation and commitment) were detrimental to the creation of value for the customer. In both scenarios, the organisational factors remained the same and were mostly a constant. However, the situational factors, in conjunction with the personal factors (an interaction effect), had a greater effect on the outcomes. From a co-creation of value perspective, it is evident that the service agent in the second scenario was not willing or able to engage in information processing other than that absolutely necessary by listening to the customer and acknowledging his request. However, this was not done with the intent of arriving at a solution that led to the creation of value, and specifically experiential value, for the customer. Here, the agent's behavioural orientation and commitment, in conjunction with the situational factors (an interaction effect of behaviour and situational variables), influenced the outcome. In the second scenario, the agent may perhaps not have responded as he did if the flight had not been at full capacity. However, even in such an instance, the agent could have been influenced by his behavioural disposition, which acts in conjunction with situational factors in determining the response.

The above reasoning could also be extended to the first scenario in that if the flight was full, the agent might have responded to the customer negatively. However, it can be concluded that in the second scenario, the agent's non-response and absence for a prolonged period of time indicated that the factors in the person, including motivation and commitment to assist the customer, were clearly lacking. This is further supported by the fact that if the agent in the first scenario faced the same situation (situational factors are kept constant) as the agent in the second scenario, the information processing and employee engagement would not have been the same, which could be attributed to attitude/behavioural orientation (motivation- and commitment-related factors in the person). This is because there was no attempt by the service agent in the second scenario to find a solution to meet the customer's need. In this case, the customer had to suggest an alternative based on his previous experience. Notably, the employee's motivation to engage in the co-creation of value could have been influenced by burnout as a result of the service load factor, all else being constant.

Based on the above, it could be concluded that the agent was not involved/engaged in the service to come up with a solution. The agent in the second scenario lacked the willingness and propensity to co-create value compared to the first. In the first scenario, the customer and agent co-created value to the extent that the agent was able to specifically address the situation by using the information provided by the customer with the willingness and commitment (attitude/behaviour-related) to find a solution. In both scenarios, operant resources were used by the agent and the customer to co-create value. However, in both scenarios involving the same firm and customer, different outcomes materialised in terms of the employees' role in the co-creation of value. The two factors that underlie this are the employees and the situation/environment in which the value was co-created, even if the firm was a constant in both scenarios. The employee's commitment and willingness to co-create (motivation), influenced by his/her attitude and behaviour, clearly influenced the relationship between the service-related input and output variables related to value co-creation.

Here, emphasis needs to be given to the fact that personal factors can either facilitate or impede the co-creation of value. In particular, the deployment of resources and the facilitation of the service process through the use of operant resources, such as customer/employee knowledge and skills, can be restricted or enhanced if the personal factors are managed effectively. Indeed, situational and organisational factors play a role in terms of having an effect on the employee's personal orientation to a service transaction. However, all else being equal, a service employee is able to co-create value to a higher degree when his/her personal orientation is better managed. In essence, this is supported by the fact that the flight attendant in the first scenario was able to manage outcomes in a better way based on intrinsic (personal) factors than in the second scenario. Even if the outcome in both situations had led to the same level of customer satisfaction, the flight attendant in the first scenario would have been better equipped to co-create value than the flight attendant in the second.

Moreover, the ability of the agent to think outside of the box and interact with the customer with the objective of obtaining and processing additional information is an integral part of co-creation (Prahalad & Ramaswamy, 2004b). In the first scenario, situational factors in conjunction with behavioural factors assisted the agent to think outside of the box. However, in the second scenario, the agent's propensity to find a solution was marred by the situational factors. Nonetheless, the attitude/behavioural orientation of the agent influenced the agent's disposition to think outside of the box. This is a function of the level of commitment related to the psychological state of the agent (the second approach outlined in the literature on employee engagement).

The first approach, which uses organisational motivational schemes and resources as factors that influence engagement, are important and could be considered at the higher end of the spectrum for this successful airline firm. Moreover, this is assumed to be a constant across both scenarios, given that the organisation was the same. Situational factors could also include the supervisor's role, which was a variable in this case. While the third approach related to employee engagement cannot be assessed in this situation, it can be indirectly concluded that the employee in the first scenario had a higher motivational state than the employee in the second scenario, given the behavioural orientation of each agent.

The above factors relate to the effect of employee engagement on the co-creation of value in a service scenario. In this case, firm-related factors are a constant as it is assumed that both employees were exposed to the same firm-specific resources, such as empowerment, training and orientation, reward systems, engagement platforms, and so on. Also, the utilitarian value of operant resources from a co-creation perspective (in John's case) was restricted in the second scenario as the flight was operating at full capacity. In both scenarios, input, throughput and output related variables influenced the outcome of the service transaction. According to Chathoth et al. (2016), firms would need to use engagement platforms to interface the firm's resources with those of the customer during the input, throughput and output phases. In the case where information on the customer was not received prior to boarding (as was the case with John), the firm would need to enhance customer engagement (organisation-related) by motivating employees (both organisation- and person-related) to process information and meet the customer's need.

The question that arises here is why an airline, with the resources to feed hundreds of customers at a time, was not able to co-create a product with a low likelihood of occurrence (say, 1:50). In other words, perhaps 1 out of every 50 customers may face a situation where they did not order a special meal beforehand. The fact that John had to suggest a solution in the second scenario itself reveals that the employee was not focused (motivated and committed) to get involved in such a transaction. Perhaps the employees' attitude/behaviour (individual) and orientation (including training from a system perspective) towards economy class passengers is one that is based on standardisation for the most part. In such arrangements, the capacity of the system is given more importance and employees are trained to not entertain customers who may have extraordinary requests because this could burden the employees (who already have a heavy load in a flight operating at full capacity) and in turn put undue pressure on the service system.

The business model and the standard operating procedures defined by the airline management would define the norms of exchange that would influence how co-creation could be considered in such a system. Here, employee engagement becomes a function of the first approach identified in the literature (Bakker & Schaufeli, 2008). The fact that the employees in the second scenario did not see any value associated with serving John in itself shows that the employee would have been considered to be "going out of his/her way" to solve the problem if a solution was found. In the first scenario, the employee's commitment and motivation is at a personal level and reflects engagement going by the second approach in the literature (see Bakker & Schaufeli, 2008). However, the employee's response to co-creation is at a personal level and would vary based on situational factors and the level of employee motivation/commitment.

118   *Prakash K. Chathoth et al.*

If both scenarios are taken in conjunction, the airline's policy to serve a customer where information on their needs had not been received *a priori* is dependent on the employee's situation-specific motivation/commitment, and hence engagement. There is perhaps no emphasis on an airline-wide approach to engage with customers in economy class (to whatever extent possible) for value co-creation. While this cannot be generalised, as only two transactions have been analysed here using a longitudinal scenario, questions could be posed as to the approach taken by airline firms across the board to meet the needs of customers in a given scenario (such as the one John faced) and the co-creation of value in such transactions.

According to Payne et al. (2008), the operant resources used by the airline firm to create value would need to be examined and questions would need to be posed as to how some level of flexibility could be included in a service system to meet the basic needs of customers, which may be considered "extraordinary" by the airline staff even though they are not out of the ordinary by global standards. For instance, what would it take for the airline firm to serve food to 15 or 17 customers on a flight with approximately 850 passengers (for A380 capacity going by the 1:50 ratio used earlier) as a worst-case scenario? Can the airline not use previous service requests and come with a probability scenario for such "extraordinary" requests happening on a particular flight that operates a given route? Would the airline not be better off by doing a cost-benefit analysis of using such operant resources to co-create value and to assess the effect of positive outcomes on customer life-time value? If Etgar's (2008) co-creation-related factors are taken into account, the cost/benefit of using key resources for creating value for all stakeholders involved needs to be analysed. Note that extraordinary costs are not incurred if the airline prepares itself for co-creation-based scenarios (i.e., operant resources), if this is considered in conjunction with customer life-time value. However, for this to happen, a reorientation of the firm's resources, including the role of employees, would be required. Accordingly, the overarching question is: Could the airline not prepare for co-creation by upgrading the operant resources if indeed such a service orientation is of the essence?

**Conclusions and implications**

This chapter explores the intrinsic and extrinsic factors that influence the hospitality and tourism industry's employees in the process of value co-creation. It also responds to the call for studies on the process in multiple stakeholder networks (Frow & Payne, 2011; Hatch & Schultz, 2010), especially from the point of view of employees (Yi & Gong, 2013), who are important internal stakeholders. Understanding the employees' role in co-creating customer experiences is critical to the successful process of co-creation. Without the active involvement of employees, especially guest-contact staff, the potential of becoming a co-creative service organisation is, in all likelihood, impossible.

The literature reveals that the role of employees in the process of co-creation is mainly influenced by situational, organisational and personal factors. Although situational factors, normally considered as extrinsic, are more difficult to control, a service firm should not neglect the importance of organisational and personal factors to facilitate the value-creation process. For instance, to successfully interact with customers to co-create a unique service experience, front-line service staff should be empowered and allowed to deliver services/solve a problem using their own professional judgement. Therefore, from an organisational perspective, senior managers should commit more to engendering mutual trust and management accountability to create a corporate culture of transparency and empowerment in the workplace. To make the empowerment process a success, personal factors, such as knowledge, attitude, enthusiasm, skills and relational network with other service providers, are required. Therefore, greater importance should be given to providing employees with the necessary training or education about their roles and responsibilities in the co-creation of value. Selecting employees with the right attitude is of utmost importance if managers really want their employees to follow their company's orientation towards co-creation. At a broader lever, this relates to a company's mission, vision, goals and objectives.

This chapter also identifies that the information processed by employees about service suppliers and customers can influence the level, quality and outcomes of co-creation. Communication with senior management to understand the company's co-creation culture and policy clearly, the background information about the customers (i.e. to better understand past, present and future dispositions [Chandler & Lusch, 2015]) and information about related service-providers are all essential to make the co-creation experience a unique and valued one.

As the customer's interaction with company employees and the service encountered will eventually determine the overall co-creation experience and the brand value, internal branding is an important element in co-creation. Therefore, employees, who are at the heart of service and corporate brands (Balmer, 2010) must understand and share the brand vision of a company because their behaviour can make or destroy the company brand. However, the ability of employees to transfer a company's brand values to customers through their behaviour could be a very challenging task for managers in the industry. This task requires a clear communication of co-creation as a service model, and processes would need to be in place to address the organisational, situational and personal factors that may limit or enhance a co-created experience. Brand-based communication, including internal branding, is a key element that helps build relationship platforms with internal and external stakeholders alike.

Figure 10.1 summarises the key factors that influence employees in the co-creation of value with customers. These influencers are listed under three categories of factors, namely, organisational, situational and personal factors. Organisational factors include the mission, vision, goals and objectives of the organisation; its strategies and policies; culture and service climate; and collaborative mechanisms of value creation. These factors all have an influence on transactions at a given time and across time periods, as they relate to the co-creation of value. Moreover, organisation-wide engagement platforms to create stakeholder involvement; norms of exchange; and organisation-specific operant resources to facilitate co-creation will influence the outcomes related to such a process. Systems and processes that enable employee engagement will also be influential, such as employee-specific incentives and reward systems, empowerment, internal branding (including relationship marketing), organisational structure and resource allocation systems that enable the use and mobilisation of resources, transparency, flexibility and efficacy in managing resources, and the measurement and management of output. These are linked to control systems that will be influential at the organisation level in the facilitation of co-creative processes.

Situational factors include service load, which could influence employees at the transaction level; the availability and deployability of resources; the flexibility of the system as it relates to a specific transaction; the level of support from supervisors and co-workers in a specific situation; and customer needs and wants, which influence customer participation and engagement. Moreover, the customer's demeanour, attitude and behaviour, in terms of how they engage in co-creative systems, would influence the outcomes. Importantly, the customer's knowledge and skills that become operant resources in a given transaction in the creation of value needs to be given due emphasis. Likewise, the customer's trust, openness and willingness to participate and share information in a given situation influences the co-creation of value. Moreover, the engagement platform available to engage the customer in a particular situation would influence the outcome from a co-creation perspective. The outcome is also influenced by customer–employee communication as it relates to a particular transaction.

Personal factors, which relate to a given employee, can be summarised as the goals and objectives of the incumbent, the knowledge and skills that he/she possesses (this is a key operant resource in co-creation) and his/her ability to process information (including level and type). Such factors also include the employee's demeanour, attitude and behaviour; his/her level of motivation and commitment; openness, enthusiasm and willingness to participate in co-creative processes; vigour and pride shown towards work; and his/her experience and exposure in managing co-creation-based transactions, including the level of training that he/she has received that is specific to co-creative systems and processes. Additionally, skills related to the employee's resourcefulness and level of flexibility, in addition to the employee's ability to communicate, influence outcomes related to the co-creation of value.

It should be noted that an interaction effect exists across the three categories (i.e., organisational, situational and employee factors), as previously detailed in the chapter. Essentially, such an effect could exist across multiple factors across the three categories. Therefore, it is imperative that the categories are not only considered separately, but also as part of a system that interacts across category influencers, as indicated by the arrow at the bottom of Figure 10.1.

To conclude, this chapter extends previous research by investigating the role of employees in the co-creation of value, while highlighting the employees' role in the process through a real-life longitudinal case. The objective is to provide theoretical and managerial insights into the process to elucidate the role of various factors, namely, situational, organisational and personal factors, which influence

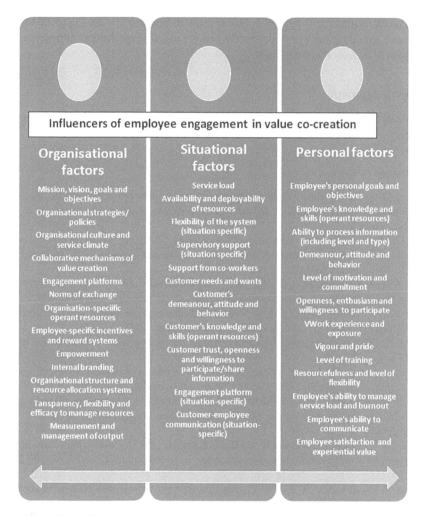

| Influencers of employee engagement in value co-creation | | |
|---|---|---|
| **Organisational factors** | **Situational factors** | **Personal factors** |
| Mission, vision, goals and objectives | Service load | Employee's personal goals and objectives |
| Organisational strategies/ policies | Availability and deployability of resources | Employee's knowledge and skills (operant resources) |
| Organisational culture and service climate | Flexibility of the system (situation specific) | Ability to process information (including level and type) |
| Collaborative mechanisms of value creation | Supervisory support (situation specific) | Demeanour, attitude and behavior |
| Engagement platforms | Support from co-workers | Level of motivation and commitment |
| Norms of exchange | Customer needs and wants | Openness, enthusiasm and willingness to participate |
| Organisation-speciific operant resources | Customer's demeanour, attitude and behavior | Work experience and exposure |
| Employee-specific incentives and reward systems | Customer's knowledge and skills (operant resources) | Vigour and pride |
| Empowerment | Customer trust, openness and willingness to participate/share information | Level of training |
| Internal branding | | Resourcefulness and level of flexibility |
| Organisational structure and resource allocation systems | Engagement platform (situation-specific) | Employee's ability to manage service load and burnout |
| Tansparency, flexibility and efficacy to manage resources | Customer-employee communication (situation-specific) | Employee's ability to communicate |
| Measurement and management of output | | Employee satisfaction and experiential value |

*Figure 10.1* Influences of employee engagement in value co-creation

the involvement of service employees in co-creating customer experiences. It should be noted that employees with better person-specific resources and more information on the firm's service value have higher levels of motivation and brand commitment. Further, if service staff are adequately empowered by the company, they appear more likely to participate with vigour, enthusiasm and absorption in the process (Chandler & Lusch, 2015).

It is important for future research to further explore the advocates. An investigation could also be conducted to explore more intrinsic factors that could help employees in the hospitality and tourism industry cultivate a more enjoyable experience from their participation in the co-creation process. Specifically, additional research on issues such as the role of (1) time, (2) actors, (3) context, (4) institutions and (5) meaning-making is essential. This appears to be currently lacking in the literature and would further our understanding of the role and motivation of frontline employees in the co-creation of value.

## Acknowledgement

This research project (1-ZVGR) was funded by the Hong Kong Polytechnic University.

## References

Abraham, D. S. (2012). Development of employee engagement programme on the basis of employee satisfaction survey. *Journal of Economic Development, Management, IT, Finance and Marketing, 4*(1), 27_37.

Alves, H., Ferreira, J. J. & Fernandes, C. I. (2016). Customer's operant resources effects on co-creation activities. *Journal of Innovation and Knowledge,* http://dx.doi.org/10.1016/j.jik.2016.03.001.

Bakker, A. B., & Schaufeli, W. B. (2008). Positive organizational behavior: Engaged employees in flourishing organizations. *Journal of Organizational Behavior, 29*(2), 147–154.

Balmer, J. M. T. (2010). Explicating corporate brands and their management: Reflections and directions from 1995. *Journal of Brand Management, 18*(3), 180–196.

Bandura, A. (2001). Social cognitive theory: An agentic perspective. *Annual Review of Psychology, 52,* 1–26.

Bitner, M. J. (1990). Evaluating service encounters: The effects of physical surroundings and employees responses. *Journal of Marketing, 54*(2), 69–82.

Bitner, M. J., Faranda, W. T., Hubbert, A. R., & Zeithaml, V. A. (1997). Consumer contributions and roles in service delivery. *International Journal of Service Industry Management, 8*(3), 193–205.

Campos, A. C., Mendes, J., Valle, P. O. D., & Scott, N. (2015). Co-creation of tourist experiences: A literature review. *Current Issues in Tourism,* doi:10.1080/13683500.2015.1081158.

Chandler, J. D., & Lusch, R. F. (2015). Service systems: A broadened framework and research agenda on value propositions, engagement, and service experience. *Journal of Service Research, 18*(1), 6–22.

Chathoth, P. K. (2007). The impact of information technology on hotel operations, service management, and transaction costs: A conceptual framework for full service hotel firms. *International Journal of Hospitality Management, 26*(1), 395–408.

Chathoth, P., Altinay, L., Harrington, R. J., Okumus, F., & Chan, E. S. W. (2013). Co-production versus co-creation: A process based continuum in the hotel service context. *International Journal of Hospitality Management, 32*(1), 11–20.

Chathoth, P. K., Ungson, G. R., Altinay, L., Chan, E. S. W., Harrington, R., & Okumus, F. (2014a). Barriers affecting organizational adoption of higher order customer engagement in tourism service interactions. *Tourism Management, 42*(1), 181–193.

Chathoth, P. K., Ungson, G. R., Harrington, R. J., Altinay, L., Okumus, F., & Chan, E. S. W. (2014b). Conceptualization of value co-creation in the tourism context. In N. Prebensen, J. Chen & M. Samil (Eds.), *Creating experience value in tourism* (pp. 33–47). Wallingford: CAB International.

Chathoth, P. K., Ungson, G. R., Harrington, R. J., & Chan, E. S. W. (2016). Co-creation and higher order customer engagement in hospitality and tourism services: A critical review. *International Journal of Contemporary Hospitality Management, 28*(2), 222–245.

Etgar, M. (2008). A descriptive model of the consumer co-production process. *Journal of the Academy of Marketing Science, 36*(1), 97–108.

Frow, P., & Payne, A. (2011). A stakeholder perspective of the value proposition concept. *European Journal of Marketing, 45*(1/2), 223–240.

Galvagno, M., & Dalli, D. (2014). Theory of value co-creation: A systematic literature review. *Managing Service Quality, 24*(6), 643–683.

Grewal, D., Levy, M., & Kumar, V. (2009). Customer experience management in retailing: An organizing framework. *Journal of Retailing, 85*(1), 1–14.

Grönroos, C. (2008). Service logic revisited: Who creates values? And who co-creates? *European Business Review, 20*(4), 298–314.

Grönroos, C., & Voima, P. (2013). Critical service logic: Making sense of value creation and co-creation. *Journal of the Academy of Marketing Science, 41*(2), 133–150.

Harter, J. K., Schmidt, F. L., & Hayes, T. L. (2002). Business-unit-level relationship between employee satisfaction, employee engagement, and business outcomes: A meta-analysis. *Journal of Applied Psychology, 87*(2), 268–279.

Hatch, M. J., & Schultz, M. (2010). Towards a theory of brand co-creation with implications for brand governance. *Journal of Brand Management, 17*(8), 590–604.

Kumar, D. P., & Swetha, G. (2011). A prognostic examination of employee engagement from its historical roots. *International Journal of Trade, Economics and Finance, 2*(3), 232–241.

Kruse, K. (2012). What is employee engagement? Retrieved from Forbes.com *http://www.forbes.com/sites/kevinkruse/2012/06/22/employee-engagement-what-and-why/#2eefe0464629*, March 1, 2016.

Maslach, C., Schaufeli, W. B., & Leiter, M. P. (2001). Job burnout. *Annual Review of Psychology, 52*, 397–422.

Meyer, C., & Schwager, A. (2007). Understanding customer experience. *Harvard Business Review, 85*(2), 116–126.

Mitchell, C. (2002). Selling the brand inside. *Harvard Business Review, 80*(1), 99–105

Mullins, L.J. (2007) *Management and organizational behaviour* (8th ed.). Upper Saddle River, NJ: Pearson Education.

Olsen, M. D., West, J., & Tse, E. C. (1998). *Strategic management in the hospitality industry* (2nd ed.). New York, NY: John Wiley and Sons.

Payne, A., Storbacka, K., & Frow, P. (2008). Managing the co-creation of value. *Journal of the Academy of Marketing Science, 36*(1), 83–96.

Prahalad, C. K., & Ramaswamy, V. (2004a). *The future of competition: Co-creating unique value with customers*. Boston, MA: Harvard Business School Press.

Prahalad, C. K., & Ramaswamy, V. (2004b). Co-creation experiences: The next practice in value creation. *Journal of Interactive Marketing, 18*(3), 5–14.

Punjaisri, K., Wilson A. M., & Evanschitzky, H. (2009). Internal branding to influence employees' brand promise delivery: A case study in Thailand. *Journal of Service Management, 20*(5), 561–579.

Ramaswamy V., & Guillart F. (2010). Building the co-creative enterprise. *Harvard Business Review,* October, 100–109.

Schaufeli, W. B., Bakker, A. B., & Salanova, M. (2006). The measurement of work engagement with a brief questionnaire: A cross-national study. *Educational and Psychological Measurement, 66*, 701–716.

Shaw, G., Bailey, A., & Williams, A. (2011). Aspects of service-dominant logic and its implications for tourism management: Examples from the hotel industry. *Tourism Management, 32*(2), 207–214.

Terglav, K., Ruzzier, M. K., & Kaše, R. (2016). Internal branding process: Exploring the role of mediators in top management's leadership-commitment relationship. *International Journal of Hospitality Management, 54*, 1–11.

Vargo, S. L., & Lusch, R. F. (2004). Evolving to a new dominant logic for marketing. *Journal of Marketing, 68*(1), 1–17

Vargo, S. L., & Lusch, R. F. (2008). Service-dominant logic: Continuing the evolution. *Journal of the Academy of Marketing Science, 36*(1), 1–10.

Verhoef, P. C., Lemon, K. N., Parasuraman, A., Roggeveen, A., Tsiros, M., & Schlesinger, L. A. (2009). Customer experience creation: Determinants, dynamics and management strategies. *Journal of Retailing, 85*(1), 31–41.

Yi, Y., & Gong, T. (2013). Customer value co-creation behavior: Scale development and validation. *Journal of Business Research, 66*(9), 1279–1284.

# 11 Co-creating the sightseeing experience with and without a guide

*Anita Zátori*

## Introduction

Value and experience co-creation has gained an increased attention in tourism marketing. Lately, the attention of the industry has also turned towards how consumers are co-creating value and their experiences together with the company, brand and/or other consumers (Fischer & Smith, 2011), and the value co-creation concept is seen as a competitive strategy.

Management and marketing concepts, tools and methods can be considered as experience-centric only if consumer experience is at the locus of the value-creation process. Although the concept of staged experience (Cohen, 1988; McIntosh, 1999; Pine & Gilmore, 1998, 1999) and experience co-creation (Prahalad & Ramaswamy, 2004) are different, both concepts aim to create an experience value. They consider experience as a content formable and developable, and not only as a part of a product.

Although, it is important to highlight that we do not solely refer to co-creation as a marketing and management concept, but also as a type of value-creation process taking place between two or more consumers, or between consumer(s) and the service provider. The experience co-creation is a process directed by the consumer, which can start any time when the consumer is emotionally, mentally, and physically available, and is capable of controlling the situation in which the experience is formed (Prebensen & Foss, 2011), while the service provider creates opportunities to engage itself in the tourists' value-generating process (Grönroos, 2008). While Prebensen and Foss (2011) analysed the co-creation process during a vacation from consumer perspective, Sørensen and Jensen (2015) studied co-creation between frontline employees and customers in a hotel.

Despite the increased research interest, we know little about how the process of co-creation is enhanced by service providers during the on-site service provision. There is even less discussion on how a customer co-creates value with other customers in tourism settings. This issue is identified as a gap which is in need of more empirical findings. Sightseeing tours were chosen as the context of the study as they represent a field in tourism where co-creation processes take place relatively often between the participants of an individual sightseeing group, or between the participants and the guide. For example, Jennings and Weiler (2006) suggested that guides can facilitate a quality experience only if the tourist's desires and expectations are met, therefore a two-way communication is needed to hear the tourist's perspective.

A consumer can participate in a sightseeing tour with or without a guide or other forms of guiding (e.g. a mobile app), alone, in a formal or informal group. Facilitating meaning for visitors is very much affected by the guide's ability to connect with what the tourist knows and cares about, hence informal brokers may in some cases be in a much better position to do this (Weiler & Ham, 2001). Although a variety of guided tours are popular, the majority of tourists do not participate in guided tours, they realize the sightseeing by themselves – in smaller or larger informal groups – and co-create the experience together; however tourism literature knows little about them. The purpose of the study is thus to find out how the sightseeing experience is co-created in the context of guided and non-guided tours, while also uncovering the differences in tourist experience formation in these two distinct sightseeing types, and the role of a guide in this process.

Observation, short interviews and diary method were applied for primary data collection. During guided tours, unstructured 'mini interviews' (conversation between two stops) were carried out. In the case of non-guided sightseeing, the observation and short interviews would have hardly been possible without interrupting the group dynamics as an outsider (researcher). Thus this type of tour was organized with invited participants, who were asked to write a diary after the tour.

Guided tours have received little attention in academic literature, despite being seen as having an important role in exploring the destination (Wong & McKercher, 2012). The core value of the sightseeing tour is heavily dependent on both aesthetic and verbal/written content, while interaction is also important. After the provision of a brief theoretical insight about sightseeing tours and the concept of co-creation, the chapter will present the case studies of the two different sightseeing tours and analyse the findings with the aim to explore the process of value co-creation.

### Sightseeing tour trends

While the main attractions play an important role in the itinerary of many sightseeing tours of a destination, less typically visited sights, or sights with a lower level of awareness or attractiveness, provide an opportunity for tourists to gain deeper insights into the destination (Leiper, 1990; McKercher, Ho, & du Cros, 2004).

Traditionally sightseeing tours have been over-directed, and tourist experiences heavily mediated, especially in the case of cultural tourism (Smith & Richards, 2013). On the other hand, there is an increasing number of tour providers who design flexible tours while encouraging spontaneity and co-creation (Zátori, 2016a). These are tour providers and guides who are using experience-centric methods and tools, putting the customer into the centre of the business process, and consciously or unconsciously applying the management concept of co-creation.

Another trend indicates that increasingly more guided tours are designed for locals (Zátori, 2015; Rátz, 2016). These tours are themed – for example, focusing only on one theme or district – not interpreting the major tourist attractions, but atypical sites or themes, especially in bigger towns and cities. Because of the themed character, the participants tend to be involved in the theme and have a personal interest in the topic, so might even have a certain level of prior knowledge.

### Guides as destination experience mediators

Tour guides influence the experience creation of the tour participants by interpreting the cultural and natural heritage of an area. Both tour guiding and tour managing (managing the itinerary and the realization of the program) are seen as activities of the tour provider (either providing it internally as a service provider, or outsourcing it to a subcontractor). The Economic Planning Group of Canada (EPGC, 1995) refers to sightseeing tours as typically being built around a destination's primary attractions, meanwhile it also argues for the experiential character of such tours. Therefore, it can be stated that guided sightseeing tours enhance the destination's experience value.

Wong and McKercher (2012, p. 1,362) describe how past studies have defined tour guides' roles as 'performers, interpreters and cultural mediators' and have analysed how their actions affect visitor experience and satisfaction. Ooi (2005) considers tour operators, tour and program providers, tourism promotional authorities, tour guides, travel reviews, guidebooks, and friendly locals as destination experience mediators. Tour providers and tour guides influence the destination experience of the tourists by selecting and interpreting tourist attraction, because they direct the tourists' attention.

Tour providers make a decision about what to show and how to interpret it, therefore they are not only mediators of the destination experience, but they have a creative power over it. Some destination experience mediators play an active role in tourist engagement, thus they do not simply mediate a destination experience, but co-create it together with the tourist. Therefore, these can be referred to as destination experience co-creators. One of the main differences is that compared to destination experience mediators, destination experience co-creators do not only influence but enhance the tourist experience and the formation of quality and memorable experiences. The sightseeing tours can vary a lot based on the guide's person. Involving interpretation and performance (unless the tour is using a script), the guide's personal style, preferences and taste is driving what and how it is interpreted and their performance largely influences the consumer's destination experience formation. It was found that the guiding performance contributes to the memorable experience formation to the largest extent. Thus, it is argued that instead of the term 'destination experience mediator', 'destination experience co-creator' is more relevant. It suggested that not only tour providers and guides but rather guidebooks reviews, friendly locals and so on should be regarded as destination experience co-creators.

*Creating the tour experience*

Tourists have different experiences, and they pay attention to different things, even if they all participate in the same activity at the same time and place (Ooi, 2005). The tour providers help to direct their attention, which is seen as a scarce resource (Davenport & Beck, 2000). When visiting a destination, tourists have limited time and lack local knowledge, so to consume more and better experiences during their stay, they are seeking a shortcut to experience the place, and this shortcut is offered by tour providers (Ooi, 2005).

To gain an insight into tour experience formation, we should acknowledge what the two most basic travel motivation types are: experience seeking and escaping. It was found that the experience seeking behaviour is more important to the one-day sightseeing tourist than the escaping one (Dunn Ross & Iso-Ahola, 1991). Experience seeking behaviour presupposes the tourist's willingness and interest in experience formation and, if the conditions are offered by the tour provider and the guide, also their active enrolment in experience co-creation. Tourists participating in a sightseeing tour are looking for local knowledge and to experience the local atmosphere. Although tourists construct their experiences based on their own background (social, cultural, etc.) and interest (Aho, 2001; Prebensen & Foss, 2011; Walls, Okumus, Wang, & Kwun, 2011), tour guides contribute to this process.

Guiding with passion, creating pleasant group atmosphere, a first-hand insight of participants' viewpoints, narrative storytelling, interesting stories and humour, and last but not least an active engagement of the tour participants (which is a prerequisite of co-creation) were identified as factors of high-quality tour guiding based on interviews with guides and tour providers (Zátori, 2015).

While designing the tour experience, factors such as tour guiding, tour content and schedule, experience environment (e.g. vehicles, technology, issues of comfort) and issues relating to customization should be considered by the service provider. Out of all these factors, tour guides have the biggest influence on tourist experience, bigger than other elements of service provision – for example experience environment, methods and level of customization (Zátori, 2015). These findings highlight the role of personal contact and interaction in experience co-creation and quality experience enhancement. Despite the fact that tour providers and guides direct the tourists' attention and gazes, and help to inform the tourists' interpretations of sights and sites, tourists construct their experiences based on their personal resources (Prebensen, Vitterso, & Dahl, 2013a; Chen, Prebensen, & Uysal, 2014).

## The concept of co-creation

By applying the concept of value co-creation companies and service providers might be able to engage consumers as co-creators and also to customize their offers (Vargo & Lusch, 2004). Some researchers link the co-creation to S-D logic (Vargo & Lusch, 2004), not considering that it was criticized by Prahalad (2004, p. 23) that Vargo and Lusch 'do not go far enough' because value co-creation should be experience-centric and not service-dominant. Consumers co-create value with other consumers and service providers while they remain active in searching and creating value (Prahalad & Ramaswamy, 2004). Customer experience and value co-creation are defined by encounter processes rather than by the product itself, which is why co-creation should pervade tourists' active involvement and interaction with the supplier in each and every aspect – from service design to consumption (Payne et al., 2008). Within this perspective, consumers are assumed to create value-in-use and co-create value with organizations, thus realizing their potential to utilize consumption to demonstrate knowledge and expertise; but also to construct, represent, and maintain their identity (Firat & Venkatesh, 1995). The context and the level of consumer involvement contribute to personal meaning formation and the perceived uniqueness of experience co-creation (Prahalad & Ramaswamy, 2004).

Tour providers using methods of the experience co-creation approach aim to engage the customer by forming possibilities for experience co-creation through interaction, experience environment, and level and possibilities of customization. Interaction has a central role in the concept, thus the firm should enhance interaction with a special focus on dialogue, access, transparency and risk sharing (Prahalad & Ramaswamy, 2004).

The firms have to innovate the experience environment effectively to enable an optimal diversity of experiences (Prahalad & Ramaswamy 2004). Service environment design has an extended literature (e.g. Bitner, 1992; Otto and Ritchie, 1996), however lately the term 'experience environment' is preferred (Prahalad & Ramaswamy, 2004; O'Dell, 2005). During the phase of service and experience design (including the creation of experience schemes and the application of certain methods and techniques), the previously obtained knowledge – concerning the possible main interests of the consumers (Stamboulis & Sayannis, 2003) and the future experiences assumed by the consumers (Ooi, 2005; Wirtz, Kruger, Scollon, & Diener, 2003) have to be implemented.

Otto and Ritchie (1996) highlight the importance of customization in tourism and event services. By enabling customization, an optimal degree of freedom is created for the tourist's experience involvement. Meanwhile, the consumer can decide to what extent and how they wish to be involved in the experience creation. This requires a higher degree of activity and participation from the tourist.

Tour providers applying the experience-centric approach, such as the concept of co-creation, to establish a higher level of consumption involvement, the so-called 'experience-involvement' (Zátori, 2015). Tour providers who offer only customizable services, but do not support co-creation, are not able to involve consumers in the experience to the same extent as those who allow both customization and co-creation during the service provision (Zátori, 2015).

### On-site co-creation in the context of guided tours

A distinction is made between the value co-creation as a strategy (which is a theoretical approach and managerial perspective) and as process of on-site co-creation. The on-site co-creation is characterized by simultaneous production and consumption of experience, and this co-creative process enhances value for both sides. Previous research highlights that guides believe they provide their best performance if it is done with passion, which assumes high experience involvement on both sides. Co-creative tours may enhance experience value for both parties: tour participants and guides.

The on-site consumer involvement, that is experience involvement, is not only a crucial aspect of experience co-creation, but also one of its main conditions (O'Sullivan & Spangler, 1998; Mossberg, 2007; Prebensen, Woo, & Uysal, 2013b). Both tour guiding and tour managing are seen as activities of tour providing. The service of tour guiding is either provided internally or outsourced to a subcontractor tour guide. The competencies belonging to these activities are managed in various ways, and differ in the case of different tour companies (Zátori, 2015). Thus even guided tours where tour providers do not apply the co-creation concept as a management approach can lead to experience and value co-creation if the tour guide enhances it. It was found that staged and co-creative elements are often mixed during the guiding (Zátori, 2015), although we must highlight that if a tour manager implies the concept of co-creation as a management approach, it should also make sure that the tour guide applies it. The service provider is capable of enhancing co-creation if the customer is willing to participate in the co-creation process. Prebensen and Foss (2011) support this notion by pointing out that the consumer has to be available and capable of controlling the situation in which the experience is formed. Aiming for this, the service provider needs to provoke the consumer's attention by generating active participation and/or attracting the interest of consumers. This way, the service is able to involve the consumers in the experience, however co-creation is not accomplished unless a value is formed, and thus service providers should 'make' the consumers find a value as an outcome of the experience (e.g. a new meaning).

Experience co-creation may be evoked through three stages as suggested by the 'AIM-model' (Zátori, 2016b). That is, it occurs in a sequential path in which service providers are capable to (1) draw the tourist's attention to the desired object or activity, then (2) involve him/her mentally and/or emotionally in the experience consumption, and finally, (3) make him/her discover things of interest, that is enhance their value creation – as an outcome of the process.

The entertaining elements (such as humour) attract attention ('A') and support mental, social, and emotional involvement in a guided tour. The guide aims to involve the consumer by transforming his attention into an interest ('I') – narrative stories serve as an excellent tool for that. Another one is if during tours the participants are encouraged to comment, to give feedback or add supplementary information. This type of knowledge sharing results in co-creation of value between the participants and the tour provider. Interactivity is not only realized through dialogues, but also with the contribution of brainstorming questions and tasks. By making ('M') the participants proactive the experience of discovery is encouraged. Case studies are presented next with the aim to investigate the co-creation process on guided and non-guided tours.

## Cases

### Case study 1: co-creation in guided tours

The aim of the observation was to observe the process of experience co-creation on a guided tour. The sampling was not random; a tour was chosen which was complex enough to analyse co-creation in various circumstances. A previous study (Zátori, 2015) identified tour providers in Budapest (Hungary) whose tours were characterized by co-creation. The observation of the tour (provided by BUPAP) was realized on January 29, 2016.The observation focused on the interaction between the guide and the tourists, the experience environment provided by the operator and the guide, the tourists' level of experience involvement and the opportunities of customization.

The subject of the observation was BUPAP, an alternative tour provider. This type of tour provider typically organizes special themed tours for which a particular demand has formed. Some of their customers are local, some of them are tourists. Local sightseeing tours provide novelty even for local tour participants for two reasons: they are guided in less well-known parts of the city and they uncover rare pieces of information and hidden stories. The tours are themed around a certain topic of history, literature, architecture, ethnic minority, just to name the most typical ones. They pay more attention to non-typical tourist attractions and focus on the hidden aspects of the story. They are 'alternative' because they apply different methods and tools than traditional tour providers. Referring to urban legends, stories and gossip typify the tours; performance is usually realized in a narrative style.

The thematic tour about the Zwack family was 3 hours long, it had a complex character as part of it happened by bus and part of it in the visitor centre of a factory, and it also included outdoor and indoor sights and gastronomic elements with tasting. It had 38 participants. The tour showcased the family history of the Zwacks, who have owned the Zwack factory for multiple generations. From their product line, the most famous one is undoubtedly the Zwack Unicum, a typical and traditional Hungarian spirit based on a special recipe. When visiting the factory, the guide from the visitor centre took over guiding duties.

During the tour, the observation criteria for interaction were: the quantity and quality of the dialogues, consumers' information access (the quantity of interaction points), transparency, and risk sharing. The access to the information such as the tour schedule and organizational issues (toilet opportunities and so on) were given before the tour started, so the transparency requirements seemed to be fulfilled at the very beginning. The guide also informed the participants about the rules and the makeup of the tour right at the beginning. The tour participants were asked to indicate if they had a question or if they did not hear the guiding clearly. At first, the group was rather passive, but after a while – from the second quarter of the tour – more and more questions were asked. After the first sight, the guide addressed questions to the group participants to make the tour more interactive and to engage the tour participants. The experience involvement of those who answered the questions successfully seemed to intensify. Questions addressing the tour participants and creating a dialogue between the guide and the participant(s) were found to engage the consumers' attention and also enhance their active role during the tour.

Based on the tour participants' attention level and observable experience involvement, and the content characteristics of the guidance, the guidance included an optimal balance of factual information and interesting stories (habits, gossip and so on). It is assumed that interesting stories have a double advantage; they do not only trigger attention in real-time frames but this kind of information also tends to stay more memorable. However, without factual information (depending on the theme), the guidance could lose its authenticity. The factual information was presented in the context of the sites. The guide did not interrupt the narrative while going from one sight to another, which was an advantage to maintain the experience involvement.

The observation identified the tour guide's significant influence on the group atmosphere. This finding is in accordance with results from the quantitative study (Zátori, 2015). During informal conversations with the tour participants, they highlighted the crucial role and the great impact of the guide. It was said that she had an extended knowledge, and that she was a very nice person – the tour participants developed positive emotions towards the guide. The guide was able to transform this positive impression of her into a positive group atmosphere and the participants were also very friendly to each other. At the end of the tour, the majority of the participants personally thanked the guide. The participants seemed to be very satisfied and content with the tour experience (e.g. asked the guide about other tours she was guiding).

At the end of the tour, the local guide of the visitor centre took over the guiding. A sensorial stimulus was introduced here, and the participants were able to touch and smell the herbs used as ingredients for the liquor. This was followed by the tasting experience of the ready product of Unicum. It represented a unique experience too, as it provided an exceptional occasion to drink freshly prepared spirit from a barrel. The participants seemed to be fully engaged in the activity.

The experience environment was complex due to multiple stops and different means of transport (walking and bus). The tour had included different sensorial stimuli – hearing (stories and on the bus, for example), seeing and touching (visitor centre, for example), and tasting (liquor). The experience environment was pleasant and it provided a certain diversity which added to the level of excitement because it offered a constant stream of new inputs (stimuli).

Tour participants had the opportunity to ask questions during the tour, moreover, the guide encouraged the participants to do so several times during the tour. Participants were also invited to make comments or add stories. By the end of the tour, one of the participants shared the entire history of her family, which was very similar to that of the Zwacks'. The tour participant did not only add a story to the content, but also authenticity and intimacy, which can be viewed as values of the experience co-creation.

The guide was facilitating the experience co-creation with various methods and tools (stories, questions, historic pictures, and so on). It is important to highlight that the experience environment and the sights were not always attractive themselves, but there were the stories to fill them up with interesting content, meaning and excitement. The content combined with the outstanding storytelling qualities of the guide led to consumer engagement, while the co-creative tour elements helped the experience co-creation process.

### Case study 2: co-creation in non-guided tours

The observation took place on a non-guided tour in Inner Elizabethtown, Budapest, Hungary, in October 2015. Two tours were organized, one with 13 participants, the second with 15 participants. The tour participants, as undergraduates of the same university class, already knew each other. They were first asked to prepare a tour itinerary in small groups of 2 to 3 people before the tour, and collect information about the sights and other features that they considered attractive enough to present during the tour. The aim was to create conditions similar to a real, non-guided, small group sightseeing – for example group of friends travelling together. After the tour, the participants were asked to write a report (diary) about the tour experiences – including their previous expectations and experiences of the tour and the participant's role during the tour. Twenty-eight diaries were conducted and analysed with the method of content analysis. The diaries were written in English. The researcher also participated in the tours and made notes of the observed data – primarily focusing on the circumstances, influencing factors and the process of co-creation between tour participants. The observer took a less active role in the tours, made only a few comments, and did not take a leading role or make any decisions. The participants did not know they were being observed during the tour.

The tour took place in Inner Elizabethtown, a downtown district of Budapest. Budapest is the capital of Hungary with more than 1.7 million residents and 8 million guest nights (HCSO, 2016). This particular district has a number of popular tourist attractions and is considered the hip, creative heart of the city (Zátori & Smith, 2014), hosting some popular bars, ruin pubs, thematic streets (e.g. the Design Street), murals painted on firewalls, and other pieces of urban art. At the same time, it is home to the Great Synagogue, which is a prime tourist attraction (located at the edge of the district), and other hidden gems of cultural heritage. Another unique feature: during the Second World War, the district was a Jewish ghetto. Inner Elizabethtown boasts an inimitable vibe with its narrow streets sprinkled with bars, restaurants, and small boutiques, making the district perfectly suitable for day time and night time activities. It is a gentrified area, a home of Orthodox Jews, hipsters, and also accommodating an increasing number of tourists. Due to the narrow streets, the network of public transport is rather poor in this one square kilometre area, so only those who visit the area with a purpose wander here.

For the majority of the 28 tour participants, the destination of the tour, Inner Elizabethtown, was a new place. Many of the participants had only been living in Budapest for 2 to 3 years, and had either not visited many neighbourhoods or did not do so with the purpose of sightseeing – that is to learn about the major cultural heritage or other contemporary issues, such as urban art or the creative arts scene. Only few – those locals living nearby or those maintaining a special interest in the quarter – were familiar with what Inner Elizabethtown has to offer. The schedule and the content of the tour was not set, but the participants could alter it. Only the duration of the tour (90 minutes) and the area were set in stone. The two tours were conducted on the same day, right after each other. The tours share many similarities regarding the co-creation process and the group dynamics. The difference was that in the first group, 1 participant, who had local knowledge, took a stronger leading role (not in an overwhelming manner but providing enough space for others), while during the second tour, there were 5 active participants providing most of the content, but almost everyone contributed to the content and schedule of the tour. The findings of the two tours about the co-creation process were homogenous, thus the analysis will not differentiate them. Most of the participants liked the tour concept, for example:

> I really like that there was no guide to supply us with a concrete plan so we were free to decide where to go and what to see.
>
> (PI)

or

> It was a great experience that we were in charge, it was more of a challenge this way that the group had such freedom.
>
> (TM)

However, some were unhappy with the spontaneous and unplanned character of the tour. For them, the tour was rather frustrating, and this limited their willingness to co-create with others. The tour participants felt equal in the group but the decision making was not always easy.

The findings revealed three determining factors influencing the individual's level of participation in the co-creation process, these are: involvement, previous knowledge, and personality. This is in line with previous findings (Aho, 2001; Prebensen et al., 2013a; Andrades & Dimanche, 2014). Those who were not interested in culture and history, or the co-creative concept of the tour, were less willing to experience co-creation with other participants. Factors of personality, previous knowledge and involvement also determined their chosen role during the sightseeing:

As I'm a shy and quiet person, I did not really speak up, I kind of felt like a real tourist who just sits back and blindly follows the tourist guide(s). . . . I only added my undivided attention and presence to the program.

(GD)

Four roles were identified during the tours: the 'Leader', the 'Middle Men', the 'Tourist' and the 'Outsider'. The role of the 'Tourist' was associated with being passive and just listening to others. This might originate from previously obtained knowledge, like the participant who did not look up information to feel herself competent enough to add comments, share facts or discuss the schedule. The 'Outsiders' behaviour shows that they did not participate in the experience co-creation, even if they participated in the program – these were the same participants who did not like the concept of a non-guided co-created tour. The following two quotes examine the 'Leader' and 'Middle Man' roles during the tour:

It was typical that 4–5 people of the group were speaking more than the others, but I think it wasn't a problem.

(VA)

I think I was a great listener and a participant on the one hand, because I let others show the way but on the other hand, sometimes I actually did add program points, and played the role of a leader as well. I feel like it was balanced, and I felt very comfortable in both roles.

(TM)

The process of co-creation of the schedule and content went well after the first 10 to 15 minutes. The participants were requested to collect information about the sights in smaller groups of 3 and prepare a schedule for a sightseeing tour in the district.

The co-creative character of the tour was not a good experience for everyone, some participants could not impose their will about the schedule. The majority of negative experiences noted in the written diary were not voiced during the tour, so they would have stayed hidden during observation without gathering consumer feedback. Some quotes describing the co-creation process:

Our next stop was the Szimpla Pub. I have never been there before. . . .In the group many knew this pub, and they told us funny and interesting stories about it.

(BZs)

The tour did not go as we have planned. On the other hand, it was better this way because we managed to discover places that we have not planned but the other groups have. Of course we had to agree with others on it. . . . We learnt a lot from others.

(ZF)

The group decided on where to go based on the proximity of the nice places, so we decided kind of randomly sometimes.

(MV)

I was a bit disappointed because we planned to visit the Bors Gastro Bar and the Szimpla Garden. Budapest is well-known about street food restaurants and ruin pubs. These 2 places symbolize this feeling the best. Instead of this we went to Gozsdu.

(MV)

Experiencing surprise, discovery, generating emotions and new knowledge were the identified outcomes of the co-creation process. Both emotional and mental experience involvement characterized the tour and the vast majority of the participants highlighted that they experienced surprise and discovery, which are seen as higher level of emotional and mental experience involvement.

I realized that there is so much more that I do not know about my home. For example, I pass by the Dohany Street Synagogue every day, and I did not know that this is the biggest one in Europe and the second biggest in the world.

(ZF)

The social experience involvement was an organic element of the co-created tour due to its non-guided character. The participants did not write about experiencing a flow-type on-site involvement, however few participants wrote about experiencing the state of existential authenticity. Reaching the state of 'existential self', the individual constructs a new, previously unknown meaning, or learns about self (Wang, 1999). As it satisfies a higher order need, its value is high for the individual. The findings show that emotional experience involvement led to a formation of existential authenticity:

I think it was heart-smothering when we visited the renovated wall which separated the ghetto from the town. We cannot imagine how different and cruel the life was then.

(BZs)

Many reported about increased involvement in the city, district or sightseeing tours, for example going back to the sights, entering the buildings, or showing the district to their friends and family. For some, the involvement had an emotional character, and they evaluated the tour as leading towards a stronger place attachment. Experience involvement led to a higher involvement at the outcome of the tour. This is not only a passive form of involvement; the vast majority of those showing an increased involvement expressed an intention of repeat visit and recommendation.

Gozsdu was a very positive surprise for me . . . It was love at first sight so I decided that I will visit Gozsdu at a lazy Friday night with my friends.

(PE)

This trip motivated me to go back and see, experience more of the things we have seen. I will definitely show a few more things for my friends and family too.

(GA)

However, it is important to point out that the non-guided tour did not satisfy everyone's needs and plans. Some were dissatisfied with the tour.

The findings indicate that the co-creation process between participants of a non-guided sightseeing tour are described by some common attributes. It is assumed that these attributes might not only be valid in the case of non-guided tours, but guided tours, or even other types of leisure or tourism services and activities too. These identified attributes are the following:

- The types of the co-created experience can be various, they can emerge in the form of a surprise, intellectual discovery, new skill, knowledge or feeling and so on. This variety of experiences can be described as the outcome of emotional and/or mental experience involvement, and it is also enhanced or limited by social experience involvement.
- The decision-making process in the group is an important element of the co-creation process. Contradictory wishes might lead to a negative experience for some group members, thus group dynamics and the group's consensus-forming ability are considered to be crucial factors of the co-creation act.
- The co-created (tour) experience might lead to increased involvement (e.g. place attachment), and also might enhance subjective well-being through personal development and formation of new meanings.
- The individual's participation in the co-creation process and the individually exerted value from co-creation depends on his/her chosen role in the group. This is affected by the individual's previous knowledge and skills, his/her involvement in that certain tour, destination or activity, and last but not least, personality and attitude.

## Conclusions

Comparing the findings of non-guided tours with the guided tour, it is seen that the experience involvement is more consistent among participants of a guided tour than those of a non-guided tour. This is also supported by a previous, larger sample, survey and observation-based study focusing on guided tours (Zátori, 2015). Although the data from the non-guided tours is based on observation and written diaries, it clearly indicates major differences in the participants' experience involvement. Based on these findings, the study argues that the role of the tour guide is crucial in enhancing experience and value co-creation. The guide can heighten the tour experience, even of those tour participants with a lower level of involvement or insufficient personal resources. Guides can engage the consumers' attention and also enhance their active role during the tour. The guide's influence is crucial, which is also affected by the fact of the 'formally led' group. For example, Urry (1990) argues that during guided sightseeing tours, tourists take on the 'role of children', they let the guide lead them and tell them when and what to do something. On the contrary, on non-guided tours, as formally non-directed tours, there is no person in charge of participants' experience involvement. The sightseers are in charge of their experience formation (influenced by group dynamics), whereas previous involvement, knowledge and attitudes have a bigger impact on the co-created experience.

On the other hand, during non-guided sightseeing, due to the size of the group (13–15 participants), not everyone could impose their will regarding the schedule, since decisions were made by the group. The lack of formal group leadership (the guide) also contributed to the uneven formation of experience quality and the level of experience involvement among participants. While some were highly impressed, others felt like outsiders and were unable to participate in and contribute to value co-creation. Meanwhile, in the case of guided tours, the guide directed the tour while also enhancing experience co-creation for all participants.

Spontaneity and sense of freedom are significant value propositions of the tourist experience in the case of a non-guided tour. These two contribute to experiencing a higher sense of discovery. It might be assumed that the role of discovery is bigger in the case of these tours, but the results from observations suggest that this is not always the case. The participants of the non-guided tours unknowingly ignored some interesting sites and attractions. Even if they collected information about the district prior to the tour, they did not have the same knowledge as a guide (the researcher previously participated in tours in the district). Those pieces of information (about what is worth checking out, which building's courtyard to enter, and so on) are necessary inputs for discoveries and to enhance the experiential value. On the other hand, it is certainly a different (and perhaps more intense) experience to discover something individually or without a guide than with a guide.

Mental experiences (such as learning) and emotional ones (such as surprise) are experienced on both tours, however, a larger amount of information is provided on guided tours which makes learning a more dominant value proposition than in the case of non-guided tours. The main value proposition of non-guided sightseeing is experiential learning; it provides the opportunity for participants to be in charge, to challenge themselves and moreover, it ensures optimal frames for spontaneity and being casual.

Another advantage of a non-guided tour is that there is no guide to direct the attention of the participants and provide a single interpretation. Instead, multiple interpretations can be presented on a non-guided sightseeing tour, and participants have more opportunities for self-expression. However this would not have been possible without the right personal resources (see for example Prebensen et al., 2013a).

Guided tours with an experience-centric approach either enable co-creation or they provide a staged experience. Alternatively, they build on both concepts. Traditionally, guided tours are characterized by the features of staged experience, such as staged performance, single interpretation, planned and scheduled character, the experience of entertainment, while the guide is in a role of a storyteller.

Guided tours aiming to meet the emerging consumer needs have moved towards co-created tour design and guiding – for example urban ethnic tours as such products (see Smith & Zátori, 2016). Guided tours enhancing experience co-creation are moving away from the 'traditional' tour features (e.g. single interpretation, inflexible schedule), allowing and encouraging the participant's involvement in the interpretation, increasing their sense of freedom and customization, enhancing self-expression, and, last but not least, including elements of experiential learning (e.g. tasting) which enhance the participant's more active role during the tour and the value-creation process (see Figure 11.1).

Non-guided tours can be 'supported' by mobile tour applications, destination websites or guidebooks. However, the character of these is more customizable than that of guided tours, because they offer plenty of recommendations and provide a large number of options from which the tourist can choose, but they lack the factor of personal interaction. Guided tours can also offer a certain level of customization, however their main advantage compared to the guidebooks or mobile apps lies in the interactivity (questions can be raised) and dialogue (adding personal stories and impressions), not to mention the dramaturgy and guide-performance quality as service value propositions, which have full potential to enhance the experience value of the tour. Mobile apps, destination websites and blogs, online travel communities, guidebooks, and co-creative guided tours are destination experience co-creators, which might add valuable resources to the value co-creation process of the sightseeing – they help planning and provide information for a learning experience, in the case of co-creative guided tours staged performance/storytelling and entertainment are additional inputs. The co-created experience enables consumers to be in charge (to a certain level), to have a chance of spontaneity and freedom, encourages their self-expression and enhances experiential learning. Figure 11.1 illustrates the position of co-created sightseeing between a consumer and a destination experience co-creator building on the advantages of guided sightseeing, but aiming to ensure the advantages of non-guided sightseeing.

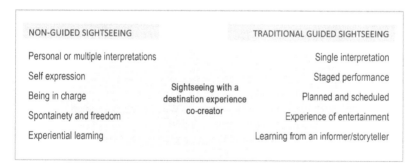

*Figure 11.1* Forms of co-creation: the destination experience co-creation with and without a guide

A limitation of the study is that the guided and non-guided tours research methodology was slightly different, thus they provide a different level of insight to the guided tour's experience co-creation. Another limitation is the exploratory and case study character of the research, working with a small sample size.

Although outside the scope of this study, the discussion on sightseeing experience cannot neglect the influence of built and natural attractions, nor the impact of local culture and organizational and business issues (tourism industry characteristics, infrastructure and so on). Some of these are managed by DMOs (Destination Management Organizations). Thus the practical implication of the findings of the study is relevant not only to tour providers, but to destination management too. The implementation of the value co-creation concept offers a great opportunity for destination management in aspects of interacting with the visitors and facilitating their destination experience. DMOs are also in charge of the formation and communication of the destination experience. It is a matter of future studies how DMOs can apply the marketing concept of value co-creation, and facilitate co-creation with visitors to enhance their experience value.

## References

Aho, S. E. (2001). Towards a general theory of touristic experiences: Modelling experience process in tourism. *Tourism Review, 56*(3–4), 33–37.

Andrades, L., & Dimanche, F. (2014). Co-creation of experience value: A tourist behavior approach. In N. K. Prebensen, J. S. Chen, & M. Uysal (Eds.), *Creating experience value in tourism* (pp. 95–112). Wallingford: CABI.

Bitner, M. J. (1992). Servicescapes: The impact of physical surroundings on customers and employees. *Journal of Marketing, 56*(April), 57–71.

Chen, J. S., Prebensen, N. K., & Uysal, M. (2014). Dynamic drivers of tourist experiences. In N. K. Prebensen, J. S. Chen, & M. Uysal (Eds.), *Creating experience value in tourism* (pp. 11–21). Wallingford: CABI.

Cohen, E. (1988). Authenticity and commoditization in tourism. *Annals of Tourism Research, 15*(3), 371–386.

Davenport, T. H., & Beck, J. C. (2000). Getting the attention you need. *Harvard Business Review,* September–October, 118–126.

Dunn Ross, E., & Iso-Ahola, S. (1991). Sightseeing tourists' motivation and satisfaction. *Annals of Tourism Research, 18(2)*, 226–237.

EPGC. (1995). *Packaging for and selling to the United States pleasure travel market.* Ottawa: Tourism Canada.

Firat, A. F., & Venkatesh, A. (1995). Liberatory postmodernism and the reenchantment of consumption. *Journal of Consumer Research, 22*(3), 239–267.

Fisher, D., & Smith, S. (2011). Cocreation is chaotic: What it means for marketing when no one has control. *Marketing Theory 11*(3), 325–350.

Grönroos, C. (2008). Service logic revisited: Who creates value? And who co-creates? *European Business Review 20*(4), 298–314.

HCSO. (2016). Tourism in Hungary 2015 with preliminary data. Retrieved from http://itthon.hu/documents/28123/8118959/MTE_4001_105x210_LA4_StatElo_2015_ENG_TELJES_web.pdf/ae097433-2c69-4893-a42c-00ee677f0865 (last retrieved 29.12.2016).

Jennings, G., & Weiler, B. (2006). Mediating meaning: Perspectives on brokering quality tourist experiences. In G. Jennings & N. Nickerson (Eds.), *Quality tourism experiences* (pp. 83–98). Oxford: Butterworth-Heinemann.

Leiper, N. (1990). Tourist attraction systems. *Annals of Tourism Research, 17*, 367–384.

McIntosh, A. J. (1999). Into the tourist's mind: Understanding the value of the heritage experience. *Journal of Travel & Tourism Marketing, 8*(1), 41–64.

McKercher, B., Ho, P. S., & du Cros, H. (2004). Attributes of popular cultural attractions in Hong Kong. *Annals of Tourism Research, 31*(2), 393–407.

Mossberg, L. (2007). A marketing approach to the tourist experience. *Scandinavian Journal of Hospitality and Tourism, 7*(1), 59–74.

O'Dell, T. (2005). Experiencescapes: Blurring borders and testing connections. In T. O'Dell & P. Billing (Eds.), *Experiencescapes: Tourism, culture and economy* (pp. 11–33). Copenhagen: Copenhagen Business School Press.

O'Sullivan, E. L., & Spangler, K. J. (1998). *Experience marketing: Strategies for the new millennium.* State College: Venture Publishing.

Ooi, C. (2005). Theory of tourism experiences: The management of attention. In T. O'Dell & P. Billing (Eds.), *Experiencescapes: Tourism, culture, and economy* (pp. 76–85). Copenhagen: Copenhagen Business School Press.

Otto, J., & Ritchie, B. (1996). The service experience in tourism. *Tourism Management, 17*(3), 165–174.

Payne, A., Storbacka, K., & Frow, P. (2008). Managing the co-creation of value. *Journal of the Academical Marketing Science, 36*, 83–96.

Pine, B. J., & Gilmore, J. H. (1998). Welcome to the experience economy: Work is theatre and every business is a stage. *Harvard Business Review, 76*(4), 97–105.

Pine, B. J., & Gilmore, J. H. (1999). *The experience economy: Work is theatre & every business a stage.* Boston, MA: Harvard Business School Press.

Prahalad, C. K. (2004). Co-creation of value, invited commentaries on 'evolving to a new dominant logic for marketing'. *Journal of Marketing, 68*(January), 18–27.

Prahalad, C. K., & Ramaswamy, V. (2004). *The future of competition: Co-creating unique value with customers.* Boston, MA: Harvard Business School Press.

Prebensen, N. K., & Foss, L. (2011). Coping and co-creating in tourist experiences. *International Journal of Tourism Research, 13*(1), 54–67.

Prebensen, N. K., Vitterso, J., & Dahl, T. I. (2013a). Value co-creation significance of tourists' resources. *Annals of Tourism Research, 42*, 240–261.

Prebensen, N. K., Woo, E., & Uysal, M. (2013b). Experience value: Antecedents and consequences. *Current Issues in Tourism, 17*(10), 910–928.

Rátz, T. (2016). 'Be global, go local': Innovation and creativity in the development of alternative guiding services in Budapest. *Journal of Tourism and Cultural Change.* http://dx.doi.org/10.1080/14766825.2016.1189558.

Smith, M. K., & Richards, G. (Eds.) (2013). *The Routledge handbook of cultural tourism.* London: Routledge.

Smith, M. K., & Zatori, A. (2016). Re-thinking host–guest relationships in the context of urban ethnic tourism. In P. Russo & G. Richards (Eds.), *Reinventing the local in tourism* (pp. 129–149). Bristol: Channel View Publication.

Sørensen, F., & Jensen, J. F. (2015). Value creation and knowledge development in tourism experience encounters. *Tourism Management, 46*, 336–346.

Stamboulis, Y., & Skayannis, P. (2003). Innovation strategies and technology for experienced-based tourism. *Tourism Management, 24*(1), 35–43.

Urry, J. (1990). *The tourist gaze: Leisure and travel in contemporary societies.* London: Sage.

Vargo, S. L., & Lusch, R. F. (2004). Evolving to a new dominant logic for marketing. *Journal of Marketing, 68*(January), 1–17.

Walls, A. R., Okumus, F., Wang, Y., & Kwun, D. J. (2011). An epistemological view of consumer experiences. *International Journal of Hospitality Management, 30*(1), 10–21.

Wang, N. (1999). Rethinking authenticity in tourism experience. *Annals of Tourism Research, 26*, 349–370.

Weiler, B., & Ham. S. (2001). Tour guides and interpretation. In D. Weaver, *Encyclopedia of Ecotourism* (pp. 549–564). Wallingford: CAB International.

Wirtz, D., Kruger, J., Scollon, C. N., & Diener, E. (2003). What to do on spring break? The role of predicted, on-line, and remembered experience in future choice. *Psychological Science, 14*, 520–524.

Wong, C., & McKercher, B. (2012). Day tour itineraries: Searching for the balance between commercial needs and experiential desires. *Tourism Management, 33*, 1360–1372.

Zátori, A., & Smith, M. K. (2014). The creative heart of Budapest. In L. Marques & G. Richards (Eds.), *Creative districts around the world* (pp. 105–110). Breda: NHTV.

Zátori, A. (2015). *Tourist experience co-creation and management.* Saarbrucken: Lambert Academic Publishing.

Zátori, A. (2016a). Experiential travel and guided tours: Following the latest consumption trends in tourism. In M. Kozak & N. Kozak (Eds.), *Tourist behaviour: An international perspective* (pp. 115–123). CABI: Wallingford.

Zátori. A. (2016b). Exploring the value co-creation process on guided tours (the 'AIM-model') and the experience-centric management approach. *International Journal of Culture, Tourism and Hospitality Research, 10*(4), pp. 377–395.

# 12 Creating value with seasonal workers through psychological contracts

*Kristin Woll*

## Introduction

The tourism industry has grown heavily and is forecast continued growth, implying an increased hiring of employees in the future (UNWTO, 2016). Companies in the tourism industry often hire employees on a seasonal basis, on what is referred to as temporary contracts in the literature (De Cuyper et al., 2008: De Jong, De Witte, Isaksson, Rigotti, & Schalk, 2008; Kalleberg, 2000). Previous studies show that temporary employment departs from the standard employment relationship in at least three dimensions (De Cuyper et al., 2008). First, temporary employment is of limited duration and often with a fixed termination date. Second, temporary employees do not necessarily work at the employer's workplace under his/her supervision. Third, temporary employees have fewer benefits and entitlements, such as a minimum wage, pensions and insurance, compared to permanent employees. It is also expected that temporary workers have less commitment and organizational citizen behaviour (OCB), also known as extra-role behaviour. This chapter highlights how organizations operating in seasonal markets may benefit from facilitating for value co-creation through developing strong psychological contracts with their employees.

When a firm experiences volatile markets or variation due to seasonality, a dilemma transpires between the need to employ a flexible workforce and the need to employ a workforce providing performance beyond the call of duty. OCB is delineated as extra-role behaviour that is optional, not directly acknowledged by the firm's reward system. However, this behaviour is key to the functioning of the organization as a system (Organ, 1988). Extra-role behaviour occurs when employees believe that such behaviour is consistent with how the organization has treated them and consistent with the degree of commitment perceived from the organization (Moorman, Blakely, & Niehoff, 1998). Based on previous research on temporary employees, the present chapter highlights this dilemma in the tourism industry. As the industry is highly dependent on seasonal workers accepting short terms contracts (e.g. shoulder seasons), it needs to ascertain how to make the seasonal workers provide extra-role behaviour and how to make them feel committed. We believe that a successful tourism industry hinges on companies' ability to understand the needs of their employees, independent of their contracts. The following research questions are therefore stated:

- To what degree do seasonal workers in the tourism industry feel committed and provide extra-role behaviour?
- If they do, why and how do they feel committed?
- Why and how do they provide extra-role behaviour?

By exploring these research questions, the present chapter will discuss how managers may promote commitment and extra-role behaviour among seasonal workers. This chapter aims to illustrate that by acknowledging what is affecting extra-role behaviour among seasonal workers such as guides within the tourism industry, and subsequently taking the right approach and developing the right types of psychological contract, commitment and extra-role behaviour will be enhanced. Consequently, the chapter will provide the tourism industry with knowledge regarding how to manage their seasonal workers more successfully, that is, co-create value for all partners involved. Furthermore, the study seeks to add to theory by testing Rousseau's assertion that workers with relational contracts tend to provide more extra-role behaviour.

## Theory

In the temporary contract literature, expectations between the employees and employers, represented by the psychological contract, have provided a useful perspective for understanding the working conditions of these employees (De Jong et al., 2008).

The psychological contract is defined as an individual's belief in mutual obligation between the person and another party such as an employer (Rousseau, 1989, 1995). A psychological contract is therefore a subjective experience based not only on the employer's behaviours but also on the actors' perception of those behaviours within a social context (Morrison & Robinson, 1997). The function of a psychological contract is the reduction of insecurity: because not all possible aspects of the employment relationship can be addressed in a formal, written contract, the psychological contract fills the gaps in this relationship. Furthermore, the psychological contract "shapes" employee behaviour. There is a range of factors that can influence employees' behaviour and hence the customer experience. Our focus is on showing how the extra-role behaviour and commitment of seasonal workers can be stimulated by developing different types of psychological contract acknowledging and meeting the employees' needs.

### *What is a psychological contract?*

The concept of a psychological contract generally describes the formation of individual perceptions by employees regarding what is owed by themselves and the organization (Rousseau, 1989), such that a psychological contract is the "subjective beliefs regarding an exchange agreement between an individual and, in organizations typically, the employing organization and its agents" (Rousseau,

2001, p. 512). Consequently, the individual's belief may diverge from what is in writing and from interpretations by other principles or a third party. All psychological contracts entail expectations that a person or a firm will act in a particular way. However, not all expectations are contractual. Rousseau and Tijoriwala (1998, p. 680) stress that "an important aspect of a psychological contract is that the beliefs compromising the contract result from promises".

To understand the content of expectations between the employees and employers, Rousseau (1995) made a distinction between transactional and relational psychological contracts. Relational contracts include terms such as loyalty (worker and employer commit to meeting the needs of the other) and stability (an open-ended commitment to the future). Rousseau (2004) emphasizes that workers with relational contracts tend to be more willing to work overtime, whether paid or not, to help co-workers on the job and to support organizational changes that their employer deems necessary. Furthermore, relational contracts involve organizations' provision of training and professional development, as well as long-term job security, in exchange for employees' fulfilment of a generalized role obligation. Employees with a relational contract contribute their commitment and involvement to the organization, often in the form of organizational citizenship behaviour (Robinson & Morrison, 1995).

A transactional contract, on the other hand, includes terms such as narrow duties and a limited or a short duration, typically working purely in exchange for money. Furthermore, employees with transactional contracts tend to do what is expected of them and little more. They also tend to seek employment elsewhere when conditions change or when employers fail to live up to their obligations (Rousseau, 2004). Table 12.1 illustrates the categories of contract by combining two dimensions: duration and performance conditions. The combination of the dimensions short duration and specified performance conditions gives us the transactional contract. The combination of the dimensions long duration and unspecified performance conditions gives us a relational contract, where trust in exchange for loyalty is vital.

Lately, a new type of psychological contract has been introduced: a value-based psychological contract, which is delineated as a credible commitment to pursue a value, cause or principle (not limited to self-interest) that is implicitly exchanged at the nexus of the individual-organization relationship (O'Donohue & Nelson, 2009, p. 258). Furthermore, it is argued that ideology plays a key role in defining and shaping the relationship between employees and employer.

*Table 12.1* Different types of psychological contract (based on Rousseau, 2004)

| *Performance conditions* | | |
| --- | --- | --- |
| *Duration* | *Specified* | *Unspecified* |
| Short | Transactional | Temporary |
| Long | Balanced | Relational |

*Psychological contracts and seasonal workers*

The psychological contract has been applied to understand the differences between permanent and temporary workers, in addition to the attitude and behaviour of temporary workers in general (Beard & Edwards, 1995). Beard and Edwards (1995) initially introduced the psychological contract to understand the working conditions of temporary workers. According to these authors, temporary workers' relationship with the organization is based on an economic exchange, and the employer makes all the decisions regarding the employees' work tasks. Hence, the temporary contract is transactional and asymmetrical in nature, and thus monitored by the employer (Beard & Edwards, 1995).

Overall, researchers suggest that transactional psychological contracts are most prevalent for temporary workers, while relational psychological contracts are most prevalent for permanent workers (Coyle-Shapiro & Kessler, 2002; Millward & Brewerton, 1999; Van Dyne & Ang, 1998). This means that temporary workers will exhibit less organizational citizenship behaviour, which again is problematic for a tourist company.

A tourist company will be dependent on workers that are providing excellent service and experiences for the customers. However, it is important to keep in mind that assessing which type of psychological contract is operating is difficult. Employment status—whether part or full time, or of brief duration or long term— does not indicate the type of psychological contract that workers will have with an employer. Part-time workers and newcomers can have relational agreements with an employer. Conversely, many full-time workers and veterans report only limited commitment between themselves and their firms (Rousseau, 2004).

## Methodology

This study adopted a qualitative and descriptive case study approach (Yin, 2009). It was considered the most appropriate method to adopt, given its exploratory nature and the limited availability of information on this topic.

### The case

This chapter is drawing on a case study performed with guides working for a company in Svalbard (Spitzbergen), Norway. Svalbard is situated north of mainland Europe, about midway between continental Norway and the North Pole. The three main industries on Svalbard are coal mining, tourism, and research. The study consists of interviews with Arctic guides and their managers employed by an Arctic tour operator in Svalbard. The tour operator offers guided tours with snowmobiles and cross-country skiing that last between one and three days. The Arctic guides are hired on a seasonal basis, typically lasting from February to May. The middle managers are hired on permanent contracts and are responsible for hiring the Arctic guides. We conducted interviews before and after the season with guides, fourteen interviews in total. In addition, we interviewed two of the middle managers and the CEO. In our case—Spitsbergen Travel—the working contracts between the company and the guides are short-term contracts (two to three months' duration in the winter season). The formal working contract primarily emphasizes the duration of the employment, in addition to salary and requirements for overtime, and guidelines for taking responsibility for the customers on the tours.

### Data collection

Data collection for this study was obtained through in-depth interviews with three managers and ten tour guides (seasonal workers) at a nature-based tourist company offering snow scooter safaris (winter tourism). Each interview lasted approximately one hour. An interview guide was developed and applied, including questions regarding working conditions, motivation, loyalty, relationships, and so forth, based on the theory of psychological contracts and extra-role behaviour. The purpose of these in-depth interviews was to solicit detailed information, opinions and insights on practices and issues relating to tour guiding, seasonality and the relationships between the guides, and between the guides and the firm.

## Findings

### What types of psychological contract do we find?

We explored the type of psychological contract between the Arctic guides and their managers at three different hierarchal levels. We will start by presenting our findings regarding transactional elements, then relational elements and subsequently we will present findings about value-based elements.

### Transactional elements

In general, the guides, like temporary workers in general, do not know if they will get a new labour contract next season (winter). In this specific case, we found that the company starts working on the staffing plan just a couple of months before the winter season. Furthermore, this study shows that the guides get no information about the company's staffing plan for next season, so they know nothing about their own possibility of being rehired. However, it seems that the guides do not expect more job security than the company offers today and that no seasonal workers at Svalbard have plans for next winter. Our interpretation is that this is a part of the lifestyle among the Arctic guides. The transactional contracts content works on exchange of salary. This study also indicates that the firm does expect the guides to work overtime, and that they help and cover if somebody get sick. Other transactional elements we found are about the expectation the guides have when it comes to housing and a wish for a degree of variety in tasks and guided trips. It seems that all these expectations are fulfilled, except for the expectation the guides have when it comes to variety in the assigned tours. Some guides tell that they want to have more variety in tasks and tours, and they wonder about the logic behind the working plan sat up by the managers. One guide put it like this: "I do not understand much of the principles of the working plan; there is not much variation." Another guide follows up on this by saying: "They [managers] could have more control and a better system regarding the working plan. They should spend some more time on getting it right." Asking the manager the same question, it seems that the manager believes that the working plan meets their expectations: "The guides know very well that the distribution of trips is based on principles of working experience and seniority." Overall, the results from this study indicate that some elements in the transactional contract are fulfilled and others are not.

In summary, the transactional contract in this case does not concern expectations about job security, as theory indicates and previous studies have shown. Asking the guides about job security and plans for next year, they all relate that they do not know what will happen next season or next winter, and that is just fine. As one guide said: "This is Svalbard, so nobody expects that the companies have decided already in May if you get a new contract next year." Another guides says: "We don't even know what is happening this summer, and nobody asks questions about what happens next winter." These quotations illustrate that the transactional contract between the employees does not contain job security.

### Relational elements

In the present case, we find relationships based on trust, both when it comes to the relationships among the guides and trust among/between the guides and the guide manager. The guides tell of a fantastic work environment based on trust and support: "We work very independently, and I take my own decisions. As a guide, you are responsible for any situation." Another informant says that "I can do whatever I feel is the right thing to do in any situation, and if I need advice, I ask for it." Overall, findings from this study regarding relational elements challenge previous research, which indicates that only permanent workers develop relational psychological contracts. We also see that the guides do trust each other, and that they counsel one another. This is also very important because of the working conditions. The weather conditions at Svalbard can be really tough, and it can be really challenging to bring so many different guests on the guided tours. The guides feel that the challenging working conditions make it important that they can support one another by seeking and giving advice. We interpret these mutual expectations among the guides as horizontal relational psychological contracts.

However, we also find vertical psychological contracts, such as mutual expectations between the guides and different managers at different levels in the company. These relational contracts between managers and their subordinates contain elements of trust and support.

> I have previously worked for a lot of different companies in the tourism industry. I cannot say much positive about the working conditions and working environment in previous places . . . I would say that previous experiences are about exploitation. . . . Where you don't mean anything to the manager,

you get fired if you ask for pay rise. I am coming back to work here and for this company because of the positive working environment; I feel that I am taken care of. It is the first time I have experienced this kind of care in this industry.

This quotation illustrates that relationships between the employees and the employer are experienced as positive. We find that the manager delegates autonomy to the guides and the guides offer loyalty in return.

*Ideological elements*

When it comes to ideological contracts, these often relate to the individual employees' and the employer's morals and values. Therefore looking for contracts with ideological elements indicates that we must search for some shared values between the employee and the company. The Arctic guides show great care for the nature and the wild animal life at Svalbard. They also show great commitment to the customers. We find that the company shares the same values as the Arctic guides. Values say something of priority and correct behaviour. Both managers and the company's strategy emphasize their responsibility to take care of the nature, and the environment, as well as taking care of the customers. In addition to the values of caring, we find safety to be another shared value. The company expects that the guides will follow safety principles, and the guides expect that the company will provide them with the right equipment so that they are able to follow the safety guidelines and principles. However, some of the tourist companies in the Arctic are facing challenges in the future. Companies are becoming more profit-based and more commercialized, but the Arctic guides are not supporting these new up-coming values. One guide put it like this: "The company I work for has grown, and it feels like I work for a money-maker. It gives me the feeling of mass tourism; however, the company is great in the way they facilitate the working conditions." We believe that this could be a challenge in the future for several reasons, including when it comes to shared values between the guides and the firm. The theoretical assumption is that the fulfilment of the psychological contract depends on shared values: based on this assumption, there is reason to believe that there will be a breach in the psychological contract if a company develops values that are not supported by the guides.

### Psychological contracts that provoke commitment among seasonal workers

Employees with transactional contracts tend to do what is expected of them and little more. They also tend to seek employment elsewhere when conditions change or when employers fail to live up to their obligations. Having a transactional contract might not be problematic if it exists between an individual contractor and a company: performance can be explicitly monitored and there is a little need to coordinate with others. However, employers who want to hire workers with high levels of organizational commitment in terms of identifying with the employer, and who want and intend to stay long term, need to understand the mechanism of the psychological contract.

We find that the guides in our case feel higher levels of commitment to those with whom they interact more (customers and colleagues within the guiding team) rather than the organization itself. The guides in this case tell that they feel highly committed to each other and to the customers; hence, they are also very committed to the task they perform. Our conclusion is that the company profits greatly from the strong commitment of the guides. In order to ensure strong commitment and OCB among seasonal workers, the tourism firms should focus on facilitating for including and involving the employees to create value together with colleagues and customers.

As a psychological contract is a subjective experience based not only on the employer's behaviours but also on the actors' perception of those behaviours within a social context (Morrison & Robinson, 1997), a relational focus should be in focus. The function of a psychological contract is the reduction of insecurity: because not all possible aspects of the employment relationship can be addressed in a formal, written contract, the psychological contract fills the gaps in this relationship. Furthermore, the psychological contract "shapes" employee behaviour. There is a range of factors that can influence employees' behaviour and hence the customer experience. Our focus is on showing how the extra-role behaviour and commitment of seasonal workers can be stimulated by developing different types of psychological contract acknowledging and meeting the employees' needs.

Furthermore, relational contracts involve organizations' provision of training and professional development, as well as long-term job security, in exchange for employees' fulfilment of a generalized role obligation. Employees with a relational contract contribute their commitment and involvement to the organization, often in the form of organizational citizenship behaviour (Robinson & Morrison, 1995).

### *Psychological contracts that provoke organizational citizenship among seasonal workers*

Organizational citizenship behaviour (OCB) refers to employee behaviour that provides extra-role behaviour and that further promotes organizational effectiveness. It is widely believed that organizations could not survive unless employees were willing to engage occasionally in OCB (Barnard, 1938; Katz, 1964; Katz & Kahn, 1978). It is believed that employees engage in OCB to the extent that they believe their organization is treating them fairly. However, this extra-role behaviour is not formally recognized by an organization's reward system (Organ, 1988). Robinson and Morrison (1995) suggest that psychological contracts are an especially important lens through which to view organizational citizenship behaviour. Employees with relational contracts tend to work overtime and provide extra service.

In this case study, we find that the guides work overtime without being paid. Their performance is recognized as effective and quality-based, which have a positive effect on extra-role behaviour. The guides explains how they always provide the "extra", especially towards the customers. As one Arctic guide states: "If we have time left, I always let the tourist see some beautiful places that they did not pay for or that are not included in the 'product'." They try to customize what the customers want: "I really try to catch what the tourists want from the trips, and I always give my customers an additional round with the scooter, if we have the time. I try to take them to places where they can enjoy the great view." Another guide tells us that she always tries to be available for the other guides, and that she always supports and helps colleagues if they need it. Most of the guides are willing to engage in extra-role behaviour and want to provide the best experience for the tourists. This could be interpreted as an outcome of mutually developed relational psychological contracts, both horizontal and vertical. Statements such as "the manager's door is always open, and I can ask for anything" tells of the freedom they are given by the managers. Likewise, the managers delegate a lot of responsibility to the guides. The middle manager says: "I give my employees full autonomy because I trust them." We interpret this quotation as a relational element. At the same time, the guides show mutual support and trust, providing even more relational elements. Altogether, it seems that that the manager, by building confidence in the employees, gets extra-role behaviour in return.

## Discussions and implications

### *How to facilitate the guides*

This study shows that strong relational ties recognize the relationship between the guide team members and make the guides very committed to each other. Relational elements also promote extra-role behaviour. This indicates that it is very important to put together the right team of guides. In facilitating the guides, the managers at all levels must see the importance of trusting the guides, and that this will give them loyalty in return. Furthermore, it is important that the top manager delegates and give full autonomy to the guide manager. This is because the guide manager is the one that understands the mechanisms between the guide team members. The implication of these findings is that the guide manager must have responsibility for the process of recruitment every season. Facilitating the seasonal workers in the Arctic is very much about putting together the right team that will follow and share the firm's values—guides that are dedicated to the wild nature and who love to be outdoors all day and take responsibility for the safety of the guests, and who will also share the company's values.

### *Is the psychological contract worth taking seriously?*

The psychological contract seems to provide a useful understanding of how managers can facilitate seasonal workers to be motivated, committed and give extra service to the customers. In the absence of rich formal contracts and long-lasting relationships, the logic of the psychological contract illustrates how to overcome challenges with seasonal workers.

As the tourism industry is growing, we will see an increasing number of workers getting contracts on a seasonal basis. Therefore, we need to develop theories and an understanding of how to manage this type of employee. As seasonal workers are a type of temporary worker, we applied a psychological contract perspective to understand the mutual expectations in the employment relationship between employees and the employer, and to understand how seasonal workers can provide high-quality services to the customers of companies in the tourism industry. Our case study shows that the company promises a sensational nature experience, and a positive work environment including trust, to the Arctic guides in exchange for extra-role behaviour. This can be described in terms of the transactional, relational and ideological elements of the psychological contract, which is a surprising finding when it comes to seasonal workers and psychological contracts.

Previous research on the psychological contract (of permanent workers) shows that companies should develop relational contracts with their employees to invoke organizational citizenship behaviour and commitment. In a short-term contract context (seasonal work), previous studies have shown that these employees develop transactional rather than relational contracts, implying that organizational citizenship behaviour is difficult to evoke. However, our findings show that the seasonal workers are willing to engage in organizational citizenship behaviour, and that this is based on a relational and ideological type of contract. Most of the guides seem to be committed to pursuing the value of giving the tourist an extraordinary experience in nature. In addition, they all pursue values such as safety. Co-creation strategies ensuring interactions between employees, and employees and customers are expected to result in stronger loyalty among the seasonal workers, in which will result in positive returns for the companies as well.

This means that they agree on common values, meaning that the psychological contract between the guides and the company consists of values such as safety and an extraordinary experience. In return, the guides expect that they will get great trips and meet new people every day. The study shows that the managers promise the guides great wildlife experiences in Svalbard, as well as offering that the guides will be part of a great team of guides.

Our study shows that the workers offer extra-role behaviour (OCB) in different ways, especially towards the guests, but also to their colleagues. The study shows that the guides have ways of providing a little extra within the team of guides. They talk about the importance of supporting each other and inviting each other on social events or trips in their leisure time, as examples of OCB.

## Limitations and further research opportunities

This study implies that more research should be carried out to understand the nature of psychological contracts between seasonal workers and their employers. Furthermore, we also need to explore what kind of psychological contract leads to OCB. According to previous research, relational-based psychological contracts affect OCB positively. This study implies that ideological psychological contracts also have a positive influence on seasonal workers' OCB, but future studies should further test these assumptions.

## Conclusions

Our overall findings show that seasonal workers have developed all three types of psychological contract: transactional, relational, and value-based psychological contracts. This reveals that the guides are coming back each winter, working for the same company under the same conditions. In addition, the study shows that the guides feel commitment towards the customers and their department. The study also gives strong indications that the guides provide what we call extra-role behaviour or organizational citizenship behaviour. This is unexpected, since seasonal workers have been characterized as less motivated, less committed, less reliable, lower skilled and lower performing than permanent workers (De Gilder, 2003). The present chapter reveals that tourism companies working under challenges such as seasonality may build loyalty and commitment among their seasonal workers through relational psychological contracts.

## References

Barnard, C. I. (1938). *The functions of the executive.* Cambridge, MA: Harvard Press.

Beard, K. M., & Edwards, J. R. (1995). Employees at risk: Contingent work and the psychological experience of contingent workers. *Journal of Organizational Behavior (1986–1998), 109.*

Chambel, M. J., & Alcover, C.-M. (2011). The psychological contract of call-centre workers: Employment conditions, satisfaction and civic virtue behaviours. *Economic & Industrial Democracy, 32*(1), 115–134. doi: 10.1177/0143831x10376421.

Coyle-Shapiro, J. A. M., & Kessler, I. (2002). Contingent and non-contingent working in local government: Contrasting psychological contracts. *Public Administration, 80*(1), 77.

De Cuyper, N., De Jong, J., De Witte, H., Isaksson, K., Rigotti, T., & Schalk, R. (2008). Literature review of theory and research on the psychological impact of temporary employment: Towards a conceptual model. *International Journal of Management Reviews, 10*(1), 25–51.

De Jong, J., De Witte, H., Isaksson, K., Rigotti, T., & Schalk, R. (2008). Literature review of theory and research on the psychological impact of temporary employment: Towards a conceptual model. *International Journal of Management Reviews, 10*(1), 25–51.

De Gilder, D. (2003). Commitment, trust and work behaviour: The case of contingent workers. *Personnel Review, 32*(5), 588–604.

Kalleberg, A. L. (2000). Nonstandard employment relations: Part-time, temporary and contract work. *Annual Review of Sociology, 26*, 341–365.

Katz, D. (1964). The motivational basis of organizational behavior. *Behavioral science, 9*(2), 131–146.

Katz, D., & Kahn, R. L. (1978). *Social psychology of organisations.* New York, NY: Wiley.

Millward, L. J., & Brewerton, P. M. (1999). Contractors and their psychological contracts. *British Journal of Management, 10*(3), 253–274.

Moorman, R. H., Blakely, G. L., & Niehoff, B. P. (1998). Does perceived organizational support mediate the relationship between procedural justice and organizational citizen ship behavior? *The Academy of Management Journal, 41*, 351–357.

Morrison, E. W., & Robinson, S. L. (1997). When employees feel betrayed: A model of how psychological contract violation develops. *Academy of Management Review, 22*(1), 226–256.

O'Donohue, W., & Nelson, L. (2009). The role of ethical values in an expanded psychological contract. *Journal of Business Ethics, 90*(2), 251–263.

Organ, D. W. (1988). *Organizational citizenship behavior: The good soldier syndrome.* Lexington, MA: Lexington Books.

Robinson, S. L., & Morrison, E. W. (1995). Psychological contracts and OCB: The effect of unfulfilled obligations on civic virtue behavior. *Journal of Organizational Behavior, 16*(3), 289–298.

Rousseau, D. M. (1989). Psychological and implied contracts in organizations. *Employee Responsibilities & Rights Journal, 2*(2), 121–139.

Rousseau, D. M. (1995). *Psychological contracts in organizations: Understanding written and unwritten agreements.* Thousand Oaks, CA: Sage.

Rousseau, D. M. (2001). Schema, promise and mutuality: The building blocks of the psychological contract. *Journal of Occupational and Organizational Psychology, 74*(4), 511–541.

Rousseau, D. M. (2004). Psychological contracts in the workplace: Understanding the ties that motivate. *Academy of Management Executive, 18*(1), 120–127.

Rousseau, D. M., & Tijoriwala, S. A. (1998). Assessing psychological contracts: Issues, alternatives and measures. *Journal of Organizational Behavior, 19*(s1), 679–695.

Thompson, J. A., & Bunderson, J. S. (2003). Violations of principle: Ideological currency in the psychological contract. *Academy of Management Review, 28*(4), 571–586.

UNWTO. (2016). *World Tourism Organisation.* Retrieved from http://www2.unwto.org/.

Van Dyne, L., & Ang, S. (1998). Organizational citizenship behavior of contingent workers in Singapore. *Academy of Management Journal, 41*(6), 692–703.

Yin, R. K. (2009). *Case study research: Design and methods.* Los Angeles, CA: Sage.

Zhao, H. A. O., Wayne, S. J., Glibkowski, B. C., & Bravo, J. (2007). The impact of psychological contract breach on work-related outcomes: A meta-analysis. *Personnel Psychology, 60*(3), 647–680.

# 13 Challenges and research directions in co-creating tourism experience

*Joseph S. Chen, Muzaffer S. Uysal and Nina K. Prebensen*

## Introduction

This work takes inspiration from an early publication titled *Creating Experience Value in Tourism* authored by Prebensen, Chen and Uysal (2014). This book strives to augment the research path on tourist experience creation, which may help instigate further investigations on tourist experience creation. Consequently, the preceding chapters depict some issues of significance in relation to tourist experience creation using theoretical, empirical and translational lenses as epistemological apparatuses. Several innovative thoughts furthering the practices and research on tourist experience creation have surfaced, specifically, those chapters offering scholarly discourses on tourist experience co-creation from both demand and supply viewpoints. They may be divided into three thematic coverages including (1) tourist psychology (i.e. Chapters 2–4), (2) product development (i.e. Chapters 5–9) and service delivery (i.e. Chapters 10–13).

   Throughout the book, innovative undertakings in scientific research in the realm of tourism have been linked to tourist-experience-creation cases from both developed and emerging economies represented by France (i.e. Chapter 3), Australia (i.e. Chapter 4), Finland (i.e. Chapter 5), Japan (i.e. Chapters 5 and 7), Norway (i.e. Chapters 6 and 12), China (i.e. Chapter 10) and Hungary (i.e. Chapter 11). Although refreshing thoughts emanating from those chapters may be considered rudimentary notes on the subject of tourist experience creation, they furnish timely and valuable contribution to the body of knowledge by stimulating scholarly debates while advancing the relevant theories and practices. As a summary, the following section highlights the illuminating points of thoughts presented in the preceding chapters.

## Highlights in tourist experience co-creation research

In the study of tourist behaviors, the subject of tourist experience has received relatively limited attention in comparison to other issues of significance such as destination image, tourist motivation and trip satisfaction. Recently scholars have further disentangled the complexity of tourist experience creation and co-creation in a systematic fashion as presented in the book of *Creating Experience*

*Value in Tourism* (Prebensen, Chen, & Uysal, 2014). The first chapter "Tourist experience creation: An overview" by Nina K. Prebensen, Joseph S. Chen and Muzaffer Uysal, covers the valuable contribution of collective thoughts such as the significance of the dynamic process of tourist experience formation which has been recently brought to prominence. From a different viewpoint, it further draws the process of tourist experience creation involving motivation, perceived value, satisfaction and loyalty as moderating and outcome variables. As for experience co-creation, the chapter advocates ways of facilitating the process of co-creation. Using a dramaturgy metaphor or perfecting physical environment dimensions and human interaction dimensions in relation to tourist experience creation, is an example of facilitation. Lastly, while recognizing tourist interaction as a facilitator of experience co-creation, the first chapter tackles the concept of interactivity. Dealing with the level of interaction, as a pragmatic conduit in service delivery, it suggests a critical direction for further study as this concept has not been fully explored by tourism researchers.

Emotion is a fundamental subject of study in psychology. In the realm of tourism, this subject has been overly linked to widely examined behavioral variables such as destination image, motivation, trip satisfaction and wellbeing. Sandra Gountas, the author of the second chapter, "Creating emotional platforms," renders additional insights on the role of emotions in tourist experiences and effects of emotions in relation to the tourist, travel companies, other tourists and service staffs. The chapter instigates further understanding of the concurrence and effect of emotional contagion during the service delivery. This enables the service providers to cope with issues confronting the tourist and consequently enhance the tourist satisfaction. In achieving the above aim, the chapter proposes five strategies in perfecting the effect of emotional contagion in a positive way. Sincerity and authenticity of service provision is another aspect emphasized by the author that could also moderate tourist satisfaction significantly. Consumer studies have vividly documented the attitude of servers as a defining factor impacting customer satisfaction. This chapter audaciously embraces the notion of sincerity and authenticity as a mechanism in manipulating the tourist's perception of the quality of service staffs. Towards the end, the chapter paves four pragmatic paths fostering the optimal level of service delivery during the process of emotional interaction.

Marketing literature underlines investigative agendas with respect to customer experiences from three aspects: before, during and after the consumption. In tourism settings, it is clear that the experiences evoked during the consumption stage have not been well examined. In an attempt to supply the aforementioned void, Isabelle Frochot and Dominique Kreziak take a revolutionary method to trace the development of tourist experiences during the trip in the third chapter titled "Designing and managing co-constructive process in a holiday environment: The case of French Northern Alpine ski resorts." They deployed daily interviews that enabled the authors to collect rich insights on experience co-creation process among ski resort guests interviewed. It is also observed that the image of mountains has a strong association with the tourist experience co-creation. For example, the redeposited image of mountain as an agriculture site (e.g. cheese production) allows the tourists to co-create their experience by immersing themselves in pursuing highly symbolic activities. In addition, the scenery of the mountain is also seen as a driving force promoting positive tourist experiences. This chapter suggests comparative study between mountain and other settings regarding the effect of both general (e.g. scenery) and symbolic (e.g. food production) dimensions on tourist experience co-creation. In sum, this chapter adds into the Tourist Experience Driver Model (Chen, Prebensen, & Uysal, 2014) that the environment (i.e. mountain) is considered as an interactive driver moderating the tourist experience.

Self-motivation is a salient determinant of experience creation and co-creation. The participants with a strong desire to achieve their goal of activity participation are likely to immerse themselves in the activities they engage and create positive experiences afterwards. As presented in the fourth chapter "Staging for value co-creation in nature based experiences: The case of surfing course at the Surfers Paradise" by Nina K. Prebensen further explicates the factors influencing self-motivation. The chapter discusses how the pundits of surfing are motivated by a sense of autonomy, competency and relatedness. By deploying two qualitative methods of inquiry (1) observations on the interactions between the host and guest and (2) in-depth personal interviews which are undertaken at a surfer strip, this chapter takes a holistic approach to examine how tourists enhance their overall satisfaction. The examination includes the destination and journey and enhances the felt wellbeing by looking at various aspects of the course: the instructor, the setting including the surrounding nature, and other course participants. Moreover, the chapter suggests ways of enhancing value by motivating, involving and teaching the customer to partake in the value-creation process (Before-During-After) through mental and physical participation in an activity or event.

When designing new services to sustain their operations, the providers ought to consider a myriad of factors harnessing the success of service delivery. In the context of tourism, tourist motivation is considered as one of the defining attributes for product development from the market-driven perspective. In other words, what motivates the tourists to the services provided is a pivotal subject of investigation for service development research. Raija Komppula and Henna Konu have vividly implemented such a viewpoint in the fifth chapter "Designing forest-based wellbeing in tourism services for Japanese customers: A case study from Finland." They particularly look at Japanese potential tourists for forest-based wellbeing tourism in Eastern Finland. Their study first undertakes a field trip to Japan to understand the needs of Japanese tourists in relation to forest-based tourism and then invites groups of tourists to experience the virtual and real services catering to the Japanese tourists as a way of testing viability of the potential of services and products. A high point of the study is the use of ethnographic technique to sketch the underlying service experiences encountered by tourists that allows the providers to align their service strategies whenever appropriate. While indeed filling the void of literature, this study benchmarks the practices in service development with respect to tourist experience creation.

As a reflection of the sixth chapter "Innovation potentials through value proposals: The case of a museum in northern Norway" by Nina K. Prebensen, individual experiences may include experiential consumption practice and shared experiences with real or virtual platform to learn, enjoy, and express themselves. This chapter conducts an empirical study at the Rock Carving Museum in Alta, Norway to develop strategies to motivate, involve and teach tourists to participate in creating value. Although a museum is traditionally not a profit-oriented entity, this chapter suggests adopting the Business Model Canvas (Österwalder & Pigneur, 2010) to determine value propositions for customer segments to utilize human and financial resources in an effective way. Following the steps of business model development, three viable groups of participation are identified which includes children, international tourists and researchers. Then, it draws a blueprint of value co-creation for the museum under investigation from the aspects of networking, empowerment of customers, use of internet and social media. In aggregate, while addressing the issue of tourist experience creation, the chapter renders a new concept of operations for government-funded institutes in an era when competition and diminishing government funding prevail.

Culture-related products and service are considered as valuable highlights enticing tourist demand. The seventh chapter "Value co-created in geothermal tourism: The case of the 'Ryokan' Industry in Japan" by Timothy Lee showcases how geothermal tourism draws tourists and adds value for tourist experience creation. Ryokan, a traditional Japanese-style inn, is the premise under investigation. The study site Beppu is the most famous destination city for hot spring baths in Japan that provides an ideal research platform to assemble updated and in-depth insights on issues hindering the development of spa tourism in Japan. Ryokan is a small-scale establishment and typically owned and operated by family instead of a large business firm, so it has faced challenges financially and managerially. Ryokans in general follow one of two growth strategies. First, they go to high-end market, second, they undergo a transformation to a modern property similar to a hotel in appearance. Those targeting the high-end market maintain the traditional look and away from the crowd while actively integrating local food and local heritage into the service scope. Such a setting allows the tourists to amply immerse in spa and accommodation stays facilitating the process of tourist experience co-creation. As for the modernized Ryokan properties, they provide better accessibility with modern hotel amenities as well as accommodating a much larger groups of tourists. In summary, this chapter portrays the Japanese spa tourist segments in the years to come.

The eighth chapter "Value creation through heritage and identity" by Ruhet Genc is inclined to construct a mathematical model of experience value creation through culture and identity. The chapter articulates that the perceived value could be viewed from three perspectives: monetary, experience and social. As stated in the chapter, heritage is viewed as physical objects and places that endure various strength of transformation from time to time as a dynamic mark of culture in general and locality in specific. Further, identity is perceived as an individual sense of self in relation to social and interpersonal functions. The chapter stresses the importance of linking the participations in cultural elements to produce a positive experience. Since both heritage and identity drive the needs and wants of tourists, it is vital not to ignore one of the two factors (i.e. heritage and identity) when developing service strategies for experience creation. The chapter suggests the timeline of service efforts that should embrace a long-term goal in garnishing services for culture heritage and identity in the process of experience value creation. As a concluding remark, recognizing the interplay between culture heritage and identity in the process of experience creation, the chapter urges further deployment of quantitative study to refine the current theories.

The scope of experience creation in cuisine and gastronomy is also rich. There are tourist activities that exclusively focus on cuisine tour experiences where individuals actively partake in menu designs and implementations of their menu during their trips. A study by Kivela and Crotts (2006) found support that gastronomy plays a major role in the way tourists experience the destination, and indicate that some travelers would return to the same destination to savor its unique gastronomy, further attesting to the importance of gastronomy as a source of experience value creation. The ninth chapter "Gastronomy in a co-creation context" by Ruhet Genc explores the creation of value in food experience and brings the concept of the slow food service into the discussion. The chapter provides a useful chronological discussion on the position of gastronomy in tourism and demonstrates how the concept of co-creation is infused in the relationship between gastronomy and tourism experiences. The chapter uses Cittaslow/Slow Food movement as a successful example of creating tourist experience in gastronomy with a reference of Cittaslow movement for Seferhisar in Turkey. It is argued for further empirical investigation and methodological rigor for substantiating anecdotal evidence and story sharing.

One of the key stakeholders of the production system of tourism and hospitality are the employees as providers of good and services. Tourists usually interact with employees throughout the duration of their stay or trip experience regardless of the setting, whether it is a hotel, destination or attending an event such as festivals. This interaction certainly influences the process and outcome of the experience. The tenth chapter "Co-creating customer experience: The role of employees in tourism and hospitality services" by Prakash K. Chathoth, Eric S. W. Chan, Robert J. Harrington, Fevzi Okumus and Zibin Song explores the important role employees play in creating experiences with customers as visitors and patrons. Using a real-life case study with two longitudinal service scenarios, they bring out how employees' attitude and behavior can affect customer value creation. The chapter delineates three influencers of employee engagement in value co-creation, namely: organizational factors, situational factors, and personal factors with respect to the role employees assume as co-creators of customer experiences. These factors can independently, in combination or collectively influence the co-creation of value in experiential consumption. The authors of the chapter encourage further exploring issues such as the role of passage of time, context, motivation of frontline employees and the likes. In addition, they suggest that the employees need to be adequately empowered by the tourism enterprise for creating value in experiences. There is ample opportunity to explore both the role of frontline employees and how the tourism enterprise can facilitate the process and protocol of co-creation in experiences with respect to different settings in hospitality and tourism.

Tourism experiences are formed throughout the duration of different phases of a trip experience. More research needs to be undertaken to explore how different phases (anticipation and planning, travel to site, on-site, travel back and, post reflective phase of travel experience, and post-trip) of tourism service and good consumption can be enhanced by service providers. The eleventh chapter "Co-creating the sightseeing experience with and without a guide" by Anita Zátori gives a great example of how the process of co-creation is enhanced by service providers during the on-site service provision in the case of walking tours in Budapest, Hungary. The on-site co-creation is characterized by simultaneous production and consumption of experience, and that the setting as a process enhances value for both the visitors and the guides. However, the distinction is drawn by two types of tours; namely, guided and non-guided tours. The chapter concludes that the experience involvement shows consistency with the members of the guided tour than the non-guided tour members. By this observation the author of the chapter points out that the role of tour guide is crucial in enhancing experience co-creation and value. The guide plays an important role as a facilitator in heightening the tour experience and involvement. However non-guided tours can take advantage of technological devices such as appropriate apps that would enable participants to actively engage and create value in their own self-guided tours, further supporting the notion that technological devices can also be utilized to facilitate experience value creation. There is a tremendous amount of research potential in this area of experiential tours and guided and non-guided tourist activities.

We have known for a long time that tourism activities can be seasonal in nature. The erratic nature of demand imposed on certain destinations can create both financial burden and inefficient ways of personnel management, for example, not being able to maintain qualified employees and providers of services year around due to high fixed expenses. Nevertheless, some companies have to work with seasonal employees in certain businesses because of location or strong dependency on climatic change. The twelfth chapter "Creating value with seasonal workers through psychological contracts" by Kristin Woll highlights how organizations operating in seasonal markets may benefit from facilitating for value co-creation through the development of psychological contracts with their employees. The chapter uses a case study performed with guides for a company in Svalbard, north of mainland Europe, about midway between continental Norway and the North Pole. Drawing on the three types of psychological contract: transactional, relational and value-based psychological contracts, the case study reveals that co-creating strategies as supported by organizations can ensure meaningful and rewarding interaction not only among the employees of the tourism enterprise but also between employees and customers in general. These psychological contracts may then result in stronger loyalty and organizational commitment among the seasonal workers, thus further positively influencing visitor experiences. Relational physiological contracts can be used from the perspective of different stakeholders to facilitate and enhance the process of creating better experiential value tourism offerings.

## Suggestions for future research

As seen, the area of experience creation is gaining further momentum and concerted efforts from researchers. No matter what kind of tourism product or service we have in mind, the tourist will be influenced by the experiencescape (Mossberg, 2007). Binkhorst and Den Dekker (2009) also assert that product- and firm-centric innovations are now being taken over by the co-creation experience as a basis for value and as the future of innovation. We believe that in the next decade or so we will continue to see more focused case specific studies in this area. There is also a need for engaging in cross-sectional and longitudinal studies of best practices that would be goal, target, and activity oriented.

One of the areas that needs constant monitoring and future attention is the notion of lifespan of consumers and lifecycle of destination and experience settings. Monitoring and juxtaposing these concepts could be of immense value in understanding tourist experience creation designating how these experiences may be influenced and managed. We wholeheartedly encourage researchers to engage in studies that could lead to effective monitoring and understanding of change in experience creation over time as a function of maturity of both individuals as consumers and destinations as the sphere of experience consumption. Managing attractions with this point in mind would enable the tourism enterprise to meet ever changing needs of the more engaging visitor market. There is ample opportunity to conduct research in this vein.

It is equally important to challenge us as researchers to further develop measures and indicators to be reflective of best practices that could have a high degree of transferability to other similar settings and cases. Again, we strongly believe that this is an area that is ripe with research challenges and opportunities in tourist experience creation. Furthermore, linking experience creation to performance measures at the firm level could yield tremendous benefits for sustainable and profitable business practices while maintaining a high degree of customer loyalty and engagement. By doing so, we are better positioned to contribute to society and thus to social sciences in general.

The role of social media in the digital age of the Fourth Generation of the Industrial Revolution would no doubt force researchers of consumer behavior to be more innovative and creative in the way we approach both basic research and applied research in examining the salient aspects of tourist experience creation, designs and platforms from the perspectives of the firm, tourists and the experience setting. There is no question that we will see more research at the intersections of the three dimensions of experience creation for experiences to be valued.

Sirgy and Uysal (2016) point out that as tourism plays a central role in the lives of many people across the globe, its expected benefits would include not only economic measures but also non-economic value of tourism measures such as quality of life (QOL) and wellbeing of participants at different levels of units of analysis. Most of the activities tourists and visitors participate in are experiential in nature (Uysal, Sirgy, Woo, & Kim, 2016; Sirgy & Uysal, 2016). Such activities have the potential to induce happiness and satisfaction, which in turn may contribute to the wellbeing of individuals. Experience creation has to be at the crux of new discourses in our future research efforts. One of the research challenges we may face is that we need to acknowledge the fact that individuals, collectives, and societies frame and construct their own reality of what they may experience. At the individual or group level, the existing behavioral differences of individuals and their responses to the levels of differences should be considered and we as researchers should be cognizant of such existing behavioral differences in creating and forming tourist experiences. The more challenging question is how the tourism enterprise would fulfil its role as a facilitator of experience creation, knowing that variations in markets need to be heard and paid attention.

## References

Binkhorst, E., & Den Dekker, T. (2009). Agenda for co-creation tourism experience research. *Journal of Hospitality Marketing & Management, 18*(2–3), 311–327.

Chen, J. S., Prebensen, N. K., & Uysal, M. (2014). Dynamic drivers of tourist experiences. In N. K. Prebensen, J. S. Chen, & M. Uysal (Eds), *Creating experience value in tourism* (pp. 11–21). Oxfordshire: CABI.

Kivela, J., & Crotts, J. C. (2006). Tourism and gastronomy: Gastronomy's influence on how tourists experience a destination. *Journal of Hospitality & Tourism Research, 30*(3), 354–377.

Mossberg, L. (2007). A marketing approach to the tourist experience. *Scandinavian Journal of Hospitality and Tourism, 7*(1), 59–74.

Österwalder, A., & Pigneur, Y. (2010). *Business model generation: a handbook for visionaries, game changers, and challengers*. New Jersey, NJ: John Wiley & Sons.

Prebensen, N. K., Chen, J. S., & Uysal, M. (2014). *Creating experience value in tourism*. Oxfordshire: CABI.

Sirgy, M. J., & Uysal, M. (2016). Developing a eudaimonia research agenda in travel and tourism. In *Handbook of eudaimonic well-being* (pp. 485–495). Switzerland: Springer International Publishing.

Uysal, M., Sirgy, M. J., Woo, E., & Kim, H. L. (2016). Quality of life (QOL) and wellbeing research in tourism. *Tourism Management, 53*, 244–261.

# Index